DEVELOPING
AS A
PROFESSIONAL

A GUIDE FOR
CONTEMPORARY
PARAPROFESSIONALS

DEVELOPING
AS A
PROFESSIONAL

A GUIDE FOR
CONTEMPORARY
PARAPROFESSIONALS

MARY D. BURBANK

THOMSON

DELMAR LEARNING   Australia   Brazil   Canada   Mexico   Singapore   Spain   United Kingdom   United States

THOMSON
*
DELMAR LEARNING

Developing as a Professional:
A Guide for Contemporary Paraprofessionals

Mary D. Burbank

Vice President,
Career Education Strategic
Business Unit:
Dawn Gerrain

Director of Learning Solutions:
John Fedor

Managing Editor:
Robert L. Serenka, Jr.

Acquisitions Editor:
Christopher M. Shortt

Product Manager:
Philip Mandl

Editorial Assistant:
Alison Archambault

Director of Production:
Wendy A. Troeger

Production Manager:
Mark Bernard

Content Project Manager:
Steven S. Couse

Technology Project Manager:
Sandy Charette

Director of Marketing:
Wendy E. Mapstone

Channel Manager:
Kristin McNary

Marketing Coordinator:
Scott A. Chrysler

Marketing Specialist:
Erica S. Conley

Art Director:
Joy Kocsis

Cover Design:
David Arsenault

Cover Image:
Getty Images

For permission to use material from this text or product, submit a request online at http://www.thomsonrights.com
Any additional questions about permissions can be submitted by email to thomsonrights@thomson.com

Library of Congress Cataloging-in-Publication Data

Burbank, Mary D.
   Developing as a professional : a guide for contemporary paraprofessionals / Mary D. Burbank.
      p. cm.
   ISBN 1-4180-6150-6
   1. Teachers' assistants—Professional relationships—Handbooks, manuals, etc.   I. Title.
   LB2844.1.A8B867 2008
   371.14'124—dc22

                                                    2007030037

NOTICE TO THE READER

To Matt, M, G, & D.

CONTENTS

4

CHAPTER FOUR

STUDENTS AND THEIR EDUCATIONAL NEEDS
73

5

CHAPTER FIVE

THE LEGAL RIGHTS AND RESPONSIBILITIES OF THOSE WORKING IN SCHOOLS
97

6

CHAPTER SIX
EFFECTIVE COMMUNICATION AS AN EDUCATIONAL TEAM MEMBER

115

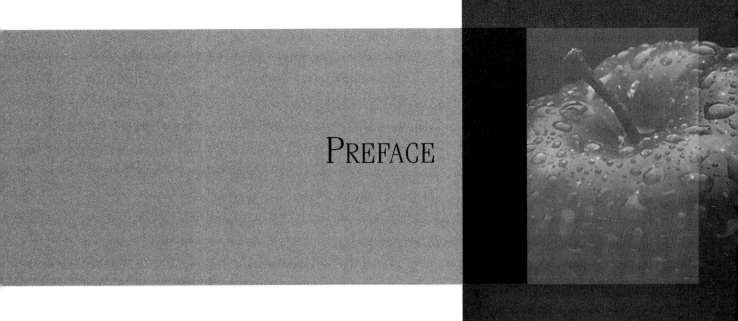

PREFACE

During the past 40 years, the number of paraprofessionals in public schools has increased steadily. Current estimates identify approximately 500,000 paraprofessionals working in a number of positions within school settings. Paraprofessionals have very specific job descriptions. The federal government defines a paraprofessional as any person who works under the guidance of a classroom teacher in an early childhood, elementary, or secondary school. Paraprofessionals may work in traditional classrooms or with language education teachers, with special educators, or in immigrant education programs. Because the work of paraprofessionals is becoming more technical, requiring increased training and evaluation, those employing paraprofessionals are in need, now more than ever, of professional development resources that are current and reflect the changing work responsibilities of paraprofessionals and the communities in which they work.

NATIONAL MOVEMENTS

Developing as a professional: A guide for contemporary paraprofessionals is a text designed to meet the needs of those working as paraprofessionals as well as those employing and mentoring them. Changes in the responsibilities of paraprofessionals have brought an increase in the accountability standards required of those working in these positions. Mandates under No Child Left Behind (2001) require that paraprofessionals meet highly qualified standards in a number of ways including: completing coursework, passing a nationally based exam, and demonstrating competencies in reading, writing, and math, in addition to possessing a high school diploma.

MARKET NEED

Of the texts currently available on paraprofessional training, mentoring, and advising, a small number are written specifically *for* paraprofessionals. The existing texts combine content for mainstream and special educators, and typically reference general legal issues related to the needs of students receiving special education services as described in the Individuals with Disabilities

Improvement Education Act (IDIEA). Limitations of the existing texts include fairly dense content and limited attention to the needs of English Language Learners in contemporary classrooms

Developing as a professional: A guide for contemporary paraprofessionals provides an introduction to general policies in education and offers a comprehensive discussion of the work of paraprofessionals working in today's classrooms and schools. In 2004, a district administrator and a university professor created a course for paraprofessionals interested in developing professionally. The course was designed by a district as a first step to respond to the highly qualified standards for paraprofessionals under the No Child Left Behind Act (NCLB). Some paraprofessionals took the course with the long-term goal of completing a licensure program. Others continued in the same positions they held. All class members completed a professional portfolio as a capstone to the year-long course on their road toward meeting the highly qualified criteria. The data gathered from the year-long study informed the development of this text. The text links the day-to-day experiences of paraprofessionals to the mentoring support provided by classroom teachers. The text encourages empowerment and professional ownership among those within the paraprofessional community.

ORGANIZATION OF THE TEXT

Developing as a professional: A guide for contemporary paraprofessionals provides readers with the fundamentals for working in contemporary classrooms. Key content features:

- an orientation to the American educational system;
- an overview of the work of paraprofessionals in United States classrooms;
- suggestions for classroom management;
- strategies for teaching students with special academic and language needs;
- a discussion of the legal issues related to working in schools;
- guidelines for effective communication with parents and other professionals;
- suggestions for instruction and assessment;
- tips for portfolio development;
- references to electronic resources.

Each chapter is divided into sections describing major content themes, portfolio suggestions, and questions for future discussion. The breakdown of each chapter includes:

Introduction	Checking for Understanding
Objectives	Points of View
Preview Questions	Portfolio Corner
Key Terms	Sample Portfolio Framework
Day-to-Day Dilemmas	Spanish Translations (*En español*)
Summary	References

SPECIAL FEATURES

This text provides users with a *reader friendly* format that invites readers into the text in meaningful ways. Influenced by the *real world perspectives* of paraprofessionals, the text includes applied examples of concepts related to educational settings. A rolling case study guides readers through the text, offers tips on professional portfolio development, and provides a section on professional references. Guides and tips are provided in both English and Spanish.

A ROLLING CASE STUDY AND A DAY-TO-DAY DILEMMA

Readers travel through *Developing as a professional: A guide for contemporary paraprofessionals* experiencing the work of Maria and Tracy, two paraprofessionals who share their thoughts, successes, and questions regarding their work in contemporary classrooms. Narratives and quotes from these paraprofessionals are included throughout the text. Questions to paraprofessionals and suggestions from the field are additional components of each chapter.

SPANISH TRANSLATIONS *(EN ESPAÑOL)*

In many communities across the United States, the number of paraprofessionals who are non-native English speakers far exceeds native English speakers. In many major urban and rural communities, 60–75% of paraprofessionals are from racial and linguistic minority groups. Due to the pronounced presence of Spanish-speaking paraprofessionals, a portion of each chapter includes a section on key vocabulary, portfolio development, and reflection questions that are presented in both English and Spanish.

PORTFOLIO DEVELOPMENT AND EXAMINATION PREPARATION

In response to the mandates under the No Child Left Behind legislation, educational communities are requiring paraprofessionals to meet the "highly qualified" paraprofessional standards in a number of ways. Successfully completing an exam developed by the Educational Testing Service (ETS) provides one avenue for meeting the stipulations for highly qualified paraprofessionals. Another option is the completion of a professional portfolio. While not every district requires a formal portfolio, portfolio development provides both an opportunity to meet NCLB standards and a forum for professional growth.

The portfolio section of each chapter includes strategies for gathering portfolio artifacts such as lesson plans, classroom management plans, certificates from training programs, ideas for working with diverse populations of learners, and communication tools such as letters and memos. The portfolio framework is subdivided into four sections based upon the Praxis standards and addresses key areas of the ETS paraprofessional examination.

ANCILLARY MATERIALS

Instructor's Manual

The teaching aids and suggestions in the Instructor's Manual (IM) are organized by chapter. Each chapter includes the following components:

Chapter Overview:	A short description of the chapter content
Chapter Goals:	A description of the major learning goals for the chapter
Chapter Outline:	A detailed description of chapter topics organized by headings
Teaching Strategies:	Concrete ideas to present topics in thoughtful and interactive ways
Icebreakers:	Strategies to begin each lesson
Journal Entries:	Reflection questions on chapter-related content
Activities:	Ideas for small and large group work
Assessment:	Questions for assessing student learning
Increasing Understanding:	Guides for reviewing in-text tables and worksheets
Day-to-Day Dilemma:	Suggestions for discussing an in-text dilemma
Portfolio Discussions:	Suggestions for building portfolio contents

 The CD-Rom that accompanies this text contains electronic versions of the Portfolio Framework forms found in each chapter as well as checklists, worksheets, and journal tables. For your convenience, the forms are provided as MS Word documents so you can easily edit and print the documents whenever they are needed.

 The student Online Companion to accompany *Developing as a Professional: A Guide for Contemporary Paraprofessionals* contains additional resources to aid students in their studies such as: a "Tips from Maria and Tracy" section, Selected Readings and electronic resources for paraprofessionals, and chapter by chapter *PowerPoint* slides. The student Online Companion can be found at www.earlychilded.delmar.com.

ACKNOWLEDGMENTS

Special thanks, from the author, are extended to the following people: Michelle Bachman and the Salt Lake City School District, Clif Drew, Irene Fisher, Don Kauchak, Rickie McCandless, Becky Owen, and Marshall Welch and the Community-Based Research Project. Spanish translations were prepared by Betty Jeanne Moffett. The author and Thomson Delmar Learning would also like to thank the following reviewers, whose valuable feedback and suggestions helped to shape the final text:

- Elaine Boski-Wilkinson, M.Ed, Collin County Community College, Texas
- Katy E. Whittingham, BA, MPA, Bridgewater State College, Massachusetts

- Lisa Thomas, BA, MA, Jack London Middle School, Illinois
- Gail Goldstein, BA, M.Ed., Central New Mexico Community College
- Nancy L. Picart, BS, MS, Executive Director, Education, Bright Beginnings Child Care Center, New York
- Elizabeth A. Jenkins, BA, M.Ed., Orlando Tech, OCPS, Florida
- Lois Oestreich, BA, M.Ed., Salt Lake Community College, Utah
- Tracey Bennett, B.S., M.S., Vance-Granville Community College, North Carolina
- Judith Piskun, M.Ed, Villa Maria College of Buffalo, New York
- Aileen Donnersberger, B.A., M.A., Moraine Valley Community College, Illinois
- Susan C. Lane, Ed.D., University of Massachusetts Dartmouth

ABOUT THE AUTHOR

Mary D. Burbank has been a Clinical Faculty member in the University of Utah's College of Education for the past 13 years. She teaches pre-service and in-service teachers in secondary education. She works in collaboration with the University Neighborhood Partners to promote access to higher education for traditionally underrepresented students and families.

INTRODUCTION

Welcome to 21st century education! Whether you are new to your position as a paraprofessional or whether you have been working in schools for years, this is an exciting time to be working in classrooms. As a paraprofessional you are an important member of a team whose job is to prepare students for the future. In addition to working closely with professional educators and administrators, paraprofessionals assist children as they learn more about the world around them. Like others working in your school, you bring a unique set of life experiences, education, and knowledge to your classroom, school, and district.

Paraprofessionals are among a growing group of people working in the field of education. In 2004 there were approximately 1.3 million paraprofessionals working in public schools. Of that group, 75% were employed in elementary schools where over half of the paraprofessionals worked in classrooms with children receiving special education services (United States Bureau of Labor's Occupational Outlook Handbook, 2007).

The work of paraprofessionals varies. In some schools paraprofessionals tutor and help children under the direct guidance of their classroom teacher. Paraprofessionals also provide support to children at recess, in the cafeteria or hallways, or in other settings within the school. They might also help with paper work, special projects, or provide physical or academic support for children with different disabilities.

The qualifications for paraprofessionals may differ across states. However, recent legislation under the No Child Left Behind Act has explicit requirements. For example, in some schools paraprofessionals are only qualified when they hold at least a two-year degree from a community college, have a minimum of two years in college, or pass a state test.

Maria and Tracy are two paraprofessionals who have worked in schools for many years. They have a lot of experience and are a part of the education teams in their classrooms. Over the years they have learned a lot about supporting the learning that takes place in classrooms. Like many educators in today's classrooms, they want to grow professionally and they want to know how to respond to changes in classrooms and schools. Most of all, they want to give students the best education possible. Even with all their experience, Maria and Tracy still have questions about their work.

This book was written especially for paraprofessionals. The views of Maria and Tracy are based on the stories of real paraprofessionals who have worked in education for years. Like others across the nation, Maria's and Tracy's stories will give you ideas about working in classrooms and will help you as you develop professionally. We hope that like Maria and Tracy you will share your knowledge and experiences with others! Let's find out a little bit more about Maria's and Tracy's backgrounds and what they bring to the classroom.

Tracy's Story: If you asked me what I love best about my work as a paraprofessional, I'm not sure if I could pick just one area. Sure there are days where I come home completely exhausted, but for the most part my job is great! I've been a paraprofessional in my school for seven years. I work with students and their families as a part of a team in a special education classroom. When I first started in my position, I had plenty of questions. My classroom teacher has helped me learn a lot about giving kids with special needs a great education! She keeps me updated on all the changes in teaching and helps me become a better paraprofessional by learning as much as possible. I guess the very best part of my job is helping students read, write, and become good learners.

Tracy, *Elementary teaching/classroom aide*

Maria's Story: The best part of my job as a paraprofessional is that I'm able to work with a team of teachers. In my classroom we teach students who are new to the United States and also kids whose families have been here for generations. The neat part about my work with the kids is that each child is like a package with different ideas, interests, and talents. You never know what's going to happen from one day to the next! When I came to the US I had a lot to learn about American schools. My own kids were in the 2nd and 4th grades and I had all kinds of questions as a parent. I can't tell you how great it was to work with both a classroom teacher and a paraprofessional who helped me learn about education in the US. Their support made all the difference for my family. Based on my own experiences I try to help other immigrants as they learn about life in American schools.

Maria, *elementary school, English as a Second Language teaching/classroom aide*

The stories of Maria and Tracy are like those of other paraprofessionals. As members of educational teams they give students the skills necessary for success in school and in life. Maria and Tracy are also growing in their roles as education professionals. New requirements for highly qualified educators bring challenges and opportunities for all educators. The stories of Maria and Tracy will guide you in your work with students in classrooms and in your own professional development.

TIPS FOR USING THIS TEXT

Developing as a professional: A guide for contemporary paraprofessionals is based on the experiences of real life paraprofessionals who work in public elementary, middle, and high schools. Three years ago a group of paraprofessionals in special education and English Language classrooms spent one year in a professional development class that was created especially for them. Some of the paraprofessionals took the class because they planned on becoming certified teachers some day. Others took it because they wanted to learn about the new standards under the No Child Left Behind Act (NCLB). No Child Left Behind is an important law because it spells out professional standards for all educators, including paraprofessionals. After they completed their course, these paraprofessionals shared their advice with other paraprofessionals. They came up with the following list of important information for anyone working in today's classrooms and schools. Working in today's classrooms requires:

1. an understanding of public schools;
2. an understanding of the needs of students with disabilities and language differences;
3. an ability to identify effective instruction and tips when tutoring students or small groups;
4. an understanding of the legal rights and responsibilities of those working in schools;
5. an ability to communicate as a part of a team—including writing professionally;
6. an understanding of how No Child Left Behind affects educators.

Preview Questions

As you begin reading *Developing as a paraprofessional: A guide for contemporary paraprofessionals,* consider the following:

1. What are some of the questions you have about your work as a paraprofessional?
2. Is there a mentor teacher at your school who will serve as a professional colleague?
3. What are some of your questions about American classrooms and schools?
4. What are the skills and special qualities you bring to a classroom that will benefit students?

UNDERSTANDING PUBLIC SCHOOLS IN THE UNITED STATES

LEARNING OBJECTIVES

After reading and reflecting on this chapter you will understand:

- The history of public schools in the United States

- How public schools are organized

- The roles of paraprofessionals in today's schools

- The decision-making process in public schools

As you read this chapter, ask yourself these questions:

1. How are decisions about school policies and procedures made?

2. Who decides what to teach and how to teach?

3. How does your role as a paraprofessional fit into the education system?

4. What type of artifacts will you include in your portfolio to demonstrate your knowledge of the educational community?

KEY TERMS

accountability standards

administrators

artifacts

Bureau of Indian Affairs (BIA)

charter schools

cultural frame of reference

curriculum

district

federal government

local level

No Child Left Behind Act (NCLB)

Office of Indian Affairs (OIA)

paraeducators

portfolio

school boards

state level

---

school boards
Locally elected officials who determine policies and procedures within a district.

Juntas escolares
Funcionarios localmente elegidos que determinan reglamentos y procedimientos dentro de un distrito.

---

administrators
School district personnel who oversee the work of the teachers, staff, and students within districts and schools.

administradores
Personal del distrito escolar que supervisa el trabajo de los maestros, del personal, y de los estudiantes en los distritos y las escuelas.

INTRODUCTION

The work of paraprofessionals is just one part of the educational system. Many people influence what goes on in schools. They include those who work in your school as well as members of state and national communities. Teachers, parents, and members of local businesses also play active roles in decision making. While it may seem like paraprofessionals are only a small part of such a big system, paraprofessionals bring a lot to classrooms. Their work is based on research on the best ways to work with many different kinds of students. As members of professional teams, paraprofessionals and other educators work to improve the ways in which children are educated in today's classrooms.

Public education is organized in the United States based on ideas of people from all over the country. National and state leaders create laws and set policies that are put into practice by individual states. Members of local **school boards** decide how new laws and policies will play out in schools. **Administrators** and educators at each school also make sure that the goals of the nation and state are put into action through work in classrooms. Educators and policy-makers work together. School educators build an educational system that intends to serve the citizens of our nation for the present as well as for the future.

The goals of early Americans included: establishing a firm leadership, developing a strong workforce, and educating knowledgeable citizens. While these very broad goals have stayed the same over time, America has not always existed as it does today. Different perspectives have led to discussion, debate, and changes in the education of children in schools. The diversity of ideas and the needs of different people within our country can be traced throughout America's history.

UNDERSTANDING THE DIVERSITY OF A NATION

If you were asked to describe the population of the United States, what would you say? Many people would respond that the US population includes people who immigrated from around the world. Others would say there are people whose families have lived in the US for thousands of years. For the families who have lived in the US for generations or for those who have recently arrived, their historical roots stem from many areas around the world. The largest group of

Education in the United States is influenced by the history of immigrants from around the world as well as from people living in the Americas for centuries.

American immigrants includes people of European descent. Many communities also have a large number of immigrants from Asia and Africa. Each group brings a history that is unique, with many customs, traditions, and beliefs. The American Indians are a group whose history is oftentimes dismissed from our historical memories. American Indians have populated North America for thousands of years. Today more than ever, educators recognize the influence of American Indians as one of many groups of people who have shaped our country's past. This recognition helps educators understand the important contributions of *all* of America's ancestors.

Of the groups of people who immigrated to America, many came to the US voluntarily, looking for religious freedom, political opportunities, or wealth. The majority of European immigrants, for example, looked for religious, political, and economic freedoms they hoped would exist for them in North America (Spring, 2006). Much like early US immigrants, many present-day immigrants from the Middle East, East Asia, and Africa also arrive for religious, social, economic, and/or political reasons.

For other immigrants, their journey to the US took place under very different circumstances. The vast majority of African immigrants arrived in this country as involuntary immigrants (Ogbu, 1995). These immigrants did not arrive in the US because of economic and religious freedom. The labor demands in the 1700s led to the transportation of Africans to the US. The early years of our country's history involved the inhumane transportation of hundreds of thousands of Africans who were taken from their native homes and families. For hundreds of years, the lives of African Americans included slavery and service. African immigrants had limited access to education and basic resources such as health care.

The economic, social, and political opportunities of many voluntary immigrants were not available for the African immigrant population in the 1700s and 1800s (Ogbu, 1995). Historians believe that for many African Americans, their

cultural frame of reference
A way of viewing the world based upon one's life experiences, culture, and history.

marco cultural de referencia
Manera de ver el mundo basada en las experiencias, cultura e historia personales.

Bureau of Indian Affairs (BIA)
An organization responsible for making changes in American Indian education. The BIA is a group responsible for the administration and management of 55.7 million acres of land held in trust by the US for American Indians, Indian tribes, and Alaska Natives.

Comité de asuntos de habitantes nativos
Organización responsable de hacer cambios en la educación de los habitantes nativos. El BIA, según sus siglas en inglés, es el grupo a cargo de administrar y manejar los 55.7 millones de acres mantenidos por los Estados Unidos que pertenecen a los habitantes nativos, tribus indígenas y nativos de Alaska.

Office of Indian Affairs (OIA)
An organization whose goal was to promote federal laws in the 1970s and 1980s that supported educational programs that were developed, monitored, and operated by American Indian communities.

Oficina de asuntos de habitantes nativos
Organización cuya meta era promover leyes federales en las décadas de los años 70 y 80 que apoyaban programas educativos que desarrollaban, mantenían y operaban comunidades de habitantes nativos.

histories in the US have created a **cultural frame of reference**, or way of viewing the world, that is quite different from groups who came to the US voluntarily (Spring, 2006). A number of present-day researchers believe that the unequal experiences of early African Americans are still in place within American culture today and continue to affect the education of African American children (Spring, 2006).

An important exception to the idea of America as a country of immigrants is seen in the history of the American Indians. The American Indians were the first people who lived in North America. They lived untouched by outsiders for thousands of years before European and African immigrants started arriving in the 1400s. The impact of European settlers on American Indians has been far-reaching. European settlers brought with them to the Americas differences in language, religion, and general ways of life. European settlers and ultimately the US government, viewed American Indians as a people to be "civilized" and educated in ways that matched their worldviews. Attempts to change the cultures, languages, and ways of life of American Indians by European immigrants led to divisions that exist to this day. These divisions are still hotly debated by educators and policy makers (Spring, 2006).

In the 1960s many people from across the nation were concerned about how American Indians had been treated throughout the history of the United States. Groups of people met to take action to improve the quality of education for American Indian students. In 1974 the **Bureau of Indian Affairs (BIA)** became a strong leader in making changes in American Indian education. The BIA is a group responsible for the administration and management of 55.7 million acres of land held in trust by the United States for American Indians, Indian tribes, and Alaska Natives. In 1974 the BIA set up policies and procedures designed to protect the legal rights of American Indian students. The work of BIA members and others created a federal **Office of Indian Affairs**, whose goal was to set up federal laws. In the 1970s and 1980s, programs for American Indians were created, checked, and operated by American Indian communities (Spring, 2006). For more information on the BIA, go to the Department of the Interior website (http://www.doi.gov) and click on Bureau of Indian Affairs.

The actions of the BIA show how options for diverse educational opportunities can be given to different groups of students. Private schools, including religious schools, are other examples of schools that improve the school experience of students looking for options besides traditional public education. Some people believe that today's **charter schools** give choices that have never existed before in public education. Charter schools are often independent and have state-funded programs that give families more choices in education. Recent changes in government, business, and political leadership have made the concept and the use of charter schools a new option in American education.

United States history helps us understand how the past influences current-day practices in education. Our review of immigration and the alternatives to public schools in the US are just two examples of the events that have changed education in our country. Just like in the past, world, national, and local events in the twenty-first century will affect the lives of future students and educators alike. The question we must also ask is, how do all of these world events influence what happens in everyday classrooms?

charter schools
Schools that exist as independent and state funded programs that operate as alternatives to public education.

escuelas de carta y estatuto o escuelas charter
Escuelas que existen en forma y con programas independientes subvencionados con fondos estatales; funcionan como alternativas a la educación pública.

Dear Maria,

I tried to find you after school today, but you'd already left the building. I thought an e-mail would be quicker than trying to find you tomorrow morning. OK, so here's my question. I need your help trying to figure out a problem I'm having in my classroom. I thought it would be a fun idea to do some projects with the students about Christmas holidays around the world. I talked to my classroom teacher and she said that we can't start lessons on our own without looking at what the state says we can teach. She also said that we have to make sure the books we read are on an approved book list from the school board. I can't figure out who is in charge of what! Did you know about all these rules? Do you know what the school board does and why do they get to make all of the decisions?

Tracy

Hi Tracy,

I had the same thing happening in my classroom a couple of years ago. We were going to do a lesson in our science class on how the earth was formed, and we were going to talk about when people first showed up on earth. We planned to use some really fun books my classroom teacher found on prehistoric people. The books were really exciting and we were going to take the kids on field trips and talk about different views on how the earth was formed. Little did we know what a big deal this was going to be! We had to look at the topics the state said we could teach, we had to see which books we could use, and we even had to tell parents and our administrator if we wanted to use books that weren't on the book lists. I couldn't believe all the people who had to get involved! All we wanted to do was read some new books and do activities we thought the kids would like.

Maria

Maria,

Thanks for your answer. It's hard to believe you had to do all that checking just to teach some lessons with your classroom teacher! I can't believe how many people get to decide what we do in the classroom. I keep hearing about all the state rules and district reports, not to mention the memos I get each week from the principal and my classroom teacher on different policies and decisions from the state office of education. It's really hard to keep track of everything and of all the people who make decisions. I guess we need to keep up on all of this information, but some days it's too much!

Tracy

Like Tracy and Maria, two students in a paraprofessional program, you may have questions about the things that affect how schools operate. You may wonder who makes the decisions, and have questions about why certain decisions are made.

Like Maria and Tracy, it's important for educators to know how policies and decisions are made. The first steps in understanding how decisions in schools are made include studying the history of education, understanding why certain topics are included in schools, and looking at how schools are run. Let's look at a few examples of how history in the United States has influenced the work of today's educators.

THE IMPACT OF HISTORY ON EDUCATION

People who work in classrooms and schools may wonder if history has affected what goes on in schools today. A number of educators believe that what takes place in US schools today is based on the ideas of people who lived more than two hundred years ago. Those who study history tell us that early European immigrants believed that certain people should be educated and that certain types of schools should exist. In the early years of American history, only the male children of white landowners were educated. Females, minorities, and the poor were not educated (Spring, 2006). At other times in American history, schools helped some students develop job skills to work as laborers, while others students went to schools that would prepare them for college. In fact, there are a number of practices in today's schools that were originally affected by ways of life in the nineteenth and twentieth centuries. Curriculum choices and the way schools are organized are the result of our country's past. Let's take a look at the impact of America's history on curriculum development and how grade levels in schools came to be.

THE PURPOSES OF THE CURRICULUM

Many people believe the reason children attend school is to prepare for the future. Preparing children for the future is important. The problem is there are many different beliefs about what an education should include. The **curriculum**, or what is studied in school, is like a road map or guide that helps teachers know the exact content they are required to teach their students. Some people believe the curriculum from kindergarten through high school should prepare students for future jobs. Other people believe the curriculum should teach bigger lessons about life and not just job skills. Be aware that there are many different ideas on how schools should educate students. Decision makers also think about what to teach students. Not only does the curriculum need to be important and related to students, it needs to meet the needs of *all* students.

Every few years administrators, educators, and parents—and, in some cases, students—meet to make curriculum decisions. These people make sure that the topics studied in schools are correct and cover many different viewpoints. As you might imagine, people from different walks of life have different views on how schools should run and what should be taught—a person in business might have a view of education that is very different from the view of an artist.

curriculum
The course of study defined by local and national decision makers which includes specific skills, values, and attitudes identified as important by local and national communities.

currículo
Plan de estudios determinado por las personas que toman decisiones a nivel local y nacional que incluye habilidades, valores y actitudes éspecíficos consideradas importantes por las comunidades locales y nacionales.

Among all of the topics studied in schools, religion has played a very important role in American education. Because many American immigrants arrived as religious and political refugees, they hoped life in a new country would give them the freedoms they felt they did not have in their home countries. For this reason, religion was a strong part of early public education. People in that time believed that if students could read religious books they would be protected from the evils in the world (Kauchak & Eggen, 2005). Many communities also believed that they should decide who would be eligible to teach (Kauchak & Eggen, 2005). By deciding who could teach and deciding what could be taught in schools, early settlers believed that religion would be included as a part of the education of all children. The important point to remember is that even when the curriculum matches the goals of a community, it must also match the rules of the US Constitution. In Chapter 5 we will discuss the legal issues related to the curriculum, particularly that of religion in public schools.

The curriculum in today's schools provides students with information on the world around them.

The study of religion is just one example of the influence of history on what is studied in American education. To this day, our nation's focus on studies of patriotism, civics, immigration, and economics is part of life in the classroom. The Pledge of Allegiance, civics classes, and even character education programs are present-day programs that help build citizenship in America's schoolchildren.

Just like curriculum decisions, the way schools are set up is also influenced by what has happened in the past. Let's take a look at how people decide what our schools will look like and how the content will differ from grade to grade.

The goals of public education include providing students with a broad education, preparing them for the world of work, and teaching them about the history of the United States. This classroom's flag reflects a tribute to patriotism.

The Development of Grade Levels in Public Education

For a moment, think about the school you are working in. Have you ever wondered why grade levels exist as they are? Maybe you have had questions about why some schools include grades K-5 and others 6–9. Just like the ways in which history has affected curriculum choices in schools, grade levels in today's schools are influenced by social and economic events in American history.

If you have worked in a public school, you are aware that students of different ages are in different grade levels. While it may seem obvious that these grade levels are based on learning abilities, interests, and overall development, there may be other reasons why grade levels exist as they do. In the 1800s leaders believed it was good for the community for children to be educated in the same areas of study. Leaders believed that education prepared children for important decision making related to leadership, jobs, and strong communities. In order to prepare well-educated students, the leaders believed that schools should focus on the different needs of children. Early leaders often thought that groups of children would follow certain pathways in their lives; some would be laborers, some farmers, and some professionals. In those days, students were chosen early, based on their potential, and they were given a certain type of education that educators believed would be best for their life goals. High schools were created for those students who were believed to have greater abilities and potential for college. Children who would work as laborers attended vocational schools where they learned a specific trade or skill. This view of learners led to students being divided into different types of schools based upon grades. What do you think of the idea of deciding the future of a student when he or she is in the early elementary grades? Should the curriculum be different for some students and not others? Many educators believed, and still believe, that tracking students through school in their early years may limit their future potential. Chapter 7 will include additional information on how teachers adapt their teaching and testing practices to their students' needs.

As our nation changed and the needs of the work force changed, views on education also changed. While students in the 1800s were often tracked into certain kinds of schools, the type of schools students attended also changed. In time, more children began attending public schools. Leaders realized that a basic form of education was needed for *all* students (Kauchak & Eggen, 2005). As a result, public education changed the type of children that were educated. Public education was expected to prepare all children with the chance for success after high school. To meet this goal, different grade levels were created, based upon standards and on the developmental needs and abilities of students. Elementary, middle, and high schools were formed to meet student needs.

The Education of Young Children

The education provided for children in the early grades (typically, kindergarten through grade 5) often includes basic skill development in content areas such as reading, writing, mathematics, and science. Children also learn basic socialization skills and participate in activities involving movement and hands-on work. Early childhood and elementary education programs focus on the developmental needs of children at their age (Kauchak & Eggen, 2005).

Grade levels in American schools are designed to meet the developmental needs of children. This student is involved in a hands-on activity common in many early grade elementary classrooms.

Middle Level Education

Junior high schools and middle schools were developed to meet the needs of the public work force. In the early nineteenth century Americans became dependent on specialized skills related to automation and more complicated work. Schools responded by including special skill training and content as part of the junior high school curriculum. Like their name implies, junior high schools are designed to prepare children for the more content-focused environment of a high school. In time, some educators believed that junior high schools were placing too much focus on content areas too early in a child's life. As a result, middle schools came about in the mid-1900s. The middle school philosophy pays more attention to the emotional, social, and intellectual changes that take place in the lives of adolescents. While content is certainly an important part of middle schools, the developmental needs of students in grades 6–8 are the focus of middle level education (Kauchak & Eggen, 2005).

High School Education

American high schools have existed for many reasons. In the eighteenth and nineteenth centuries, some high schools focused on training students for specific vocations or trades. Others prepared students for specialized studies in colleges and universities.

The problem with some of these early high schools was that groups of students were tracked into programs based upon qualities such as their English skills, their socioeconomic status, or their family history of college attendance. Today, high schools are designed to meet a range of students' needs and deliberate tracking is less common, although critics believe that the curriculum in many high schools is still meant to track students into different career directions (Kauchak & Eggen, 2005).

To this day, educators think hard about how to provide *all* children with an appropriate education. Educators believe that certain groups of students find greater success in the American school system than others. Educators still think about ways of making education equal for all students. What do you think? Are there students in your school who seem to fit into the system better than others? In what ways do they find more success than their classmates? What are some of the current trends in America that will likely affect the policies and procedures of the future?

THE GOVERNANCE STRUCTURES OF AMERICAN SCHOOLS

The public school system in the United States is made up of groups who work together to serve students and their families, in addition to the classroom teachers and administrators at your school. There are others who make decisions about what goes on in schools. State and national decision makers influence the policies and procedures. They decide how schools will operate, they figure out budget and finance information, and they make decisions about curriculum and assessment. If you're like Maria and Tracy, sometimes you feel confused by all the changes in education. Maria and Tracy feel pressured sometimes by all the information they receive, not only from people at their schools, but also from people all over their state and around the whole nation. To understand how decisions are made in schools, it's helpful to know who participates in decision making.

School leaders oversee the daily demands of a school, including organizing the physical space, managing a budget, and hiring teachers and staff. Other leaders guide and direct the larger goals of public education. Table 1-1, "Governance and Leadership in American Schools," lists all the groups involved in education in your school community. Federal, state, and local leaders each play important roles in running schools. Let's take a look at the work involved at each of these levels.

The work of the **federal government** in the US is influenced by the country's Constitution and the Tenth Amendment. The federal government includes leaders from the presidency, the Congress, and the courts. The Tenth Amendment states that the federal government is responsible for the education of citizens in each of the fifty states (Kauchak & Eggan, 2005).

The legislation associated with the **No Child Left Behind Act (NCLB)** is an example of the way in which laws through the federal government influence what teachers and paraprofessionals do in today's schools. While the federal government has to follow rules and laws that allow states to make their own decisions, states and local school districts must meet certain federal standards in order to receive specific types of funding. For example, if the federal government

---

federal government
National leaders who develop and ensure the implementation of laws and policies related to education.

gobierno federal
Líderes nacionales que desarrollan y aseguran la puesta en práctica de leyes y regulaciones relacionadas con la educación.

No Child Left Behind Act (NCLB)
Federal legislation that addresses the standards of students, teachers, and paraprofessionals working in the public school system.

"Que ningún niño se quede atrás" (NCLB)
Nombre dado a la legislación federal que trata de los estándares de estudiantes, profesores y paraprofesionales que trabajan en el sistema escolar público.

TABLE 1-1 Governance and Leadership in American Schools

Federal Government
State Legislatures and Courts
State Offices of Education
Local School Boards
District Superintendents
District Offices
Principals and School Faculty and Staff
Family and Community Members

The federal government establishes policies that guide the day-to-day operations of schools and classrooms.
© *Steve Maehl*

state level
Legal decision makers who oversee policies and practices within each state.

nivel estatal
Las personas que toman decisiones legales y supervisan reglamentaciones y prácticas dentro de cada estado.

local level
A group of elected citizens who oversee policies and practices within each school district operation.

nivel local
Grupo de ciudadanos elegidos, responsables de supervisar las reglamentaciones y prácticas de cada distrito escolar.

district
An administrative unit that is legally responsible for the public education of children within specific state boundaries.

distrito
Unidad administrativa que es legalmente responsable de la educación pública de los niños dentro de áreas específicas de cada estado.

plans to send money to a state for students in special education programs, the state and districts must agree to spend the money the way the federal government requires. Otherwise, the money will not be sent to the state. The key is that both the federal government and the states must understand who has authority when decisions are made.

At **state** and local levels, leaders have to work together. State law makers and boards of education make decisions about legal issues and how money will be spent on education-related issues. At the **local level**, school boards and administrators are responsible for the education of children within **districts**, or specific areas within communities.

School boards include elected officials from local communities. School boards have authority over district money, hiring, curriculum, students, and the school buildings. School board decisions influence salaries, class size, and the sale of and access to equipment in schools (Kauchak & Eggen, 2005). School principals, teachers, and staff are responsible for putting into action the policies and rules established by people at the federal, state, and local levels. They make sure schools follow federal and state laws. In most cases, principals, teachers, and staff members work together to build communities that best serve the needs of each and every student in their schools.

The influence of state leaders and local educators is powerful, but there are also two key groups we can't forget. Families and community members have the most important influence on the day-to-day education of young people. Chapter 6 will provide additional information on the important roles that family and community have.

THE DAY-TO-DAY WORK OF TEACHERS AND PARAPROFESSIONALS

Schools are often compared to small communities. Like small towns, schools are filled with activity and depend on teachers, students, paraprofessionals, and building staff. With all these people working together, it is understandable that policies and procedures guide activities in schools. For example, national and state standards describe what will be taught at different grade levels. In addition, each state sets professional standards for the teachers and paraprofessionals responsible for teaching the curriculum. It is important for teachers and paraprofessionals to understand job expectations for them and the standards for evaluating their work. Let's examine the qualifications of paraprofessionals in more detail.

Paraprofessionals and Their Work

The main responsibility of many paraprofessionals is to work with a mentor or classroom teacher. Paraprofessionals are asked to complete a number of different kinds of assignments on their own. The policies and laws that guide the work of educators are complex. You will learn more about legal issues in Chapter 5, but the number one rule to keep in mind is that policies and procedures are in place to provide students with the best educational experience possible. As a paraprofessional, there are clear expectations and guidelines regarding your work responsibilities. For example, paraprofessionals may:

1. work one-to-one with students providing tutorial help,
2. teach small groups of students, and/or
3. be involved in assisting with lesson planning and assessment.

These job responsibilities are important and give paraprofessionals a set of guidelines for their work. At times though, these guidelines are not always clear. In a recent lunchroom conversation, Maria and Tracy talked about the questions they have about their job responsibilities. Sometimes they feel unsure about what they can and cannot do as part of their jobs. How will you find out about the job responsibilities you have at your school?

DAY-TO-DAY DILEMMA
HOW WOULD YOU HANDLE THIS SITUATION?

Tracy: Maria, I need your advice. My classroom teacher asked me to help her make a lesson on oceans and teach it to our students next week. She wants me to make up a quiz to see if the students have learned what we've taught them. I'm not sure how much I'm supposed to help in creating lessons and tests. I have a lot of good ideas, but I want to make sure I'm doing what I should do. At a workshop I went to at the district, the personnel director gave us a list of our job responsibilities and also advised us on how to work with our classroom teachers. She said if we have questions, we should ask our classroom teacher about our job responsibilities. So, should I help the teacher on the lesson and quiz?

Maria: I know there are some parts of teaching and testing that we can help with, but there are other areas where we aren't trained. I know that I'm no expert on lesson planning for sure. Maybe she just wants you to listen to her ideas. Why don't you talk to her some more and find out exactly what she wants? You know a lot and maybe she's just interested in your ideas. In my classroom, my teacher just likes to tell me about her ideas and we work on her plans together. So, ask her and see what she says.

paraeducators
Paraeducators or paraprofessionals are educators who work under the guidance of classroom teachers to provide students with exceptionalities and language needs with the support to succeed in the classroom.

paraeducadores
Paraeducadores o paraprofesionales son educadores que trabajan bajo la supervisión de los maestros de clase para dar apoyo a los estudiantes con excepcionalidades y necesidades lingüísticas para que tengan éxito en el aula.

In 2005, the National Center for Educational Statistics (NCES) identified a number of job titles that help describe the different types of work completed by paraprofessionals, also known as **paraeducators**. According to NCES, a paraprofessional works with classroom teachers in the following ways:

assistant counselor

behavior tracker

bilingual aide

bilingual special education aide

career aide

child care giver

computer aide

extracurricular activity aide

financial aide specialist

library aide

media center aide

psychologist assistant

teaching assistant

teaching/classroom aide

tutor

As members of educational teams, paraprofessionals play important roles in today's classrooms.

As you can see, the responsibilities of paraprofessionals include a number of job duties. Under each of these job descriptions, paraprofessionals provide academic and language support, emotional and social support, and individual career development. Remember that the type of work you will be asked to complete is based upon the responsibilities of your job title. The National Resource Center for Paraprofessionals (2005) lists the work of paraprofessionals in three general areas: Levels I, II, and III. In this book we discuss the Level I responsibilities. Let's look at the specifics duties of Level I paraprofessionals. Level I job responsibilities include:

1. working with small groups of students in activities developed by teachers;
2. carrying out behavior management and discipline plans developed by teachers;
3. helping teachers with general lessons and assessment activities;
4. keeping track of information about student performance, so teachers can plan curriculum and learning activities accordingly;
5. helping teachers organize learning activities in supportive ways;
6. doing general clerical work related to copying, supervision, inventory; and
7. assisting teachers in involving parents/caregivers in their child's education.

As you can tell, the responsibilities of paraprofessionals include many important areas. However, there are also limitations to the kind of work in which paraprofessionals may be involved. Just like Tracy mentioned, there are areas where paraprofessionals must work under the direct guidance of the classroom teacher. The following descriptions are areas which are *not* part of the job descriptions of paraeducators. They may not:

1. diagnose learner needs;
2. meet with teachers or others to plan individualized/personalized programs for learners;
3. create and maintain learner-centered environments;
4. match curriculum with teaching strategies without the leadership of a classroom teacher;
5. plan lessons;
6. make changes in the content and lesson strategies that the classroom teacher has prepared;
7. test and decide whether students have actually learned content; and
8. involve parents or caregivers in all aspects of their child's education without the guidance of the classroom teacher.

There are clear limits to paraprofessionals' work. Based upon our list, you probably still have questions about areas where there is crossover between your work as a paraprofessional and the work of a classroom teacher. To answer your questions, make sure that you talk to your classroom teacher. She/he will help you figure out your roles and responsibilities, so that the expectations of your work are clear. Your classroom teacher and district human resource director can give you more information if you have questions about your job duties. In

accountability standards
Policies that ensure that students in public schools are being served by the most qualified personnel.

estándares de confiabilidad
Regulaciones que aseguran que los estudiantes de las escuelas públicas estén a cargo del personal mejor capacitado.

portfolio
A collection of work samples that showcase one's work.

carpeta
Colección de muestras de trabajo que demuestran el desempeño de una persona.

artifacts
Sample work products that demonstrate your work as a paraprofessional.

documentos
Productos de muestra que sirven como prueba del trabajo de un paraprofesional.

Chapter 2 you will learn more about the professional requirements for paraprofessionals under NCLB.

Chapter 6, on effective communication, will also help you develop questions for your classroom teacher and a plan for talking to him or her about your responsibilities in a way that will be best for the students in your classroom.

Paraprofessionals and Accountability

As a paraprofessional, it is important to understand the requirements of your job. It is also important to know how you'll be evaluated. All members of the educational community are subject to **accountability standards**. Accountability standards are policies that make sure that students in public schools are being served by qualified personnel. Paraprofessionals are no exception. Paraprofessionals must have abilities in reading, math, and writing and know how to use these skills and knowledge in classroom instruction. A popular way of evaluating work is through professional **portfolios**. A portfolio is a book where you can organize all your materials on teaching and working with children and families. A portfolio is also a place to showcase your work through **artifacts**, or pieces of work that show what you know about the work you do. Creating a professional portfolio is a way of developing as a paraprofessional. Portfolios are just one way of meeting the standards for paraprofessionals. Other ways of meeting the standards are through exams or the completion of courses. You will learn more about preparing for the exams and professional development expectations for paraprofessionals in Chapters 2 and 8.

SUMMARY

Most organizations are complex and have many layers. The education system in the US is no different. Public education depends on the help of many people and is based on the history, culture, and traditions of our country. The way schools are run, the goals of society, and the economic, political, and social events in the country's history each play a part in today's educational system. This chapter reviewed the effects of our nation's past on areas such as the curriculum in schools and grade level breakdowns. We also discussed the jobs of many different people in making schools run. Like all educators, paraprofessionals are an important part of this complex system. This chapter highlighted just some of the ways paraprofessionals participate in the system we call public education.

CHECKING FOR UNDERSTANDING

1. List the ways in which American history has affected some of the current practices in public education.
2. Who is in charge of decision making in American public education?
3. How would you explain your role as a paraprofessional to a friend who does not work in education? What do you enjoy most about your work? Why?

POINTS OF VIEW

Working with their classroom teachers and talking with other educators in their school helped Maria and Tracy learn more about the structure of American schools. Think about the people in your school who can share with you their knowledge about educational issues.

1. Find out who works in your school and ask them about the roles they have there. You will be amazed by all the different people who work together to make a school community run! Of course, there are the principal and the assistant principal. These people are the administrators who work closely with both the teachers in their school and the district leaders. Staff members at your school include secretaries, cafeteria workers, custodians, and transportation assistants. Special service providers include the librarian (sometimes called the media specialist), the special education teacher, and in some schools speech therapists and reading specialists.

2. Review your school's handbooks for teachers and students. Pay close attention to the policies and procedures for conduct, dress, and professional expectations.

3. In addition to the general information handbook found at your school, pay close attention to the policies related to safety issues and contact with students and parents. This will prove to be useful information about your rights and also about the procedures for appeal if you feel your professional rights have been violated. Check with the administrative assistant or building principal at your school for a copy of the school handbook and personnel regulations.

PORTFOLIO CORNER

As we noted at the beginning of this chapter, you will be asked to gather a number of artifacts, or sample products, to show your abilities as a paraprofessional. One of your responsibilities will be to gather these artifacts in a portfolio as a way of showcasing all your hard work. The portfolio framework used throughout this book is based upon the guidelines established for paraprofessionals under the 2001 law we've already talked about. The NCLB, as it is often referred to, is a law that addresses standards of performance for students, teachers, and paraprofessionals working in the public school system. You will learn more about the NCLB in Chapter 2. Chapter 8 will include more information on the ways in which your work as a paraprofessional will be evaluated by your classroom teacher, your building principal, and perhaps the human resources director in your district.

Table 1-2, "Portfolio Framework," describes four standards for measuring the paraprofessional's qualifications. These standards are based on the NCLB criteria for highly qualified paraprofessionals. The standards measure a paraprofessional's ability to (1) provide support for instructional opportunities within a classroom setting; (2) demonstrate professional and ethical practice; (3) demonstrate an ability to provide a supportive learning environment; and (4) demonstrate an ability to communicate effectively and participate in the

TABLE 1-2 Portfolio Framework

STANDARD I— SUPPORTING INSTRUCTIONAL OPPORTUNITIES	STANDARD II— DEMONSTRATING PROFESSIONALISM AND ETHICAL PRACTICE
a. Have knowledge of and proficiency in basic reading/writing readiness. b. Have knowledge of and proficiency in basic writing/writing readiness. c. Have knowledge of and proficiency in math/math readiness. d. Have knowledge of strategies, techniques, and delivery methods of instruction. e. Assist in delivering instruction according to teacher/provider lesson plans. f. Demonstrate the ability to record relevant information about learners to assist in the learning process. g. Organize and prepare materials to support learning and the teaching process.	a. Have knowledge of and adhere to the distinctions in the roles and responsibilities of teachers/providers, paraprofessionals, families, and other team members. b. Carry out responsibilities in a manner consistent with all pertinent laws, regulations, policies, and procedures.
STANDARD III— SUPPORTING A POSITIVE LEARNING ENVIRONMENT	**STANDARD IV— COMMUNICATING EFFECTIVELY AND PARTICIPATING IN THE TEAM PROCESS**
a. Use proactive management strategies to engage learners. b. Support the teacher's behavior management plan.	a. Serve as a member of an instructional team. b. Use effective communication skills (written, verbal, and nonverbal).

team process. It is important to note that these standards are quite similar to the standards to which licensed teachers must submit.

Chapter 1 provided an introduction to Standards II and IV of the professionals standards for paraprofessionals. The standards include: Demonstrating Professionalism, Ethical Practice, and Communicating Effectively and Participating in the Teaching Process. Table 1-2, "Portfolio Framework," is based upon the Praxis guidelines for highly qualified paraprofessionals. The framework is divided into the following four categories.

ARTIFACT SUGGESTIONS

Use the following questions as a guide in choosing some of the artifacts you will use to show your knowledge of the structure of schools.

1. Clip a notice or find an advertisement of an upcoming school board meeting in your community. What are the major themes for discussion?

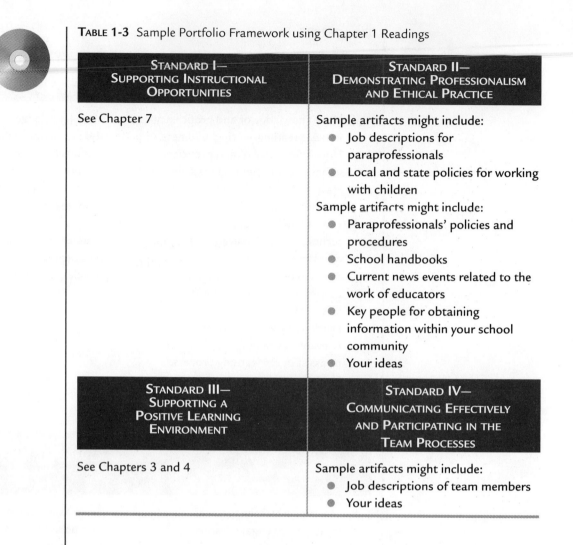

TABLE 1-3 Sample Portfolio Framework using Chapter 1 Readings

STANDARD I— SUPPORTING INSTRUCTIONAL OPPORTUNITIES	STANDARD II— DEMONSTRATING PROFESSIONALISM AND ETHICAL PRACTICE
See Chapter 7	Sample artifacts might include: <ul><li>Job descriptions for paraprofessionals</li><li>Local and state policies for working with children</li></ul> Sample artifacts might include: <ul><li>Paraprofessionals' policies and procedures</li><li>School handbooks</li><li>Current news events related to the work of educators</li><li>Key people for obtaining information within your school community</li><li>Your ideas</li></ul>
STANDARD III— SUPPORTING A POSITIVE LEARNING ENVIRONMENT	**STANDARD IV— COMMUNICATING EFFECTIVELY AND PARTICIPATING IN THE TEAM PROCESSES**
See Chapters 3 and 4	Sample artifacts might include: <ul><li>Job descriptions of team members</li><li>Your ideas</li></ul>

2. Find 2–3 news stories that show the role of the federal and state government in setting policies for schools using as sources your local television, radio, newspaper, and school or community council meetings. Which news story is the most important to you? Why?

3. Identify the people at your school who will help you learn more about decision making and policies. Identify 2–3 questions you might ask about how decisions are made at your school. List your questions below:

   a. _____

   b. _____

   c. _____

4. List the artifacts you have identified in the worksheet listed on the Sample Portfolio Framework.

   Table 1-3, Sample Portfolio Framework, includes sample artifacts that will meet Standards II and IV, based on the discussions in Chapter 1. Write down any additional artifacts you might want to include.

REFERENCES

Department of the Interior. (2006). Click on Bureau of Indian Affairs. Retrieved June 14, 2007 from http://www.doi.gov.

Kauchak, D., & Eggen, P. (2005). *Introduction to teaching: Becoming a professional* (2nd ed.). Upper Saddle River, New Jersey: Merrill Prentice Hall.

National Resources Center for Paraprofessionals. (2005). *The employment and preparation of paraeducators, the state of the art—2002.* Retrieved July 12, 2006 from http://www.nrcpara.org.

Ogbu, J. (1995). Understanding cultural diversity and learning. In J. Banks & C. Banks (Eds.), *The Handbook of Research on Multicultural Education.* New York: Macmillan Publishing.

Spring, J. (2006). *American Education* (12th ed). San Francisco: McGraw Hill.

Additional selected readings and Paraprofessional electronic resources are available as part of the student Online Companion web site: www.earlychilded.delmar.com.

EN ESPAÑOL

OBJETIVOS DEL APRENDIZAJE

Después de leer y reflexionar sobre este capítulo usted comprenderá mejor

- Las escuelas de los Estados Unidos y su historia
- Cómo están organizadas las escuelas públicas
- Las responsabilidades de los paraprofesionales en las escuelas de hoy
- El proceso de la toma de decisiones en las escuelas públicas

A medida que usted lea este capítulo, hágase las siguientes preguntas:

1. ¿Cómo se toman las decisiones sobre regulaciones y procedimientos escolares?
2. ¿Quién decide qué enseñar y cómo enseñarlo?
3. ¿Cómo encaja su función como paraprofesional en el sistema educativo?
4. ¿Qué tipo de **documentos** incluirá en su **carpeta** para demostrar su conocimiento de la comunidad educativa?

PARA VERIFICAR LA COMPRENSIÓN

1. Describa las formas en que la historia de los EE.UU. ha afectado las prácticas actuales en la educación pública.
2. ¿Quién está a cargo de la toma de decisiones en la educación pública de los EE.UU?
3. ¿Cómo le explicaría su función como paraprofesional a un amigo o amiga que no trabajara en la rama educativa? ¿Qué es lo que más disfruta de su trabajo? ¿Por qué?

PUNTOS DE VISTA

Maria y Tracy han aprendido más acerca de la estructura de las escuelas de los EE.UU. a través del trabajo que realizan con los maestros de sus clases y las charlas que tienen con otros educadores de sus escuelas. Piense en personas de su escuela que puedan compartir con usted sus conocimientos sobre temas relacionados con la educación.

1. Averigüe quiénes trabajan en su escuela y pregúnteles cuáles son sus funciones. ¡Le sorprenderá la diversidad de personas que colaboran para que funcione la comunidad escolar! Por supuesto, están el director y el director auxiliar. Estas personas son los **administradores** que trabajan de cerca con los maestros de la escuela así también como con el personal del **distrito**. Entre los miembros del personal de la escuela se incluyen secretarias, empleados de la cafetería, conserjes y asistentes transportistas. Los proveedores de servicios especiales incluyen al bibliotecario, a veces llamado el especialista en medios, al profesor de educación

---

documentos
Productos de muestra que sirven como prueba del trabajo de un paraprofesional.

artifacts
Sample work products that demonstrate your work as a paraprofessional.

---

carpeta
Colección de muestras de trabajo que demuestran el desempeño de una persona.

portfolio
A collection of work samples that showcase one's work.

---

administradores
Personal del distrito escolar que supervisa el trabajo de los maestros, del personal, y de los estudiantes en los distritos y las escuelas.

administrators
School district personnel who oversee the work of the teachers, staff, and students within districts and schools.

---

distrito
Unidad administrativa que es legalmente responsable de la educación pública de los niños dentro de áreas específicas de cada estado.

district
An administrative unit that is legally responsible for the public education of children within specific state boundaries.

especial, y, en algunas escuelas, a terapistas del habla y a especialistas de lectura.

2. Repase los manuales de la escuela para maestros y para alumnos. Preste atención a las reglas y a los procedimientos en cuanto a conducta, vestimenta, y expectativas profesionales.

3. Además del manual de información general de su escuela, preste mucha atención a los reglamentos relacionados con cuestiones de seguridad y los contactos con los alumnos y sus padres. El saber esta información lo pondrá al tanto de sus derechos así también como de los procedimientos de apelación en caso de que sus derechos como profesional hayan sido transgredidos. Pregunte al asistente administrativo o al director de su escuela si hay un ejemplar disponible del manual de la escuela y del reglamento para el personal.

PARA LA CARPETA

Como observamos al principio de este capítulo, le pedirán que presente una variedad de documentos, ideas o productos de muestra, que pongan en evidencia su habilidad como paraprofesional. Una de sus responsabilidades será organizar estos documentos en una carpeta para demostrar el arduo trabajo realizado. La estructura de carpeta modelo que presentamos está basada en las pautas establecidas para paraprofesionales por la ley **"Que ningún niño se quede atrás"** del año 2001. Esta ley llamada en inglés *No Child Left Behind Act* o, según sus siglas, NCLB, trata de estándares de funcionamiento para los alumnos, maestros y paraprofesionales del sistema escolar público. Veremos más sobre esta ley en el Capítulo 2. En el Capítulo 8 encontrará información adicional sobre cómo su trabajo de paraprofesional será evaluado por el maestro de clase, el director de la escuela y tal vez el director de recursos humanos del distrito.

La tabla 1-1, Estructura de la carpeta, presenta una descripción de cuatro estándares para evaluar las calificaciones de los paraprofesionales. Estos estándares están basados en los criterios de NCLB para paraprofesionales altamente calificados.

Los estándares miden la habilidad de un paraprofesional para: (1) apoyar toda oportunidad educativa en el entorno del salón de clases; (2) demostrar una conducta profesional y ética; (3) demostrar habilidad para ofrecer un ambiente conducente al aprendizaje; y (4) demostrar destreza para comunicarse eficazmente y participar en el proceso de equipo. Es importante observar que estos estándares son bastante similares a los estándares a los que deben ajustarse los maestros licenciados.

El Capítulo 1 ofrece una introducción al Estándar II de los estándares profesionales para los paraprofesionales: demostrar una conducta profesional y ética, y al Estándar IV: comunicarse eficazmente y participar en el proceso de equipo. La tabla 1-1, Estructura de la carpeta, está basada en las pautas Praxis para los paraprofesionales altamente calificados. La tabla está dividida en cuatro categorías.

"Que ningún niño se quede atrás" (NCLB)
Nombre dado a la legislación federal que trata de los estándares de estudiantes, profesores, y paraprofesionales que trabajan en el sistema escolar público.

No Child Left Behind Act (NCLB)
Federal legislation that addresses the standards or students, teachers, and paraprofessionals working in the public school system.

TABLA 1-2 Estructura de la carpeta

ESTÁNDAR I—APOYAR TODA OPORTUNIDAD EDUCATIVA	ESTÁNDAR II—DEMOSTRAR UNA CONDUCTA PROFESIONAL Y ÉTICA
a. Tener conocimientos y habilidad en el alistamiento básico lectura/escritura. b. Tener conocimientos y habilidad en el alistamiento básico escritura/escritura. c. Tener conocimientos y habilidad en el alistamiento básico matemáticas/matemáticas. d. Tener conocimientos de estrategias, técnicas y métodos de enseñanza e instrucción. e. Ayudar a impartir la instrucción de acuerdo al plan de lección del maestro/educador. f. Demostrar capacidad para asentar información relevante sobre los educandos para asistir en el proceso de aprendizaje. g. Organizar y preparar materiales para apoyar el aprendizaje y el proceso educativo.	a. Tener conocimientos y aceptar las distinciones en las funciones y responsabilidades de los maestros/educadores paraprofesionales, familias y otros miembros del equipo educativo. b. Cumplir con las responsabilidades de acuerdo a todas las leyes, reglamentos, políticas y procedimientos pertinentes.
ESTÁNDAR III—APOYAR UN AMBIENTE CONDUCENTE AL APRENDIZAJE	ESTÁNDAR IV—COMUNICARSE EFICAZMENTE Y PARTICIPAR EN EL PROCESO DE EQUIPO
a. Utilizar estrategias de conducción pro-activas para atraer a los educandos. b. Apoyar el plan de control de conducta del maestro.	a. Servir como miembro de un equipo educativo. b. Utilizar destrezas de comunicación (escrita, verbal y no verbal) efectivas.

Juntas escolares
Funcionarios localmente elegidos que determinan reglamentos y procedimientos dentro de un distrito.

school boards
Locally elected officials who determine policies and procedures within a district.

gobierno federal
Líderes nacionales que desarrollan y aseguran la puesta en práctica de leyes y regulaciones relacionadas con la educación.

federal government
National leaders who develop and ensure the implementation of laws and policies related to education.

SUGERENCIAS PARA LOS DOCUMENTOS DE LA CARPETA

Las siguientes preguntas pueden servirle de guía para identificar algunos de los objetos o ideas que utilizará para demostrar su conocimiento de la estructura escolar.

1. Guarde un aviso o un anuncio de una futura reunión de la **Junta escolar** de su comunidad. ¿Cuáles serán los temas principales de discusión?

2. Basándose en el periódico, las estaciones de radio y televisión locales y las sesiones de la Junta escolar o el Consejo de la comunidad, identifique dos o tres noticias que ilustren el papel del **gobierno federal** y estatal

en el establecimiento de reglamentos escolares. ¿Qué noticia le pareció más importante? ¿Por qué?

3. Identifique a las personas de su escuela que lo o la puedan ayudar a aprender más sobre la toma de decisiones y adopción de reglamentos. Piense en dos o tres preguntas que pueda hacer sobre cómo se toman decisiones en su escuela. Escriba las preguntas abajo:

a. _____

b. _____

c. _____

4. Haga una lista de los documentos identificados en la hoja de trabajo incluida en la Estructura modelo de carpeta.

La tabla 1-2, Estructura modelo de carpeta, incluye documentos de muestra relacionados con los estándares II y IV tratados en el Capítulo 1. Agregue cualquier otro documento que quiera incluir.

TABLA 1-3 Estructura modelo de carpeta

ESTÁNDAR I— APOYAR TODA OPORTUNIDAD EDUCATIVA	ESTÁNDAR II— DEMOSTRAR UNA CONDUCTA PROFESIONAL Y ÉTICA
Vea el Capítulo 7	Los documentos de muestra pueden incluir: • Descripciones de puestos para paraprofesionales. • Reglamentos locales y estatales respecto al trabajo con niños. • Reglamentos y procedimientos para paraprofesionales. • Manuales escolares. • Noticias reales de eventos relacionados con el trabajo de educadores. • Nombres de personas que puedan proveer información dentro de su comunidad escolar. • Sus propias ideas.
ESTÁNDAR III— APOYAR PUN AMBIENTE CONDUCENTE AL APRENDIZAJE	ESTÁNDAR IV— COMUNICARSE EFICAZMENTE Y PARTICIPAR EN EL PROCESO DE EQUIPO
Vea los Capítulos 3 y 4	Los objetos o ideas de muestra pueden incluir: • Descripciones de los puestos de los miembros del equipo. • Sus propias ideas.

NO CHILD LEFT BEHIND AND THE ROLES
OF PARAPROFESSIONALS

CHAPTER OUTLINE

The No Child Left Behind Act

    NCLB and Standardized Assessment

    Educational Assessment—Why the debate?

Measuring Success through Annual Measurable Goals and Adequate Yearly Progress

    Title I Schools

The Impact of the No Child Left Behind Act on Paraprofessionals

Scoring Well on the Praxis Exam

Test Preparation for the Praxis ParaPro Test

    Understanding Question Types

    Preview the Content

    Use Different Strategies

    Practice

    Online Testing

KEY TERMS

achievement gap

Adequate Yearly Progress (AYP)

Annual Measurable Objectives (AMO)

Educational Testing Service (ETS)

LEARNING OBJECTIVES

After reading and reflecting on this chapter you will understand:

- The policies and regulations related to NCLB
- The impact of NCLB on paraprofessionals in today's schools
- The impact of NCLB on the teaching profession

As you read this chapter, ask yourself these questions:

1. What does NCLB say about the standards for highly qualified paraprofessionals?
2. What steps will you take to meet the standards for highly qualified paraprofessionals?
3. How will you prepare to take a test required of paraprofessionals who want to meet the highly qualified standards under NCLB?
4. What kind of artifacts will you include in your portfolio to reflect your knowledge of NCLB?

high stakes testing

No Child Left Behind Act (NCLB)

Praxis ParaPro Test

standardized tests

Title I Schools

Introduction

Changes in the field of education take place for many different reasons. Some changes take place because of movements in politics and business. Other changes take place because of the arrival of new people in existing communities. Today, the changes in education are the result of efforts to improve quality and to make sure that people are accountable for teaching and learning. In 2001, the **No Child Left Behind Act (NCLB)** set up new standards for teachers and others working in schools. At no time in the history of American education has one law had such a dramatic impact on so many different people involved in education (Hardy, 2002). NCLB affects three groups of people: children in schools, people hoping to be teachers, and educators currently working in schools. Specifically, NCLB spells out expectations for the way children perform in school. NCLB guides colleges and universities in preparing future educators, and the law defines expectations for teachers and paraprofessionals.

Tracy and Maria are educators who try to keep up-to-date with the changing policies in their schools. Like Tracy and Maria, you will have questions about laws such as NCLB. In a recent e-mail exchange following a day at work, Maria and Tracy share their feelings about NCLB policies for paraprofessionals.

No Child Left Behind Act (NCLB)
Federal legislation enacted in 2001 that defines standards along three areas: teacher preparation; standardized test performance of children in public schools; and professional development of practicing teachers.

"Que ningún niño se quede atrás"
Legislación federal aprobada en el año 2001 que define estándares en tres áreas: preparación del maestro; rendimiento estandarizado de exámenes para los alumnos de las escuelas públicas; y desarrollo profesional de maestros practicantes.

Day-to-Day Dilemma
How would you handle this situation?

Maria,

Sorry I didn't get back to you this afternoon. I'm so busy these days that I don't even have five minutes to talk with you. E-mail is the only way I can keep up with everything! You said you had some questions about the NCLB flyer we got in our boxes. If you're like me, you feel like there's too much information to keep track of. All the rules, standards, and professional development policies we're supposed to know about are giving me a headache! Don't you get tired of hearing about all this new information? The workshop we went to last week helped me a little, but I still have a ton of questions. What did you think of the meeting?

Tracy

Hi Tracy,

I'll share with you the information I got at the meeting when I see you, but the district workshop leader and your classroom teacher probably are the best people to talk to. I also found this really cool Internet site that has a lot of information. They have information in Spanish too! It's from the US Department of Education. Go to www.ed.gov and you'll find a ton of resources on NCLB and paraprofessionals.

Maria

Maria,

Thanks for your answer. I'll take a look and see what I can find, but getting information on the web is always hard for me. Maybe we could meet after school one day in the library and look at this information with either your classroom teacher or mine. I'm not sure how to keep track of all this stuff.

Tracy

Hi Tracy,

I know what you mean about keeping track of information. I've come up with a system that works pretty well for me. I started keeping a journal list that helps me with information that I need to remember. The journal is also a place where I keep notes and questions that I'll ask my classroom teacher when we have time. Even when I think I'll remember new words, I still have questions. This chart is a good first step to organize all the new information we hear about. Once I write down new terms, the next thing I do is to find out exactly what each of the new words mean. I usually write down the official definition, but then I also write my own definition so I can really remember what the words mean to me. I'll show you my vocabulary journal tomorrow.

See you then.

Maria

Table 2-1, New Information and Vocabulary Journal, helps Maria and Tracy keep track of information on NCLB. Copy the table, and then add any additional terms you find useful.

TABLE 2-1 New Information and Vocabulary Journal

VOCABULARY TERMS	FORMAL DEFINITION	EVERYDAY LANGUAGE DEFINITION
No Child Left Behind (NCLB)		
Adequate Yearly Progress (AYP)		
Annual Measurable Objectives (AMO)		
Standardized Tests		
Title I School		
Educational Testing Service (ETS)		
Praxis Test for Paraprofessionals		

The No Child Left Behind Act

Just like Tracy and Maria, you may wonder about all the new information related to laws and policies in education. As you learned in Chapter 1, governance and leadership in American education are based on the ideas and the histories of a lot of different people. People from political groups, businesses, and communities come together to decide the best way to educate children in American schools. Today, as in the past, people make decisions based on different social, political, and economic events in the world. Just like the laws that came before it, the No Child Left Behind Act of 2001 (Pub. L. 107-110, NCLB) was shaped by political and social events in the 1990s. Let's look at an example. Testing is very common activity in most classrooms. Educators give tests to learn about their students, to evaluate their teaching, and sometimes to respond to the needs of the community. Over time, educators and researchers found that the test scores of children weren't always the same. To address the issue of difference in student performance, political leaders in the 1990s thought that educators should figure out why some students did well on their tests while others did not. They also thought that communities should decide if their educators had adequate training. The result of all these questions was that schools and districts started to pay closer attention to national standards for educators and students. NCLB was created to improve education standards for different groups of people.

As with any law or policy, there are supporters as well as opponents. Since its official beginning in 2002, NCLB has caused a lot of talk about its strengths and weaknesses. Some of the weaknesses of NCLB include not having enough funds to put the policies into practice. Some people believe that there isn't enough money and support available for teachers. They also question whether the testing standards under NCLB are the best way to measure students' learning. Supporters of NCLB believe that testing will be a source of more information and the basis of better standards for new teachers. Whether you are for or against NCLB, the major goal of the law has been to provide all American schoolchildren with opportunities and resources for greater success in school. Let's look at the ways in which NCLB's testing practices take place in many communities.

NCLB and Standardized Assessment

NCLB sets guidelines for teachers and other people working in schools. These guidelines set standards for educators to teach in ways that help all children perform at about the same levels. Right now, there are big differences in how groups of students perform on their **standardized tests**. Standardized tests are types of exams where the scores of one person are compared to a collection of scores from other people who took the same test. The goal of comparing different people's scores is to decide if there are groups of students whose scores show that they have had a weaker education.

Educational Assessment—Why the debate?

Educational assessment is a controversial topic. Supporters of standardized tests believe that test results give a better picture of a student's abilities in

standardized tests
Examinations where the scores of an individual student are compared to a group score that has been developed through a comparison of scores from many people who have taken the same test.

Exámenes estandarizados
Exámenes en los que las calificaciones de un estudiante se comparan con un resultado establecido a través de comparaciones con las calificaciones de varias personas que han tomado el examen.

achievement gap
Differences in the test performance among groups of people taking standardized tests.

Brecha de rendimiento
Diferencias en los resultados de los exámenes entre los diversos grupos de personas que toman exámenes estandarizados.

high stakes testing
Assessments used to measure students' performance in school related content areas. Performance results determine if students move from one grade to the next or if a school gets funding.

Exámenes de alto riesgo
Evaluaciones que se usan para determinar el rendimiento de los estudiantes en las materias escolares. Los resultados de los exámenes determinan si los estudiantes pasan de un grado a otro o si la escuela obtiene fondos.

Standardized assessment provides educators with a picture of students' understanding of school-based content. © *Dana Heinemann*

reading, writing, science, and mathematics. The results of standardized tests are used to create plans that best suit students' needs. Supporters of NCLB believe that past test performance among different groups of students indicate that not all children in the US succeed in the same way. European Americans tend to score higher on standardized tests when compared to other groups. Children who are members of major racial and ethnic groups and many children from poor homes tend to score lower on some types of standardized tests. For this reason, the supporters of NCLB believe the law will be helpful in pinpointing which children need additional support. Supporters believe that test scores will give educational leaders information that will help teachers educate in ways that build success for all students. Educators and policy makers who support NCLB believe that if the policies of the law are put into action, the **achievement gap**, or differences in performance between groups of test takers, will be reduced, thereby making the education of all children equal.

Some people don't like to use standardized tests because they may not let all learners show their best work. Those against standardized tests believe that they measure only a small part of students' abilities. They believe that the tests may be biased against those who have not had the educational and financial resources necessary for success in schools. They also know that when children have taken a lot of tests they are more comfortable taking tests than when they haven't. Comfort and experience in taking tests may influence how well a student will perform. When students are stressed when taking a test, they may not show their true ability in that area.

Students are not the only ones who feel the pressure of taking standardized tests. Many classroom teachers feel the pressure of what is referred to as **high stakes testing**. Teachers who feel pressured to make sure their students do well on tests may teach only the content that is on the tests, possibly ignoring other valuable information (Cuban, 1996; Kauchak & Eggen, 2005). Critics of standardized tests believe that the type of knowledge measured on standardized tests is limited to the memorization of facts, and not all children are exposed to the same type of instruction. These opponents believe that it is very difficult to find a person's true ability through a test score. They also question whether the kind of knowledge that is "essential" can be gathered through a test score (Gutiérrez, 2002). Tests that give a well-rounded picture of a student are suggested as another choice to traditional standardized tests. Supporters of alternative assessments suggest educators use other ways to measure students' abilities. Portfolios and project-based assessments are not exactly the same as standardized tests, but they give a description of students' abilities in different areas.

The viewpoints of both supporters and opponents of standardized testing are certainly important. However, educators must not forget that we live in a time where performance on a wide range of tests is valued by political leaders, school personnel, and families. Wherever you stand on the issue of assessment—either in full support of standardized assessment, in opposition to standardized assessment, or from a perspective that values a range of testing—the

Annual Measurable Objectives (AMO)

Annual Measurable Objectives (AMO), describe the minimum percentage of students who must score well on tests in reading and mathematics. Based upon their students' performance and ability to meet the AMO goals, schools are evaluated to determine if the annual measurable objectives are met.

Objetivos anuales mensurables (AMO)

Los objetivos anuales mensurables describen el porcentaje mínimo de estudiantes que deben obtener buenas calificaciones en lectura y matemáticas. Se hace una evaluación de las escuelas para determinar si se han alcanzado las metas del AMO basada en el rendimiento de los estudiantes.

No Child Left Behind has established policies and procedures for educating America's children.

assessment discussion is alive and well, and will continue to raise many questions and answers in the years to come.

Paraprofessionals, and all of those working in today's schools, must know the policies and practices related to effective assessment. They must study both the strengths and weaknesses of the tools used to measure students' abilities. One point to keep in mind is that people have very different ideas about the strengths and limitations of NCLB and the discussions can be very emotional! Your own experiences with NCLB will help you decide if the law has met its goals in your school and community. Chapter 7 will provide additional information about assessment, and the connection between instruction and effective assessment.

MEASURING SUCCESS THROUGH ANNUAL MEASURABLE GOALS AND ADEQUATE YEARLY PROGRESS

One of the questions you might have is how are schools compared or measured. This is an important question because one of the goals of NCLB is that all students will have to meet the same standards of performance by the years 2013–2014. This means that students' test performance must be compared on some level. **Annual Measurable Objectives (AMO)** describe the lowest percentage of students who must score well on tests in reading and mathematics. Based upon their students' performance and their ability to meet the AMO goals, schools are evaluated to see if the annual measurable objectives are met. Once again, students' tests scores are used as a way to compare how well educators are teaching and students are learning.

What happens if students in a school do not reach their AMOs? This is also a valuable question. As a part of each school's NCLB agreement, the school must show that all its students, regardless of their racial, ethnic, and economic background, meet a standard that represents **Adequate Yearly Progress** or AYP. Perhaps you have even heard educators ask the question, "Did your school meet its AYP?" Adequate Yearly Progress is another term that is very important and shows the growth each school must make on meeting its goals for student performance on standardized tests. If a school is not able to show an appropriate level of growth during two consecutive years, the school is rated as being "in need of improvement." In this case, the school must come up with a plan to show improvement in their test performance. If the school is unable to produce improved test scores, it may suffer additional penalties.

If all the talk about NCLB leaves you feeling overwhelmed, remember there are many different parts to the law. Today's educators know that NCLB is at the center of many educational decisions. Figure 2-1, NCLB Framework, shows the relationship between NCLB, AYP, and AMO. Which of the parts of NCLB makes most sense to you? Which areas seem more confusing? Make a plan to meet with your classroom teacher to discuss the specific questions you have about NCLB and its different parts.

Adequate Yearly Progress (AYP)
A part of NCLB that represents the growth each school must demonstrate toward meeting its goals for student performance on standardized tests. If a school is not able to show an appropriate level of growth during two back-to-back years, it is given a rating that indicates its "need of improvement."

Progreso anual adecuado (AYP)
Un componente de la ley "Que ningún niño se quede atrás" que representa el crecimiento que cada escuela debe demostrar hacia el logro de sus objetivos de rendimiento estudiantil en los exámenes estandarizados. Si una escuela no puede alcanzar un nivel adecuado de crecimiento durante dos años consecutivos, recibe una evaluación que indica "la necesidad de mejoramiento académico."

Title I Schools
A federal education program that provides funding for schools with students from low-income families.

Escuelas de Título I
Programa federal de educación que provee fondos para escuelas con estudiantes provenientes de familias de bajos ingresos.

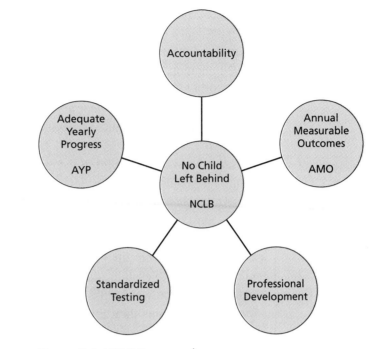

FIGURE 2-1 NCLB Framework

TITLE I SCHOOLS

The policies related to NCLB place new expectations on all schools and educators. Some schools have to follow NCLB policies in an even more detailed way. These schools are known as **Title I schools**. Title I schools are very important to paraprofessionals who are often part of the educational teams that support many of their students.

Title I schools have been around a long time. In 1965 leaders believed that some schools needed additional money from the federal government in order to serve their students. The money the federal government sent to Title I schools was for families and communities that did not have the resources to serve the special needs of children from poor homes. Today, Title I schools educate large numbers of students from low income families who often need additional services to improve their academic performance. Title I money has been used in a number of different ways, including paying for "pull out" programs. In many "pull out" programs paraprofessionals work directly with students who need support and basic skill development. Problems with the pull out model include:

1. taking children away from their school friends,
2. focusing on skills not related to the curriculum, and
3. scheduling problems for teachers when their students leave for support services (Kauchak & Eggen, 2005).

One important advantage of pull out programs is that students are given focused support in areas where they need extra attention. The one-to-one time spent in pull out programs is essential to student success, and some researchers believe that Title I schools are really helpful because their services help students from poor backgrounds succeed (Gooden, 2003). These same researchers say that giving students extra support is just one of many ways to help them succeed (Boorman, 2000).

In addition to the curriculum and instructional limitations of pull out programs, Title I pull out programs take students out of their classrooms for a segment of the school day. The clear advantage of this type of support is the increased support provided by paraprofessionals. When paraprofessionals are well trained, the support they provide is critical. The disadvantage is that paraprofessionals may not always be properly trained and that their skill levels are different. Some paraprofessionals bring a large amount of experience and training to their positions. Others have had less training (US Department of Education, 1999). In order to make sure students get the support they need, legislation under NCLB requires that paraprofessionals, and other unlicensed personnel, meet the highly qualified standards of their specific job assignments. One of the ways that Title I schools make sure paraprofessionals do their best work in the classroom is through open communication between classroom teachers and paraprofessionals. When educators work in teams they plan, deliver, and assess lessons together. Changes in the support given to paraprofessionals in Title I schools is one example of the impact of NCLB requirements for highly qualified paraprofessionals. Let's look at additional ways in which NCLB has affected today's paraprofessionals.

THE IMPACT OF THE NO CHILD LEFT BEHIND ACT ON PARAPROFESSIONALS

During the past 40 years, the work of paraprofessionals has become more technical, requiring increased training and evaluation. The standards for highly qualified paraprofessionals include: 1) completing postsecondary education; 2) obtaining an Associate's degree; and/or 3) submitting to a state or nationally based test, demonstrating abilities in reading, writing, and math (Jennings, 2002).

For many paraprofessionals, meeting the standards for being highly qualified under NCLB means taking a standardized test. The test that most paraprofessionals take was developed by a national organization known as the **Educational Testing Service** or ETS. ETS serves hundreds of thousands of people each year. People who take tests through ETS do so for many reasons. They might take exams to meet NCLB highly qualified standards, they might takes tests for admission to colleges and universities, or they may just want to learn more about standardized tests (ETS, 2006). To find out more about the exact content of the paraprofessional test, go to: http://www.ets.org. The ETS website is the first stop in learning more about how to prepare for a standardized test. The directions at the site are written just for paraprofessionals. The ETS website is helpful but you may be overwhelmed by its huge content. Before you take any sort of test, it's important to learn as much about the test as possible. If the information at the site is too complicated for you to understand, or

Educational Testing Service (ETS)
A testing company responsible for developing and implementing the standardized tests taken by individuals seeking access to educational institutions.

Servicio de pruebas educativas (ETS por sus siglas en inglés)
El servicio de pruebas educativas es la compañía responsable de desarrollar e implementar los exámenes estandarizados que toman los individuos que buscan acceso a instituciones educativas.

Scoring well on the ParaPro test requires review and practice.

it seems to be too much information, Maria and Tracy understand. They helped each other while studying the different parts of the practice test for paraprofessionals. The guides in this chapter, as well as the portfolio assignments in this book, will help you prepare for the test.

SCORING WELL ON THE PRAXIS EXAM

Paraprofessionals must show their skills and knowledge in reading, writing, and mathematics as part of the standardized testing requirements. The **Praxis ParaProTest** tests a paraprofessional's ability to apply knowledge and skills to classroom situations. The test is divided into sections for reading, mathematics, and writing as follows: a) reading skills and knowledge; b) the application of reading skills and knowledge to classroom instruction; c) mathematics skills and knowledge; d) the application of mathematics skills and knowledge to the classroom; e) writing skills and knowledge; f) the application of writing skills and knowledge to classroom instruction. Table 2-2, The Praxis ParaPro Test Guide, provides a quick reference checklist for each of the sections of the test.

The Reading Skills and Knowledge section of the Praxis exam asks you to read a series of stories that test your ability to read, understand, analyze, and interpret content. This section of the Praxis exam also has questions that ask you to read and figure out graphs, charts, and tables. Although ETS website (http://www.ets.org.) has additional information on the exam, the following points are important to keep in mind as you get ready:

1. find the main idea or primary purpose in a specific reading.
2. find supporting ideas—that is, find other information that strengthens and supports the main idea;
3. figure out how a reading selection is organized—say which section comes first, for example, according to the meaning of words or phrases in context.
4. draw meaning or implications from text—that is, after reading a passage you will have to make predictions or guess the content based on the information given;
5. indicate whether the information given is fact or opinion; and
6. extract information from tables, charts, diagrams, and graphs.

The Application of Reading Skills and Knowledge to Classroom Instruction section of the test asks paraprofessionals to apply their knowledge of reading and instruction to classroom situations. This section focuses on foundations of reading and knowledge of words. You will be asked to break down words into root words, prefixes and suffixes, and you will be also asked to tell how words are similar and different.

The second section of the exam also tests paraprofessionals' knowledge of strategies that are used to teach reading. For example, test questions assess a paraprofessional's ability to: 1) help students with prereading strategies and figure out strategies to help students understand content; 2) help students to use tools such as dictionaries; and 3) help students understand written directions.

Praxis ParaPro Test
A standardized test developed by the Educational Testing Service that assesses a paraprofessional's ability to apply their knowledge and skills to classroom situations. The test is divided into six key areas including: a) reading skills and knowledge; b) the application of reading skills and knowledge to classroom instruction; c) mathematics skills and knowledge; d) the application of mathematics skills and knowledge to the classroom; e) writing skills and knowledge; f) the application of writing skills and knowledge to classroom instruction.

Prueba de Praxis ParaPro
Una prueba estandarizada desarrollada por el servicio de pruebas educativas que determina la capacidad de un paraprofesional para aplicar sus conocimientos y destrezas a la enseñanza en el aula. La prueba se divide en seis áreas clave: a) destrezas y conocimientos de lectura; b) la aplicación de las destrezas y conocimientos de lectura a la enseñanza en el aula; c) destrezas y conocimientos de matemáticas; d) la aplicación de las destrezas y conocimientos de matemáticas a la enseñanza en el aula; e) destrezas y conocimientos de escritura; f) la aplicación de las destrezas y conocimientos de escritura a la enseñanza en el aula.

TABLE 2-2 The Praxis ParaPro Test Guide

PRAXIS TEST SECTION	CONTENT
Reading Skills and Knowledge	Identify main ideas Identify supporting ideas Identify the organization of a reading selection Draw inferences or implications Determine the differences between fact and opinion Interpret information from tables, charts or figures
Application of Reading Skills and Knowledge to Classroom Instruction	Sounding out words Breaking down words into parts Decoding words Distinguishing between types of words Alphabetizing words Prereading strategies Understanding content Observing students' ability to interpret Helping students use dictionaries and interpret directions
Mathematics Skills and Knowledge	Major Concepts in: Arithmetic Algebra Geometry Measurement Data Organization and Interpretation
Application of Mathematics Skills and Knowledge to Classroom Instruction	Apply the concepts in the Skills and Knowledge section to classroom scenarios
Writing Skills	Basic Grammar Word Use Punctuation Parts of Speech Parts of Sentences Spelling
Application of Writing Skills	Apply the concepts in the Writing Skills section to educational scenarios

The third section of the test covers content related to Mathematics Skills and Knowledge. On this section paraprofessionals show their knowledge of basic math concepts and how to apply that knowledge in the classroom. The specific content of the tests includes basic mathematics concepts (e.g., addition, subtraction, multiplication, and division), mathematical symbols and the language related to mathematics problem solving and geometry and data analysis.

Sample test questions help paraprofessionals prepare for the type of questions found on the ParaPro standardized exam.

Similar to the section on the Applications of Reading, there is in the test a section on the Application of Mathematics Skills and Knowledge to Classroom Instruction. This section tests a paraprofessional's ability to apply in the classroom the content listed in the third section of the test.

The final two sections of the test assess Writing Skills and the ability to apply them. Specific tests measure basic grammatical skills, the ability to use words, write clearly, and present information that is free from errors in spelling, punctuation, and sentence structure. The test also assesses basic elements of effective writing including the ability to help students as they create content, edit the content, and make clearly written statements from different points of view. Each of the parts of the Praxis ParaPro Test require paraprofessionals to show their knowledge of, and ability to, apply key content to classroom situations.

Reading through the last few pages may leave you feeling stressed out about taking standardized tests. Whether you have taken a lot of tests in your life or whether this is the first time you will take a standardized test, you still might feel nervous. Tracy and Maria understand how you feel. Tracy's advice to Maria in a recent e-mail will provide you with a few tips as you prepare.

Hi Tracy,

Help! Tests make me so nervous! I'm never really sure how to prepare. I understand that I need to take the Praxis ParaProTest for paraprofessionals in order to be considered highly qualified under NCLB. I know that the test will measure how well I know reading, math, and writing. I also know that part of the test requires me to show how I use my knowledge in a classroom. But I'm still nervous. Any advice?

Maria

Hi Maria,

I know how you feel. I actually get sick to my stomach when I think about taking a test. The pressure makes me feel awful. I have learned that there are ways of preparing that will help calm me down. When I was studying for my test, I took advantage of all the resources I could find. There are different books and practice tests available on the ETS website that will help you. The way I understand the categories is that the test is trying to figure out if we know how to do our jobs when we:

1. help the teacher teach the children in our classrooms;
2. work as real professionals to help our students;
3. help the children through everything we do including the way we set up the classroom, the way we work with students, and the way we communicate with other people on our teams.

It's normal to feel stressed, but the key to calming down is to prepare as much as possible for the test. Let me know what you think of these ideas.

TEST PREPARATION FOR THE PRAXIS PARAPRO TEST

If you're like Maria and Tracy, you may feel stressed by just thinking of taking a test. You're not alone. While some level of stress is helpful to increase motivation, stress can also have a negative effect on test performance. If you are too worried about taking a test you may not do your best on the exam. The following suggestions will help you prepare to take the Praxis ParaPro Test, or any other exam you might have to take. Keep these ideas in mind as you work with your own students, as they will benefit from the same advice as they prepare to take tests in their classrooms (Eggen & Kauchak, 2003).

Understanding Questions Types

Understanding the type of questions on the Praxis exam is important. You will be asked to complete a total of 90 questions within a certain amount of time. Ninety questions may seem like a lot, but the test is broken down into sections across six categories including reading, mathematics, and writing. In addition to knowing about reading, writing, and math, it is important to study different types of test questions. Researchers and teachers tell us that knowing how to take a test and finding out whether we understand the questions on the test can be as important as knowing the exact content being tested. Let's begin with the content. Studying the content ahead of time is the first step to prepare for your test.

Preview the Content

Preview the content of the test and study the test questions that will be covered. If you review the test you'll have a better sense of what to expect, areas to study for the exam, and a plan for how much time it will take to answer specific questions. Questions you might ask yourself as you review for the test include:

1. What type of information is a particular question asking me?
2. Do I feel comfortable with my knowledge of how to respond to these questions?
3. In which areas do I need to review my skills?

These questions will help you review your current test taking strengths and weaknesses.

Use Different Strategies

The form of most standardized tests includes different types of questions. Depending on the format of the question on the test, your strategy for answering the question will be different. On some of the multiple choice items, the questions are presented as short questions, and you are given a series of answers from which you must choose only one. For example, you might be asked a question like the following:

Which word is NOT spelled correctly?

a. compare
b. hardwhere
c. repair
d. scare

In this question, you are being asked to choose the answer that is misspelled. Look for the single answer that is not answered correctly. The answer is **b**. The word should be spelled hardware. For other questions, you will be given a short essay to read and will be asked to choose one answer from a list of possible choices. Different question formats require different strategies. For example, essay questions require more reading and ask you to read the text as you choose an answer. Suggestions for questions with essays include the following:

1. Read the full passage instead of skimming or quickly reviewing the passage.
2. Don't worry if there is some information that you don't understand. It's actually likely that you won't understand everything you read.
3. As you answer the questions after reading the short passage, go back through the text and revise your answer.
4. Try to answer all the questions in the reading skills section.
5. Read all the answer choices and choose the best answer.

Make sure your answer is directly related to the story. There may be more than one answer that fits, but there is only one answer that is the adequate choice (ETS, 2003).

Practice

Practicing for your test is an important part of the preparation. As you review sample tests, study the format of the questions, and focus on how the directions are worded. After you've finished the test, review the answers for both the questions where you knew the answers, and for the questions where you had problems. For each question you're having trouble with, ask yourself if the way the question is worded is confusing. Sometimes, the way a question is worded can cause confusion, even when people really know the answer. Let's look at a question where the wording is a problem:

"At what point in the day did you determine it was appropriate to leave your place of employment to return to your dwelling?"

This question may cause problems because the words are complicated, or the words may be confusing. If the sentence were written in a more simple language you'd probably know the answer. You might be surprised to know that this question asks: What time did you leave work to go home? The way the question is worded may cause confusion. In every case, make sure you know what the question is asking. First, take the question apart and put the question in your own words. Even if you don't know all of the words, you may be able to understand the more complicated parts of the sentence once you understand other parts of the question. Finally, answer the question.

The last tip is to pay attention to the amount of time it takes to complete the practice questions. If you find yourself spending too much time on any one question, you may need to move on to other questions and continue with the questions that are easier to answer. After you have finished the easier questions, go back through the test to review the questions that were more difficult. Table 2-3, Test Taking Strategies, gives you a helpful list of tips to use when taking tests.

On the Educational Testing website you'll find a helpful guide for test preparation. The study guide includes practice questions, tips for preparing for the test, and advice on how to make the best choices as you complete the test (Educational Testing Service, 2003). For more information on test preparation, go to ETS website (http://www.ets.org.)

Online Testing

A paper and pencil format is used in the current Praxis ParaPro Test. But standardized tests are becoming more and more available through on an online, computerized format. The advantage of an online format for test creators is

TABLE 2-3 Test Taking Strategies

- Preview the test's content.
- Read all directions carefully.
- Read the entire question.
- Read each answer choice carefully.
- Cross out choices that you know could never be the correct answer.
- Make sure you're not taking too much time to complete questions.
- If you have to write a longer answer or an essay, write out first a quick draft versions.
- When you write an essay check your answer for content and presentation.

that they are able to create different forms that are easier to use. Different formats let test developers change the content very quickly. Changing the format of a test reduces the potential for cheating and gives more chances to those people who need to retake the test (Borja, 2003). Quick feedback is useful because it helps test takers who are trying to meet short deadlines. Traditional paper and pencil tests take longer to be scored, and their results are usually not known for a while. A possible weakness of electronic formats is that many people have never taken a test on a computer which may cause them to score poorly.

Summary

The impact of the No Child Left Behind Act is far reaching. The law sets policies for teachers and those working in classrooms and schools. NCLB also sets guidelines for teacher education programs and professional development expectations for educators. An important result of the No Child Left Behind Act is its influence on students through standardized testing. Standardized test results show how students perform against a set of standards. Each year, schools must show how their students perform and set plans for reaching their goals. Much like the students in their classrooms, educators must also show their ability to meet performance levels through standardized testing. This chapter covered some of the strengths and weaknesses of the assessment standards linked to No Child Left Behind for students and paraprofessionals. The chapter also reviewed ideas for paraprofessionals who are preparing to meet testing requirements. Knowledge of the Praxis ParaPro Test and a plan for building test taking skills helps paraprofessionals in their efforts to meet the highly qualified standards under NCLB.

In today's schools the policies of NCLB provide educators with new standards for working with children.

Checking for Understanding

1. Develop a definition for the following terms: The No Child Left Behind Act, Adequate Yearly Progress, Title I Schools, Praxis Standards, and Annual Measurable Outcomes. Use Table 2-1, New Information and Vocabulary Journal, and read each official definition. Then, write a definition using your own words.

2. Describe three ways in which NCLB will impact you as a paraprofessional. In what ways will you show your professional abilities?

3. Describe each of the key areas of the Praxis ParaPro Test and identify the areas with which you're more familiar. Next, list the areas where you feel your knowledge is more limited. Who will you contact at your school to learn more about the content of the exam?

Points of View

Maria and Tracy share the following suggestions on how to learn more about the effects of NCLB on public schools.

1. Find out how teachers and paraprofessionals can learn more about their professional development requirements. Each district has a Human Resources (HR) director whose job is to assist employees. Do you know the HR director in your district? If not, how can you find out more about him or her?

2. Each district has a technology specialist whose job is to help educators use electronic resources. Together with your classroom teacher, talk to the technology specialist at your school to find out more about the technology available to those preparing to complete the Praxis ParaPro Test.

3. Each district must share their schools, AYP performance with the public. Most state offices of education and school districts give a complete breakdown and summary of each school performance. With the assistance of the technology or media specialist at your school, review your school's AYP performance. In which content areas were the children in your school most successful? In which areas did the school fail to meet AYP? What are some of your school's strengths, as indicated on the AYP report? What are some of your school's AYP performance limitations?

4. Taking a test is only one of the ways paraprofessionals show their professional knowledge. Paraprofessionals also have the option of obtaining post-high school degrees through two- and four-year colleges. Contact your local junior or community college, or four-year college or university, and find out more about the policies and procedures for enrollment, degree programs, and financial assistance opportunities.

Portfolio Corner

As we noted earlier in the book, you will be asked to gather a number of artifacts, or sample products, that demonstrate your work as a paraprofessional. The suggestions in this chapter cover the ways you will meet the standards for highly qualified paraprofessionals under NCLB. You have also learned about the expectations for highly qualified paraprofessionals.

The portfolio framework we are using in this book is based upon the guidelines established for paraprofessionals under NCLB. These standards are quite similar to the standards to which licensed teachers must conform.

In Chapter 1 we examined a Sample Portfolio Framework. The standards listed below address four general areas regarding a paraprofessional's ability to: 1) provide support for instructional opportunities within a classroom setting; 2) demonstrate professional and ethical practice; 3) provide a supportive learning environment; and 4) communicate effectively and participate in the team process.

Read the tips Tracy gives Maria about the categories of the Praxis Standards.

Hi Tracy,

At our meeting last month at the district office, the Human Resource director told us about the four categories of the Praxis Standards. I learned that the categories help teachers and paraprofessionals keep track of their work. I think I understand why these categories were chosen—because they show the important skills and abilities that paraprofessionals need to be successful. I hate to admit this Tracy, but I still have questions about NCLB. I'm still not sure what these categories really mean. Could you help me better understand the content?

Maria

Hi Maria,

I also had a lot of questions when I was learning about the Praxis categories. Take advantage of all the information your classroom teacher can share. There are people in the district who have a lot of information as well. My best advice is to talk to the people around you and ask a lot of questions.

Tracy

Table 2-4, Sample Portfolio Framework, includes the four standards used to evaluate the qualifications of paraprofessionals. These standards are based upon the NCLB criteria for highly qualified paraprofessionals in Title I schools. Standard I refers to a paraprofessional's ability to provide students in classrooms with the necessary support to succeed in the classroom. Think about the portfolio artifacts or the lines of evidence you might use to demonstrate your knowledge in this category. Your artifacts should show your abilities in reading, writing, and mathematics, as well as your ability to deliver the lessons created

TABLE 2-4 Sample Portfolio Framework

STANDARD I— SUPPORTING INSTRUCTIONAL OPPORTUNITIES	STANDARD II— DEMONSTRATING PROFESSIONALISM AND ETHICAL PRACTICE
Sample artifacts might include: ● Video of you working with students ● Evaluation feedback from a mentor teacher ● Your ideas See Chapters 7 and 8	Sample artifacts might include: ● Praxis test scores ● Associate's or four-year degree ● Evaluations from classroom teachers or peers ● School handbooks ● NCLB policies ● Paraprofessional job description ● New Information and Vocabulary Journal ● Your ideas
STANDARD III— SUPPORTING A POSITIVE LEARNING ENVIRONMENT	STANDARD IV— COMMUNICATING EFFECTIVELY AND PARTICIPATING IN THE TEAM PROCESSES
See Chapter 3	See Chapter 6

by your classroom teacher. They might include a video of your work with students, or peer or classroom teacher feedback of your work.

Standard II asks paraprofessionals to show knowledge of their professional responsibilities in ways that match district policies and procedures. The artifacts you might include for Standard II include evaluations of your teaching from your classroom teacher, information from district trainings, course work, letters of reference, a Praxis ParaPro Test score, or interview summaries and conversations with mentors.

Standard III asks paraprofessionals to show their knowledge of how they will support student learning. Artifacts under Section III might include lesson ideas you have worked on with your classroom teacher or descriptions of the type of support you provide students in your classroom. You may also be asked to show how you put your classroom teacher's management system or curriculum plans into action.

Standard IV asks paraprofessionals to show how they communicate and work as members of teaching teams. The artifacts, or proofs of evidence, that you might share under this standard include notes you have written to parents and students. You might also want to keep a log of your time in team meetings at your school, or work samples from your work in classrooms that show how you work with students and coworkers. You could also include lesson plans and activities developed by your classroom teacher that you have implemented.

Use Table 2-4, Sample Portfolio Framework, and list sample artifacts that will meet Standards I and II based on the ideas discussed in Chapter 2.

REFERENCES

Boorman, G. (2000). Title I: The evolving research base. *Journal of Education for Students Placed at Risk, 5* (1&2), 27–45.

Borja, R. (2003). Prepping for the big test. *Education Week, 22,* 23–26.

Cuban, L. (1996). Curriculum stability and change. In P. Jackson (Ed.), *Handbook of research on curriculum* (pp. 216–247). New York: Macmillan.

Educational Testing Service (2003). *ParaPro assessment study guide, practice and review.* Princeton, New Jersey: Educational Testing Service.

Gooden, M. (2003). At-risk children: Title I almost 40 years later. *School Business Affairs, 69,* 14–18.

Gutiérrez, R. (2002). Beyond essentialism: The complexity in teaching mathematics to Latinos. *American Educational Research Journal, 39,* 1047–1088.

Hardy, L. (2002). A new federal role. *American School Board Journal, 18,* 20–24.

Kauchak, D., & Eggen, P. (2005). *Introduction to Teaching: Becoming a professional* (2nd ed). Upper Saddle River, New Jersey: Pearson, Merrill Prentice Hall.

Jennings, J. (2002). Knocking on your door. *American school board journal, 189,* 25–27.

No Child Left Behind Act of 2001. Public Law 107–110 (8 January 2002). Washington, DC: U.S. Government Printing Office.

U.S. Department of Education, (1999). *Digest of education statistics,* 1998. Washington, DC: U.S. Government Printing Office.

Additional selected readings and Paraprofessional electronic resources are available as part of the student Online Companion web site: www.earlychilded.delmar.com.

EN ESPAÑOL

OBJETIVOS DEL APRENDIZAJE

Después de leer y reflexionar sobre este capítulo podrá comprender mejor:

- Las políticas y regulaciones relacionadas con la ley **"Que ningún niño se quede atrás"** (NCLB).
- El impacto de esta ley en los paraprofesionales de las escuelas de hoy.
- El impacto de NCLB en la profesión docente.

A medida que lea este capítulo, hágase las siguientes preguntas:

1. ¿Qué es lo que la ley "Que ningún niño se quede atrás" dice sobre los estándares para los paraprofesionales altamente calificados?
2. ¿Qué pasos deberá tomar para lograr estos estándares?
3. ¿Cómo se preparará para tomar el examen para los paraprofesionales que quieren lograr los estándares requeridos por la ley "Que ningún niño se quede atrás"?
4. ¿Qué documentos incluirá en su carpeta para demostrar su conocimiento de dicha ley?

PARA VERIFICAR LA COMPRENSIÓN

1. Dé una definición de cada uno de los siguientes términos: ley "Que ningún niño se quede atrás", progreso anual adecuado (AYP según sus siglas en inglés), escuelas del Título I, estándares de Praxis y resultados anuales mensurables.
2. Lea cada definición formal del cuadro 2-1, Nueva información y Diario de vocabulario. Luego escriba una definición con sus propias palabras.
3. Describa tres maneras en las que NCLB lo o la afectará como paraprofesional. ¿De qué manera demostrará sus capacidades profesionales?
4. Describa cada una de las áreas clave del examen Praxis ParaPro e identifique las áreas que le resultan más familiares. Después, haga una lista de las áreas donde piensa que su conocimiento es más limitado. ¿A quién puede contactar en su escuela para aprender más sobre el contenido del examen?

PUNTOS DE VISTA

Maria y Tracy comparten las siguientes sugerencias para aprender más sobre los efectos de la ley "Que ningún niño se quede atrás" en las escuelas públicas.

1. Averigüe cómo maestros y paraprofesionales pueden aprender más sobre los requisitos para el desarrollo profesional. Cada distrito tiene un Director de Recursos Humanos (RH) que trabaja para asistir a los empleados. ¿Conoce usted a su director de Recursos Humanos? ¿Si no, cómo podrá encontrar más información sobre la persona que ocupa ese cargo en su distrito?
2. Cada distrito tiene un especialista en tecnología que ayuda a los educadores a utilizar recursos electrónicos. Junto con el maestro de su clase hable con el especialista en tecnología de su escuela para aprender más

---

"Que ningún niño se quede atrás"
Legislación federal aprobada en el año 2001 que define estándares en tres áreas: preparación del maestro; rendimiento estandardizado de exámenes para los alumnos de las escuelas públicas; y desarrollo profesional de maestros practicantes.

No Child Left Behind Act (NCLB)
Federal legislation enacted in 2001 that defines standards along three areas: teacher preparation; standardized test performance of children in public schools; and professional development of practicing teachers.

sobre los recursos electrónicos disponibles para las personas que se preparan para tomar el examen Praxis ParaPro.

3. Cada distrito debe hacer público el informe del Progreso anual adecuado (AYP en inglés) de sus escuelas. La mayoría de las oficinas estatales de educación y los distritos escolares ofrecen detalles y resúmenes completos de los resultados de cada escuela. Con la ayuda del especialista en tecnología y medios de su escuela, observe los resultados del AYP de su escuela. ¿En qué áreas tuvieron los niños más éxito? ¿En qué áreas la escuela no pudo lograr un progreso adecuado? ¿Cuáles son algunos de los puntos fuertes de su escuela, según lo indicado en el informe de AYP? ¿Cuáles son algunas de sus limitaciones?

4. Tomar un examen es sólo una de las maneras en que los paraprofesionales pueden demostrar su conocimiento profesional. Los paraprofesionales también tienen la opción de obtener títulos o licenciaturas después de los estudios secundarios en instituciones de enseñanza con cursos de dos o cuatro años de duración. Contáctese con la escuela técnica o la universidad local para obtener más información acerca de las regulaciones y los procedimientos para el proceso de inscripción, los programas de licenciatura, y las posibilidades de ayuda financiera.

PARA LA CARPETA

Como ya observamos antes, se le pedirá que reúna un número de documentos, o productos de muestra, que demuestren su trabajo como paraprofesional. Las sugerencias de este capítulo incluyen las diversas maneras en las que podrá alcanzar los estándares para paraprofesionales altamente calificados. También nos hemos referido a las expectativas en cuanto a desempeño.

La estructura de carpeta que presentamos en este libro se basa en las pautas que NCLB establece para los paraprofesionales. Estos estándares son muy similares a los que deben ajustarse los maestros licenciados.

En el Capítulo 1 examinamos la estructura de una carpeta modelo. Los estándares mostrados abajo se refieren a cuatro áreas relacionadas con la habilidad de un paraprofesional para 1) apoyar toda oportunidad educativa dentro del entorno del salón de clases; 2) demostrar una conducta profesional y ética; 3) ofrecer un ambiente conducente al aprendizaje; y 4) demostrar destreza para comunicarse eficazmente y participar en el proceso de equipo.

Lea lo que Tracy le dice a Maria sobre las distintas categorías de los estándares Praxis.

Hola Tracy:

En nuestra reunión del mes pasado en la oficina del distrito, el director de Recursos Humanos nos explicó las cuatro categorías de los estándares Praxis. Me enteré de que las categorías ayudan a maestros y paraprofesionales a organizar la documentación y mantener un registro de su trabajo. Creo que entiendo la razón por la cual se eligieron estas categorías, porque representan las habilidades y destrezas que un paraprofesional debe tener para tener éxito. No me gusta admitirlo, Tracy, pero todavía tengo preguntas sobre la ley "Que ningún niño se quede atrás". Todavía no estoy segura de qué significan estas categorías. ¿Podrías ayudarme a entender mejor el contenido?

Maria

Hola Maria:

Yo también tenía muchas preguntas cuando estudiaba las categorías Praxis. Aprovecha toda la información que tu maestro de clase pueda compartir contigo. En el distrito hay también muchas personas que tienen información. Mi mejor consejo es que hables con las personas de tu alrededor y que les hagas todas las preguntas posibles.

Tracy

La tabla 2-1, Estructura modelo de carpeta, incluye los cuatro estándares usados para evaluar las calificaciones de los paraprofesionales. Estos estándares se basan en el criterio de NCLB para paraprofesionales altamente calificados en las escuelas del Título I. El estándar I se refiere a la habilidad de los paraprofesionales para dar a los estudiantes la ayuda necesaria para tener éxito en la clase. Piense en los objetos o documentos que puede usar para demostrar sus conocimientos en esta categoría. Sus documentos deben poner en evidencia sus habilidades en lectura, escritura, y matemáticas, así como su destreza para enseñar la lección preparada por su maestro de clase. Entre sus documentos puede haber un vídeo de su trabajo con los estudiantes, o comentarios de sus compañeros o del maestro de clase sobre su trabajo en la clase.

El estándar II pide a los paraprofesionales demostrar conocimiento de sus responsabilidades profesionales de modo que correspondan a las regulaciones y procedimientos del distrito. Los documentos que puede incluir para el Estándar II son evaluaciones del maestro de clase, información de seminarios o talleres del distrito, trabajo del curso, cartas de referencia, calificaciones del examen de Praxis ParaPro, o resúmenes de entrevistas y conversaciones con mentores.

El Estándar III pide a los paraprofesionales demostrar conocimiento de las formas en las que apoyarán el aprendizaje del estudiante. Los documentos de la sección III pueden incluir ideas para lecciones en las cuales usted haya trabajado junto con el maestro de clase o descripciones del tipo de ayuda que usted proporciona a los estudiantes de su clase. También le pueden pedir que demuestre cómo pone en práctica su sistema de control de conducta o los planes del currículo.

Tabla 2-4 Estructura modelo de carpeta

ESTÁNDAR I— APOYO DE TODA OPORTUNIDAD EDUCATIVA	ESTÁNDAR II— DEMOSTRAR UNA CONDUCTA PROFESIONAL Y ÉTICA
Los objetos de muestra pueden incluir: • Vídeos de su trabajo con los estudiantes • Evaluación y reacción del maestro mentor • Sus ideas. Vea los Capítulos 7 y 8	Los objetos de muestra pueden incluir: • Los resultados del examen Praxis • Títulos, licenciaturas y post grados. • Evaluación de maestros de clase y compañeros de trabajo. • Manuales de la escuela • Las regulaciones de NCLB • Descripción del trabajo de paraprofesional • El nuevo diario de vocabulario e información. • Sus ideas.
ESTÁNDAR III— OFRECER UN AMBIENTE CONDUCENTE AL APRENDIZAJE	ESTÁNDAR IV— COMUNICARSE EFICAZMENTE Y PARTICIPAR EN EL PROCESO DEL EQUIPO
Vea el Capítulo 3	Vea el Capítulo 6

El Estándar IV pide a los paraprofesionales que demuestren cómo se comunican y trabajan como miembros de un equipo educativo. Los documentos o pruebas que usted puede compartir de acuerdo a este estándar incluyen las notas o mensajes que usted haya escrito a padres y a estudiantes. También puede llevar un diario de su participación en reuniones de equipo o muestras de su trabajo en clase que muestren cómo interactúa con estudiantes y colegas. Asimismo puede incluir planes de lecciones y actividades desarrolladas por su maestro de clase que usted haya implementado.

Use la Tabla 2-1, Estructura modelo de carpeta, y haga una lista de los documentos que estén relacionados con los estándares I y II, basándose en las ideas presentadas en el Capítulo 2.

ISSUES IN CLASSROOM MANAGEMENT

LEARNING OBJECTIVES

After reading and reflecting on this chapter you will understand:

- The factors affecting classroom management
- How to develop rules and consequences
- Ways of addressing disruptive behavior
- Ways of managing a diverse student body

As you read this chapter, ask yourself these questions:

1. What are your beliefs about the ways in which students should behave in the classroom?
2. What are some of the strategies teachers use to gain students' attention?
3. What are some of the strategies teachers use when they respond to students who misbehave?
4. How might cultural and language differences between educators and students impact classroom behavior and how educators respond?
5. What kind of artifacts will you include in your portfolio to reflect your knowledge of effective classroom management strategies?

KEY TERMS

behavior contracts

classroom management

contacts

extrinsic motivators

feedback

logical consequences

negative reinforcement

positive reinforcement

preventative measures

proximity

time out

token economies

Tribes Learning Community Model

"withitness"

---

classroom management
The process of creating and maintaining order in the classroom.

manejo de la clase
Proceso de crear y de mantener orden y disciplina en la clase.

INTRODUCTION

If you ask anyone working with students to name the most important part of their work in classrooms, many people will put **classroom management** at the top of the list. Classroom management, or classroom discipline, includes the ways teachers and paraprofessionals build classrooms that help students learn. Management involves different tasks including writing interesting lesson plans, learning to communicate effectively, and creating rules for the kind of behavior that allows a teacher to teach and students to learn.

Kids will be Kids

> Children these days are out of control. They don't follow their parents' rules, they eat whatever they want when they want, they don't think about their communities, and they make life for their teachers very difficult. Furthermore, all kids today only worry about their stuff. They have bad manners, don't follow directions; they sit around instead of going outside. They don't show adults the respect they deserve and they go against their parents and talk out of turn.

Many people who read this quote agree with the author's opinion. Their personal experiences working with young people lead them to agree with what the author says. There are others whose experiences with children are completely different. What about you, do you agree with the author, or are your experiences different? Some readers may feel as though children today fail to show adults, and even their friends, the respect they deserve. You might be surprised to know that this quote is very old. It was written by the Greek philosopher Socrates 2,500 years ago!

The important message to remember is that while young people can sometimes be difficult to manage, children have many wonderful qualities. Some behaviors are quite common among all children. Other behaviors are cause for more attention. Educators can begin to study classroom management by looking at the factors in classrooms and schools that influence student behavior.

Factors Affecting Classroom Interactions

Classroom management is a major topic of study for almost everyone connected with classroom teaching. In many cases, new educators fear their students will not respect them. Experienced educators report that effective classroom management is a major goal in their classrooms and principals tell their teachers that they must have more control. Even children expect the educators in their classrooms to show leadership and to manage classrooms effectively. Effective educators know that many different factors affect their students' behavior. Educators who take the time to study their classrooms understand what makes teaching and learning possible.

Sometimes when we think of "classroom management" we might imagine misbehaving students. We might think of a teacher who is tired because of the time spent preparing lessons that cannot be taught. If we think of classrooms this way, we are only thinking about a small part of life in classrooms. Classroom management is neither good nor bad, but it is *necessary* and is an important part of every classroom. Think about how your personal philosophy and comfort level affect your work in the classroom. When do you feel most comfortable working in the classroom? How do you react to students who are misbehaving? When are students most likely to misbehave? To answer these questions, think about everything that working in a classroom implies. Think about the topics taught, the ways educators teach, and the relationships between students and teachers. Ask yourself if what we teach students is interesting. How does the instruction in classrooms help students learn? Finally, think about whether students get along with their teachers and their fellow students.

Figure 3-1, Ingredients for Effective Classroom Management, shows how the different parts of classrooms fit together. Classrooms are like communities where the "ingredients" make students feel welcome and where learning takes

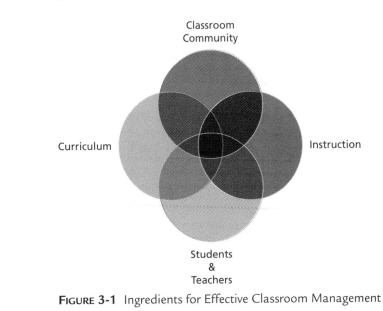

Figure 3-1 Ingredients for Effective Classroom Management

place. The ingredients for success in a classroom include the curriculum, the type of instruction used, the personal qualities of students and teachers, and the feeling of community.

In the past, people thought that each of these ingredients worked by itself and never interacted. Today educators understand that these ingredients work together to build positive classrooms. We know that if the curriculum, or the topics that are studied, are interesting to students, they are more engaged. Interesting topics keep students motivated and help them enjoy the lessons taught. Even though paraprofessionals don't create lessons, they can increase students' interest by sharing with them their excitement for learning.

In addition to an interesting curriculum, the way the teacher organizes the lessons is important. If a teacher sets up classroom lessons in ways that keep students involved, students are more likely to be interested and are less likely to misbehave. Lessons that include interesting topics and careful instruction help build a positive classroom community.

Each of the classroom management ingredients adds to what many researchers and teachers describe as the **preventative measures** in classrooms. Preventative measures are the tools that educators use to reduce the chances for management problems to occur. Preventative measures include:

1. building a positive classroom community,
2. creating an interesting curriculum,
3. using teaching strategies that keep students motivated,
4. using routines and schedules,
5. giving jobs to students,
6. organizing the room so people can move and have easy access to supplies, and
7. learning more about students.

One of the ways educators learn more about their students' behavior is by increasing **proximity** to students. Proximity implies closeness between people or objects. Paying attention to how space is used helps educators make contact with students. When educators are in close contact with students, they reduce the chances of management difficulties in the first place (Burden, 2006). Proximity gives educators the chance to move closer to students by standing near a potentially disruptive student. Moving closer to a student helps the educator figure out why the problem may have happened and gives the student a reminder to pay attention. Proximity is a tool that doesn't draw a lot of attention to a student but helps the learner focus on his or her work.

Some classroom setups make proximity easier than others. We have all been in situations where a cramped setting doesn't allow us to move about easily. Places that are cramped may cause people to become distracted or make them irritable. Classrooms are no different. Discuss how the room arrangements in Figure 3-2, Classroom Configurations, might add to student success in the classroom. In each of these classrooms formats, the way the room is organized helps being in contact with students. When might the use of small clusters of desks be most useful? When might a teacher want to include rows? When might a half circle of chairs be most appropriate?

---

preventative measures
Practices used by educators that are designed to reduce the occurrence of classroom management difficulties. Examples include building a productive classroom community, creating an interesting curriculum, and implementing effective teaching strategies.

medidas preventivas
Prácticas empleadas por los educadores destinadas a reducir las dificultades que puedan surgir en el manejo de la clase. Ejemplos incluyen la creación de una comunidad productiva en el aula, la elaboración de un currículo interesante y el empleo de estrategias de enseñanza eficaces.

---

proximity
Distance between individuals or objects that allows educators to increase their direct contact with learners by standing near a potentially disruptive student.

proximidad
Distancia entre individuos u objetos que permite a los educadores incrementar su contacto directo con los educandos al poder ubicarse cerca de un estudiante con problemas de disciplina.

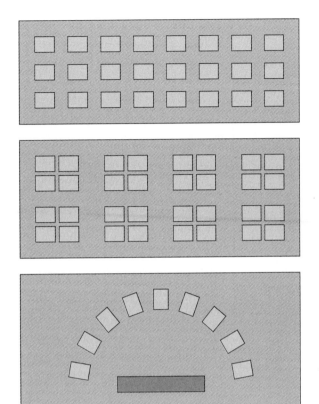

FIGURE 3-2 Classroom Configurations

The seating arrangements in a classroom can influence an educator's ability to work with a range of students.

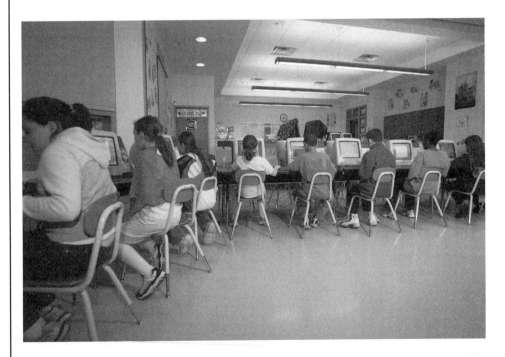

Other preventative measures that get students' attention include making eye contact, touching a student's desk to refocus attention, or repeating questions using direct language such as "Conner, I need your attention at the front of the room." Each of these ways is a reminder to students of their expected classroom behavior.

Preventative measures are an important part of an educator's classroom management plan. Preventative measures are only one part of classrooms where teaching and learning take place. Maria and Tracy are at a local coffee shop. Listen to them as they discuss their experiences in creating a productive classroom environment. Think about how you would respond if you were in their position.

DAY-TO-DAY DILEMMA
HOW WOULD YOU HANDLE THIS SITUATION?

Tracy: Pass the chocolate, Maria! I've had a rough day and could really use an extra boost of energy about now. The kids in my classroom are driving me crazy!

Maria: Here, Tracy. Take *two* pieces of chocolate. What's going on in your classroom?

Tracy: I was working with the students in one of the reading groups that my classroom teacher assigned to me. Everything seemed fine until I asked the kids to finish a worksheet. I thought I was going to pull out my hair because the kids were so difficult to manage! I told them over and over how to do the assignment and they just didn't seem to get it. They kept asking me to repeat the directions. Then, they started to laugh; they wouldn't stop playing around; and finally they started cheating by copying each other's answers. I finally had to end the lesson and told them to go back to their seats and read. I just don't know what to do with the kids when they're so difficult. I even tried yelling and told them they couldn't go to recess, but nothing seemed to work.

Maria: I know what you mean about bad days. Sometimes I want to stand in the hall and scream. If it helps, I know we're not the only people who have trouble with management. I saw this story in a magazine the other day. It said that classroom management is one of the major reasons why so many people quit teaching. The story gave some good ideas on how to make sure classes don't get out of hand. It said that we're supposed to work with the kids one-on-one, and try not to get mad at them. The guy who wrote the story said we have to know what's going on in the class all the time. When I read that I thought, 'Yeah right, how am I supposed to do that?' Anyway, he also said teachers need to make lessons where the kids are active. The guy said when the kids are interested they don't have a chance to misbehave.

Tracy: Okay, so that's good advice, but what are we supposed to do to stop problems in the first place? I can't put up with another day like this! I won't have any more hair to pull out! Give me more chocolate...

Maria: Well, I'll make a copy of the story and we can talk to our classroom teachers about it. It talked about making the classroom feel like a community and understanding each student. We're also supposed to have rules and consequences, so that the kids know what we expect from them and what will happen if they have problems. Let's at least talk to our teachers. They have a lot of experience with management. They should have good advice for us.

Tracy: Okay that's a good plan. Either that or I'll need a lot more chocolate!

CLASSROOM AS COMMUNITY

When educators work toward a common goal they are one step closer to building a classroom community. Common goals are important. Classroom communities are strongest when people care about one another and work together to help students learn and grow. Alfie Kohn is a famous writer and researcher on classroom communities. He believes educators should make classrooms places where children feel safe and supported. Kohn (2000) says that most management plans only use punishment and reward systems. He tells us that while punishment and rewards may meet short-term goals, that's not enough. Kohn thinks that classrooms should be places where decisions make students feel like they are a part of bigger communities. Punishments and rewards by themselves restrict long-term learning and limit the creation of community. Kohn (2000) suggests educators think about the following areas when building classroom communities:

1. individual needs of students in classrooms,
2. curriculum or the topics the students study,
3. type of instruction used in lessons, and
4. ways of keeping students involved in lessons.

Each of these strategies helps students feel like they belong.

The Needs of Students and Teachers

We've all been in situations where we feel emotional—maybe sad or angry. Sometimes we feel so emotional that we're unable to understand others, to follow directions, or do simple everyday jobs. When people are under stress, in a new situation, or confused it is sometimes difficult to make decisions or get along with others. Students in classrooms are no different. They need classrooms where they feel comfortable, safe, and supported. Just like adults, students' emotional needs affect how comfortable they feel and how well they learn. Effective teachers know about learners' needs and create environments where students feel accepted and encouraged to learn.

One of the ways educators build positive classroom communities is through the **Tribes Learning Community Model** (2006). The basic idea of Tribes is that educators can make students feel welcome and respected even if

Tribes Learning Community Model
A community building model includes the strategies educators implement in their classrooms in order to create an environment where students feel included and respected regardless of differences in ability, gender, language, life goals, and interests. The Tribes philosophy encourages classrooms where students are actively involved in their own learning through choices in what they learn and in their opportunities for success.

Modelo comunitario de aprendizaje de tribus
Modelo para la formación de una comunidad que incluye las estrategias que los educadores emplean en la clase para crear un ambiente en el cual los estudiantes se sientan incluidos y respetados independientemente de sus diferencias en capacidad, género, idioma, objetivos e intereses. La filosofía de este modelo fomenta clases en que los estudiantes se involucren activamente en su propio proceso de aprendizaje mediante opciones respecto a lo que aprenden y a sus oportunidades de éxito.

they have differences in their abilities, gender, language, life goals, and interests. The Tribes philosophy says good classrooms are places where students are active in their learning. Students are active because they get to make choices in what they learn and find success in many different ways (Tribes Learning Community Model, 2006). When students have choices in what they study, they feel like they have a say in their classroom community. What kind of choices do students have in your classroom? Do they get to choose the books they read? Maybe they have choices in the way they may complete an assignment. Talk to your classroom teacher about the times when students may be given choices in the classroom.

Curriculum

If students enjoy the topics they study, they are more likely to be involved in lessons. In Chapter 1 we talked about the curriculum in grades kindergarten through high school. We talked about the influence of national, state, and local policymakers on curriculum standards and the standards for educators who teach the curriculum. The curriculum is made, ideally, to help students learn the most important information in different content areas. In addition to choosing important topics to study, educators must also think about how to make the topics match students' needs. If the curriculum relates to students' lives, students feel more connected. Educators who think about the ways the curriculum affects students' behavior in classrooms tend to have fewer management problems. A curriculum that is interesting and motivating helps students enjoy what they learn. Lessons that link to students' backgrounds make the content come alive. Matching the content of lessons to students' lives is becoming more and more important as our nation changes.

Interesting lessons keep students engaged in the content of their classes.

Many educators and researchers support the idea of a curriculum that relates to students' cultures and language differences (Gaye, 2000). With an increase in the number of culturally and linguistically diverse students in today's classrooms, educators must respond. A curriculum that pays attention to different cultures and languages means teachers must ask themselves these questions:

1. Does the curriculum help students understand the importance of families and communities?
2. Does the curriculum help students see how they can have an influence in their communities and in society?
3. Do teachers help their students understand how history has shaped what we study today?

Researchers and teachers believe that today's students need to study curriculum in new ways. Today's educators understand the importance of a curriculum that celebrates all languages and cultures (Villegas & Lucas, 2002). Chapters 4 and 7 will provide additional information on culturally responsive teaching.

Methods of Instruction

Just like ways to connect curriculum and management, educators also think about how different types of instruction help their students learn the curriculum. Effective educators give guides or strategies that help students understand the purpose of lessons and how to complete assignments. They also make sure that students understand how they will be tested on what they have learned. Without these levels of instruction, students may become confused and frustrated, and in some cases, react negatively.

Effective educators share curriculum, know whether students understand the curriculum, and make adjustments when necessary. These teachers possess *"withitness"* (Kounin, 1970), or a general awareness about what is taking place in their classrooms. *"Withit"* teachers know when to change their curriculum and instruction. They have a quality described by some as an "eyes in the back of their heads" ability to tell what is going on, even when they do not appear to be paying attention to individuals or small groups. These educators are experts in their ability to teach, test, and interact with students all at the same time. No wonder educators go home tired each day! Effective teachers think about their teaching during class time. Effective teachers also reflect on whether they meet the needs of each student every day. Thinking about each student's success is key to good teaching.

Student Involvement

Strong educators create interesting lessons and use different kinds of instruction. They also think about each child as part of the teaching-learning cycle. If students are always passive, or waiting for something to be delivered to them, they are less likely to be involved in a lesson. Learners who are active in lessons and are given choices to participate through discussions, activities, or work with

"withitness"
A teacher's awareness of what is taking place in their classroom. Teachers who demonstrate *"withitness"* are aware of the happenings in their classrooms and know what students are doing within the context of a lesson; they know when to change their curriculum and instruction. They can tell what is going on in the classroom at all times, thanks to an ability described by some as "eyes in the back of their heads".

"estar con los ojos abiertos"
La total atención del maestro a lo que ocurre en la clase. Los maestros que "están con los ojos abiertos" son conscientes de lo que pasa en su clase y saben lo que están haciendo los estudiantes dentro del contexto de una lección; saben cuándo cambiar su currículo y enseñanza. Pueden decir qué pasa en la clase en todo momento, y tienen una cualidad que algunos describen como "ojos en la nuca".

others are more likely to stay focused and are less likely to be distracted. Chapter 7 provides additional information on the methods of instruction you may want to include in your work with young people. Even using the best ideas, all educators have days when their plans don't work. The big question is how do we act when our plans don't work out? How should educators react when students aren't involved in a lesson, don't follow directions, or become disruptive?

RESPONSES TO CLASSROOM DISRUPTIONS

After a long day at school, Maria began to question whether she was really cut out to be an effective paraprofessional. As she thought about her day, she tried to remember all that had taken place and wondered why the students' behavior had become so difficult to manage. Think about what you would have done in her place.

Mrs. Ramirez, Maria's classroom teacher, asked Maria to work with a small reading group in her classroom. After each child read a short section, Maria led a small group discussion where students shared their ideas on the readings. Next, the students completed a writing assignment in pairs. Finally, after working in pairs, the students read quietly until recess. As Maria thought about her students' assignments, it seemed like such an easy set of directions. She thought it would be very easy to lead the lesson and make sure students were doing what they were supposed to do. Maria could not believe the lesson had been so hard for the students to follow. The students wouldn't take turns to read from their books, they talked out of turn, and bothered others when they should have been working quietly. When Maria met with Mrs. Ramirez to discuss the day's lesson, she had to be honest and report that none of the children in the reading group had finished their assignments.

As an effective mentor and guide, Mrs. Ramirez knew just how to answer Maria's questions about the day's lesson. Mrs. Ramirez and Maria went over the lesson and paid special attention to the lesson plan and three key areas: 1) rule development; 2) participation policies; and 3) assignments steps.

Rule development, participation policies, and assignment steps are some of the tools educators use to cut down on management problems. As Maria thought about her lesson, she realized that she hadn't shown the students how to participate in the lesson. Her lesson wasn't clear and she hadn't explained what students were supposed to do. She forgot to model the kind of work she expected from students, and she was inconsistent in how she reacted to them. It is no wonder students misbehaved during the lesson! The lesson outline in Table 3-1, Lesson Plan Checklist, includes Mrs. Ramirez's suggestions for Maria's future lessons.

TABLE 3-1 Lesson Plan Checklist

Lesson Goal	Has the goal of the lesson been described? How will you measure student learning?
Lesson Objectives	Does the lesson ask students to show what they are learning in each part of the process?
Instructional Procedures	Are the directions clear and do students understand what you're asking them to do in each step?
Focusing Event	How will you get students' attention during the lesson? Are you able to motivate the students to care about what you're teaching?
Teaching Procedures	Are the expectations of assignments clear? Have you modeled what students are expected to complete?
Closure	How does the lesson end? What should students do when the lesson ends?
Reflection	What should happen next time the lesson is taught?

After her discussion with Mrs. Ramirez, Maria felt much better about her ability to work with students. Maria now understood the importance of working with her classroom teacher to set rules and procedures, to follow through with expectations, and to help students understand the consequences of actions in the classroom. Here is Maria's advice on areas a paraprofessional should think about when leading lessons:

1. rule development,
2. follow through with expectations, and
3. logical/natural consequences.

Rule Development

Rules are statements or policies that give students guidelines for acceptable classroom behavior (Kauchak & Eggen, 2005). Effective rule development includes:

1. saying rules using positive words—"Students will treat each other with respect."
2. explaining why the rules were chosen in the first place—"We treat each other with respect so everyone will feel welcome in the classroom."
3. keeping the number of rules to between 3–5—Fewer rules help students understand general expectations about behavior in the classroom, and
4. changing the rules as students learn how the policies and procedures work within a classroom. For example, once students learn how to use supplies in a classroom, they may not need to ask for permission each time they're used.

Educators who follow these tips on rule development understand that rules should be clear, short in number, and changed as students grow and develop. Talk with your classroom teacher to learn more about classroom rules and procedures.

Follow Through with Expectations

Have you ever been in a situation where the rules changed without any warning? Maybe you were traveling one morning on your usual route to work, when a detour sign forced you to make a change. If you're like most people, you may have been surprised by the sudden change. While changes happen all the time, we all rely on consistency in our classrooms. Well-run classrooms are places where students know what to expect. Consistency in the ways rules and policies are used is very important. Consistency helps students understand what is expected. Teachers and researchers know that classroom rules and policies make life in classrooms predictable and safe (Brophy, 1998; Kauchak & Eggen, 2005).

What about the times when students don't follow rules and policies? What should happen in these circumstances? At times, paraprofessionals are in a unique position in classrooms. Because they work with the classroom teacher as part of a team, students may not see their authority in the same way. Sometimes students feel the teacher is the only official authority in the classroom. As a result, paraprofessionals don't always get the respect they deserve. Students must be reminded that paraprofessionals are part of the classroom teaching team and that paraprofessionals are also leaders in the classroom. Students should understand that paraprofessionals have clear expectations and expect students to follow through with their requests. Even when students understand that paraprofessionals are part of an educational team, they don't always follow classroom rules. Many people believe that the best way to respond to students who don't follow rules is to let them deal with the natural or **logical consequences** of their actions.

Logical/Natural Consequences

Rules and policies give students a sense of what's expected from them in their classrooms. Consequences are the actions taken when students don't follow the rules. One group of researchers describes logical consequences as the natural result that happens when students don't follow the rules or procedures (Dreikurs, Grunwald, & Pepper, 1982). For example, if a student writes on a desk, the natural or logical consequence would be to have to clean the desk. Another example would be to complete an assignment before going to recess. If a student doesn't comply, he or she would have to live with the alternative consequence of missing recess (Burden, 2006).

After her conversation with Mrs. Ramirez on policies, procedures, and consequences, Maria thought about how she would reteach her lesson. Let's take a look at how Maria changed her strategies based on Mrs. Ramirez's suggestions.

logical consequences
The natural result of failing to follow the rules or procedures within a classroom.

consecuencias lógicas
Resultado natural de no obedecer las reglas o los procedimientos de la clase.

> **Maria:** Good morning, boys and girls. Today we're going to work in our reading groups. Our lesson is very interesting and it will help you learn more about the topics we've been studying for the past few days. Before we begin, I'd like to explain our goals and the procedures for the lesson so you'll know exactly what I expect.

Today we're going to start by reviewing stories on families. I'll ask each of you to read a section of our story. Next, you will have the chance to work with one of your writing buddies on an assignment. Then you will read the remainder of the story silently.

Let's review our rules for participation when we read and share answers. Who can tell me how I know if you are volunteering to read?

Student: You know when we're ready to read when we raise our hands.

Establishing policies for participation in classrooms helps reduce classroom management difficulties.

Maria: Yes, your raised hand tells me you're ready to share with the group. When your hand is raised I know that you're ready to read. By taking turns everyone's ideas are shared.

Maria: Who can tell me how you will complete the worksheet assignment with your reading buddies?

Student: First, we read each question. Then, we listen to our buddy, and then, we talk about our answers. Next, we write down our answer for each question. When we're finished we read quietly.

Maria: That's a great answer. Let's do the first answer together, so everyone understands how to share with a partner. Remember, girls and boys, if you don't use your time well in class, you'll need to take your writing assignment home.

Based upon Mrs. Ramirez's suggestions Maria adapted her lessons, so that her students had better structure. She explained her expectations and she gave students the chance to tell her what they understood about the assignment. Maria's new way of teaching the lesson reduced confusion and frustration. For students who did not complete their work in class, the logical/natural consequence was to finish their work at home.

ADDRESSING DISRUPTIVE BEHAVIOR

The preventative measures Maria implemented in her classroom are very important. Maria's strategies reduced the number of problems within her lesson. However, there are also times when educators need to respond differently. In some classrooms educators include **token economies**, **behavior contracts**, and **time-out** options when more formal measures are necessary for managing disruptive behaviors.

Token economies, behavioral contracts, and time out are procedures used in many classrooms across the US. There are many educators and researchers who support these methods and believe they provide students with clear expectations and a structure for guiding behavior. There are many other educators who believe these methods for management teach students to behave well only because they get a reward or avoid punishment (Kohn, 2000). Researchers like Alfie Kohn believe that while token systems may work in the short run, it's also important to look at the causes of misbehavior. Kohn tells us that we should also think about the curriculum, instruction, and how teachers and students get along in the classroom (Kohn, 1996). As you think about the management policies in your classroom, think about what affects student behavior.

---

token economies
Ways of managing student behavior that include the use of extrinsic motivators such as candy, points, or stickers.

premios simbólicos
Métodos para controlar el comportamiento del estudiante que incluyen el uso de motivadores extrínsecos; como dulces, puntos extra o pegatinas.

---

behavioral contracts
Written guides with specific behavioral objectives in mind that include an outline of the rules and consequences of behaving in a certain way.

contratos de conducta
Guías escritas con objetivos de comportamiento específicos que incluyen un bosquejo de las reglas y de las consecuencias de comportarse de cierta manera.

---

time out
A way of managing behavior that involves moving a student to an isolated part of the classroom or to another room.

fuera de clase
Método de controlar la conducta en la clase que implica enviar a un estudiante fuera del aula o a una parte aislada de la misma.

Remaining calm when students become frustrated helps reduce management difficulties.

Token Economies

Token economies are ways of managing student behavior that include the use of **extrinsic motivators**. Extrinsic motivators are rewards that teachers give their students when they behave positively. Tokens, often in the form of points, candy, stickers, or privileges, are given to students when they do something right. Simply put, when students follow rules they receive tokens based upon their willingness to do what they're told (Burden, 2006). Adding tokens is often called **positive reinforcement**. If a student fails to behave, a token is taken away from the student. In these cases, students experience **negative reinforcement**. When extrinsic motivators don't have an impact on behavior, stricter strategies are used.

Behavior Contracts

Behavior contracts are used when students have difficulty following the rules in the classroom. Contracts are often used when other tools don't work with a particular student. Contracts are written with a behavioral objective in mind. Most contracts include a list of the rules and consequences for behaving in a certain way. Contracts might include:

1. a definition of a behavior that is expected;
2. a time period in which the behavior will occur;
3. rewards if the contract is followed as written; and
4. punishment or consequences if the contract is not followed as written (Burden, 2006).

The content of many contracts focuses on behavior. Others include learning or social skill goals. Contracts are useful because they give learners and their teachers a clear sense of what is expected within a certain amount of time. What are some of the advantages of a contract? Are there students for whom contracts will not work?

Time Out

Time out, or time away from the group, offers students time away from the main lesson activities within a classroom. A time-out location may be a chair or a place for a break away from the other students. Time out may also be located in another room, where a student who is having difficulty following the rules spends time under the watch of another adult such as a librarian or nearby classroom teacher (Burden, 2006). Time out is a controversial practice. Time to think about actions away from the main action in a classroom might be useful for some students. However, time out is also a tool that sets students apart from the rest of the group and may cause embarrassment or isolation. Embarrassing a student is not an effective way to build a community. Many educators and researchers believe working with a student one-to-one is a better method of addressing a concern with a student, and it avoids embarrassment. Are there ways in which time out could be used as a reward where students get to take a break? Talk to your classroom teacher about how time out or time away from the group could be used in positive ways.

---

extrinsic motivators
Rewards that are paired with a positive behavior. Tokens, often in the form of points, candy, stickers, or privileges are distributed to students based on positive behavior in educational settings.

motivadores extrínsecos
Recompensas que se asocian a un comportamiento positivo. Estas recompensas, a menudo puntos extra, caramelos, pegatinas, o privilegios se les dan a los estudiantes para premiar un buen comportamiento.

positive reinforcement
A reward that maintains or increases a behavior.

refuerzo positivo
Recompensa que mantiene o fomenta un comportamiento.

negative reinforcement
An action that decreases a behavior.

refuerzo negativo
Acción que desalienta un comportamiento.

Token economies, contracts, and time out are very structured, teacher-directed management strategies. These methods are used when preventative measures fail to change behaviors. Based on your work in the classroom, are there times when students need more structure? Are there types of lessons when students require less structure? How will you provide guidance for students and at the same time keep a positive relationship with them? Will your methods of management work the same way with all students?

CLASSROOM MANAGEMENT IN DIVERSE CLASSROOM SETTINGS

American schools are filled with children from around the globe. The suggestions provided in this chapter remind educators of the importance of the wonderful differences among our students. Effective educators understand that the needs of students are different. In the area of classroom management, today's educators must think about how cultural and language differences influence how they interact with students. They must think about how their teaching matches their students' needs and whether traditional methods of management help all students the same way.

Experience and research tell us that all children grow when they are in classrooms that celebrate individual differences. Effective management strategies are those that make students feel supported and nurtured in the classroom. Educators of culturally and linguistically diverse students know that students from various cultures bring unique ways of interacting, expectations about classroom discipline, and responses to classroom policies (Echevarria & Graves, 2007; Hernandez, 2001). When students new to the US are provided

Effective classroom management includes recognizing the diverse needs of students.

with support, they experience more success as learners. Smooth transitions into American classrooms are particularly important for students learning English for the first time. For children learning English, classroom practices should be sensitive to cultural differences related to proximity, physical contacts with students, and public displays of feedback. Researchers on classroom management and multicultural education remind us that classroom policies and procedures should reflect the interaction styles and cultural differences of a wide range of students (Echevarria & Graves, 2007; Hernandez, 2001). Let's take a look at a few examples of classrooms where teacher are culturally sensitive to their students.

1. Proximity is a regularly used tool for prompting students' attention. Proximity is a useful away for educators to remind students of policies and procedures. Teachers must be sensitive to students' levels of personal space because of cultural differences in how space is viewed. For example, where an individual stands when communicating with others may show either respect or lack of respect depending upon one's cultural background. Effective educators understand cultural differences among their students when they make their management plans (Hernandez, 2001).

2. Like proximity, the appropriateness of **contacts** and interactions with students requires cultural sensitivity. Tapping a student on the shoulder as a way of focusing attention may be interpreted quite differently across groups of students (Hernandez, 2001). It is important that educators think about these cultural differences when making contacts. A verbal reminder or a tap on a student's desk to focus attention might be quite usual in some classrooms. For other children, who are not as familiar with the more subtle cues that are common in American schools, a teacher or paraprofessional may need to explain her/his expectations more clearly.

3. Public displays of **feedback** through comments made to students by a teacher or paraprofessional may be understood differently across groups of students. For some students, public comments about good work or reprimands may be quite common. For other students, these public comments may be embarrassing or may promote a spirit of group competition that is less common and acceptable in some cultures (Hernandez, 2001).

STUDENTS' PERSPECTIVES ON MANAGEMENT

In addition to your goals for making students feel welcome in the classroom, think about how you, as a part of the education team, will gather feedback from students and their families about their perspectives on effective classroom environments. With the help of your classroom teacher, develop a classroom management survey to be used with the students and families in your classroom. Include questions that ask students to explain the rules and classroom practices they find important. Parents and guardians may also share important ideas on classroom policies for students from diverse backgrounds.

---

contacts
Interpersonal or physical interactions with students.

contactos
Interacciones interpersonales o físicas con los estudiantes.

---

feedback
Information on performance that can be used to increase future learning.

reacción
Información sobre una actuación o desempeño que puede ser usada para fomentar un futuro aprendizaje.

Surveys are tools that can help educators understand more about their students. The grade level you teach and the needs of your students will affect the type of survey you develop. Tracy and her classroom teacher included the following questions on the survey they sent to the parents:

1. Describe the three most important rules for every classroom.
2. Explain why you believe classroom rules are important.
3. In what situations is your child most comfortable within the classroom?
4. Describe how a teacher should respond to a student who is following the classroom policies and procedures.
5. Describe how a teacher should respond to a student who is NOT following the classroom policies and procedures.

SUMMARY

When groups of people come together, rules and policies help them understand how to work together. Like other organizations, effective classrooms include management plans that explain expectations, rules, and procedures. This chapter explained key parts of effective classroom management including possible causes of misbehavior, steps that help reduce management difficulties, and follow-up action when problems do happen. Management is an important part of any classroom, but management is more complicated than simply responding when students misbehave. The relationships between students, teachers, curriculum, and instruction create positive communities where student teaching and learning are the goals. In these communities everyone wins!

CHECKING FOR UNDERSTANDING

1. Describe the impact that curriculum and instruction may have on classroom management. What type of curriculum do you believe children find the most interesting? What type of curriculum might be least interesting? Why?
2. Describe preventative measures that reduce the chances for disruptive behavior in the classroom. Which one are you most likely to include when working with students? Why?
3. How do the language and cultural differences among students impact their classroom experiences?

POINTS OF VIEW

Maria and Tracy share the following suggestions on how to put your personal philosophy of classroom management into action.

1. Based on what you have learned in this chapter, create a personal discipline policy for classroom management. Write answers to the following points with your classroom teacher as you create your plan.
   a. What are the responsibilities of the teacher in a classroom?
   b. What are the responsibilities of paraprofessionals in a classroom?

c. What are the roles of students in a classroom?

d. Describe your expectations for student behavior.

e. How will you prevent discipline problems in the classroom?

f. How will you support the students in the classroom?

g. What are the some of the rules that should be included in any classroom?

2. In order to learn the perspectives on management of other educators at your school, work with your classroom teacher and interview two teachers and a sample of students. Talking with others will help you learn about how other people manage a classroom. The information you learn from others will help you as you think about your own plan. Maria and Tracy suggest you use the following questions as part of your interviews:

a. Why have specific classroom management tools been chosen? Are they successful?

b. What common management problems do teachers face?

c. Are there schoolwide discipline policies?

d. What are the consequences of misbehavior?

What Do Students Think?

Ask students their opinions of the rules used in their classrooms. Identify students' views on fair and unfair classroom policies and procedures. Make sure your discussion focuses on the *rules* and **procedures** and **not** on individual teachers.

Ideas for Observations

Think about these questions during your classroom observations: Are the classroom rules posted on the walls? How does the teacher react to misbehavior? How are the seats arranged? Does the teacher demonstrate *"withitness"*? Is a routine followed in the class? Does the lesson include interesting activities?

PORTFOLIO CORNER

This chapter focused on the ways paraprofessionals assist classroom teachers as they create productive classroom environments. Productive classrooms exist when educators understand how curriculum, instruction, and individual differences influence the classroom environment. The suggestions in this chapter included ideas for creating classroom rules and ideas for how educators respond when children misbehave.

Use Table 3-2, Sample Portfolio Framework, and find sample artifacts that will meet Standard III based on our discussions in Chapter 3. Examples of artifacts from Chapter 3 might include surveys to students, parents, and other educators. You may also want to include classroom maps and seating charts. Contracts with students and notices to parents about classroom policies and procedures are other artifacts to think about.

TABLE 3-2 Sample Portfolio Framework

STANDARD I—SUPPORTING INSTRUCTIONAL OPPORTUNITIES	STANDARD II—DEMONSTRATING PROFESSIONALISM AND ETHICAL PRACTICE
See Chapter 7	See Chapter 2
STANDARD III—SUPPORTING A POSITIVE LEARNING ENVIRONMENT	**STANDARD IV—COMMUNICATING EFFECTIVELY AND PARTICIPATING IN THE TEAM PROCESSES**
Sample artifacts might include: • Classroom map and seating arrangement • Student survey • Parent/caregiver survey • Parent advocate survey • Interview questions for teachers and students Behavioral contracts • List of roles and policies • Your ideas	See Chapter 6

REFERENCES

Brophy, J. (1998). *Motivating students to learn*. Boston: McGraw-Hill.

Burden, P. (2006). *Classroom Management: Creating a successful learning community* (2nd ed.). Hoboken, New Jersey: John Wiley & Sons, Inc.

Dreikurs, R., Grunwald, B., & Pepper, F. (1982). *Maintaining sanity in the classroom: Classroom management techniques* (2nd ed.). New York: Harper & Row.

Echevarria, J., & Graves, A. (2007). *Sheltered content instruction: Teaching English Language learners with diverse abilities* (3rd ed.). Boston: Ally & Bacon.

Gay, G. (2000). *Culturally responsive teaching: Theory, research, and practice*. New York: Teachers College Press.

Hernandez, H. (2001). *Multicultural education: A teacher's guide to linking context, process, and content* (2nd ed.). Upper Saddle River, New Jersey: Pearson.

Kauchak, D., & Eggen, P. (2005). *Introduction to teaching: Becoming a professional* (2nd ed.). Upper Saddle River, New Jersey: Pearson.

Kounin, J.S. (1970). *Discipline and group management in classrooms*. New York: Holt, Reinhart, and Winston.

Tribes Learning Community Model (2006). Retrieved February 2, 2006 from http://www.tribes.com.

Villegas, A.M., & Lucas, T. (2002). *Educating culturally responsive teachers: A coherent approach*. New York: State University Press.

ADDITIONAL READINGS ON CLASSROOM MANAGEMENT

Fay, J., & Funk, D. (1995). *Teaching with love and logic: Taking control of the classroom*. Golden, Colorado: The Love and Logic Press, Inc.

Parenti, J. (2001). *First year urban teacher*. Philadelphia, Pennsylvania: Teacher for Hire.

Wong, H. (1998). *The first days of school*. Mountain View, California: Harry Wong Publications.

Additional selected readings and Paraprofessional electronic resources are available as part of the student Online Companion web site: www.earlychilded.delmar.com.

EN ESPAÑOL

OBJETIVOS DEL APRENDIZAJE

manejo de la clase
Proceso de crear y de mantener orden y disciplina en la clase.

classroom management
The process of creating and maintaining order in the classroom.

Después de leer y reflexionar sobre este capítulo podrá comprender mejor:

- Los factores que afectan el **manejo de la clase**
- Cómo desarrollar reglas y consecuencias
- Cómo tratar el mal comportamiento
- Cómo manejar un conjunto heterogéneo de estudiantes

A medida que lea este capítulo, hágase las siguientes preguntas:

1. ¿Qué piensa sobre la forma en que los estudiantes deben comportarse en el aula?
2. ¿Cuáles son algunas de las estrategias que los maestros usan para atraer la atención de los estudiantes?
3. ¿Cuáles son algunas de las estrategias que los maestros usan como reacción al mal comportamiento de los estudiantes?
4. ¿Cómo pueden las diferencias culturales e idiomáticas entre los educadores y los estudiantes afectar el comportamiento en la clase y cómo reaccionan los educadores?
5. ¿Qué documentos incluirá en su carpeta para demostrar su conocimiento de las estrategias eficaces en el manejo de la clase?

PARA VERIFICAR LA COMPRENSIÓN

1. Describa el impacto que el currículo y la enseñanza pueden tener en el manejo de la clase. ¿Qué tipo de currículo piensa que será más interesante para los niños? ¿Qué tipo de currículo será menos interesante? ¿Por qué?
2. Describa las medidas preventivas que reducen la probabilidad del mal comportamiento en la clase. ¿Cuál de ellas piensa que va a emplear en su trabajo con los estudiantes? ¿Por qué?
3. ¿Cómo afectan el idioma y las diferencias culturales entre los estudiantes sus experiencias en la clase?

PUNTOS DE VISTA

Maria y Tracy comparten las siguientes sugerencias sobre cómo poner en práctica su filosofía personal del manejo de la clase.

1. De acuerdo con lo que ha aprendido en este capítulo, elabore una política personal de disciplina para el manejo de la clase. Junto con su maestro de clase escriba respuestas a los siguientes puntos a medida que vaya elaborando su plan:

   a. ¿Cuáles son las responsabilidades del maestro en el aula?
   b. ¿Cuáles son las responsabilidades de los paraprofesionales en el aula?
   c. ¿Qué papel tienen los estudiantes en el aula?
   d. Describa sus expectativas con respecto al comportamiento de los estudiantes.

e. ¿Cómo prevendrá problemas disciplinarios en el aula?

f. ¿Cómo apoyará a los estudiantes en el aula?

g. ¿Cuáles son algunas de las reglas que deberían emplearse en todas las aulas?

2. Para saber qué piensan otros educadores de su escuela sobre el manejo de la clase, planee con su maestro entrevistas a dos maestros y a varios estudiantes. Hablar con otros lo o la ayudará a enterarse de la forma en que proceden los demás educadores. La información que obtenga le servirá para elaborar su propio plan. Maria y Tracy sugieren que utilice las siguientes preguntas como parte de las entrevistas:

a. ¿Por qué se han elegido técnicas específicas para el manejo de la clase? ¿Son o no acertadas?

b. ¿Cuáles son problemas comunes del manejo de la clase que los maestros deben confrontar?

c. ¿Hay medidas disciplinarias que impone la escuela?

d. ¿Cuáles son las consecuencias del mal comportamiento?

¿Qué piensan los estudiantes?

Pregunte a los estudiantes qué piensan sobre las reglas disciplinarias de sus clases. Identifique sus opiniones sobre lo que consideran justo e injusto en el aula. Cerciórese de que sus conversaciones se enfoquen en las reglas disciplinarias y no en los maestros.

TABLA 3-2 Estructura de una carpeta modelo

ESTÁNDAR I—APOYAR TODA OPORTUNIDAD EDUCATIVA	ESTÁNDAR II—DEMOSTRAR CONDUCTA PROFESIONAL Y ÉTICA
Vea el Capítulo 7	Vea el Capítulo 2
ESTÁNDAR III—OFRECER UN AMBIENTE CONDUCENTE AL APRENDIZAJE	**ESTÁNDAR IV—COMUNICARSE EFICAZMENTE Y PARTICIPAR EN EL PROCESO DE EQUIPO**
Los objetos de muestra pueden incluir: <ul><li>Mapa de la clase y diagrama de la disposición de los asientos</li><li>Encuesta a los estudiantes</li><li>Encuesta a los padres o guardianes</li><li>Encuesta a representantes de los padres</li><li>Preguntas para entrevistar a maestros y estudiantes</li><li>Contratos de conducta</li><li>Lista de funciones y regulaciones</li><li>Sus ideas</li></ul>	Vea el Capítulo 6

Ideas para las observaciones

Considere las siguientes preguntas durante sus observaciones de clase: ¿Están las reglas del salón de clase a la vista? ¿Cómo reacciona el maestro ante el mal comportamiento? ¿Cómo están dispuestos los asientos? ¿Cómo demuestra el maestro que "está con los ojos abiertos"? ¿Se sigue una rutina en la clase? ¿Incluye la lección actividades interesantes?

Para la carpeta

En este capítulo vimos cómo los paraprofesionales ayudan a los maestros de clase a crear un entorno productivo en la clase. Una clase productiva tiene lugar cuando los educadores comprenden cómo el currículo, la enseñanza y las diferencias individuales influyen en el ambiente de la clase. Entre las sugerencias de este capítulo se incluyen ideas para crear reglas en una clase e ideas para responder cuando los niños no se comportan.

Use la tabla 3-1, Estructura de una carpeta modelo, y haga una lista de objetos de muestra que se refieran al estándar III, de acuerdo a lo tratado en el Capítulo 3. Entre los documentos puede haber entrevistas a estudiantes, padres y otros educadores. También puede incluir planos del salón de clases y de la disposición de los asientos. Otros documentos a considerar son contratos con los estudiantes y notas para los padres sobre reglas y procedimientos del salón de clases.

STUDENTS AND THEIR EDUCATIONAL NEEDS

LEARNING OBJECTIVES

After reading and reflecting on this chapter you will understand:

- The concept of learner diversity
- The needs of students receiving special education services
- The needs of students learning English

As you read this chapter, ask yourself these questions:

1. What do educators mean by diversity in classrooms?

2. What does inclusion mean?

3. What are some of the unique needs of students in special education classrooms?

4. What is an Individualized Education Plan (IEP)?

5. What are some of the unique needs of students in classrooms for non-native English speakers?

6. How does the language of students change from the classroom to the playground? What are the differences between formal and informal exchanges? How do formal and informal language differences impact English Language Learners?

7. What kind of artifacts will you include in your portfolio to reflect your knowledge of the educational needs of students receiving special education services as well as of those learning English for the first time?

KEY TERMS

Attention Deficit Hyperactivity Disorder (ADHD)

Basic Interpersonal Communication Skills (BICS)

bilingual

cerebral palsy

Cognitive Academic Language Proficiency Skills (CALPS)

computer assistive technology

English as a Second Language (ESL)

English Language Learners (ELL)

exceptionalities

inclusion

Individualized Education Plan (IEP)

Individuals with Disabilities Education Improvement Act (IDEIA)

learning disability

Least Restrictive Environments (LRE)

mainstreaming

mental retardation

Public Law 94-142

sheltered classrooms

special education

transitional bilingual education

INTRODUCTION

Witajcie	Bienvenidos	Vel
Willkommen	Kaibu	Welcome!
Soo dhawow		

No matter what the language is, every student in a classroom wants to feel welcome and included. Today's classrooms are filled with children from around the world. Some students are new to the US and some come from families that have been in this country for generations. No matter where a classroom is located, students bring with them different abilities, languages, and life experiences. Effective educators understand and celebrate the diverse qualities of their students. This chapter provides information on learner differences and highlights ways educators can recognize, understand, and celebrate each of their students.

**Braille Alphabet
(English Braille America Edition)**

a	b	c	d	e	f	g	h	i	j
k	l	m	n	o	p	q	r	s	t
u	v	w	x	y	z				

#1   #2   #3   ...

1– ●●–4
2– ●●–5
3– ●●–6

Some students with visual differences use Braille to learn content. Recognizing their special needs makes them feel welcome in their classrooms.

Some students with hearing differences use American Sign Language. "Welcome" is an important word in any language. © *Dennis Cox*

When you hear or read the word *diversity,* what are some of the thoughts that come to mind? For some people, variety is the first word that pops up. For these people, diversity includes different ideas, experiences, and views on how to approach life. For other people, the word diversity implies confusion, struggles, and misunderstandings. A positive approach to understanding diversity recognizes each child's strengths and opportunities for building skills and abilities. As a paraprofessional in today's classrooms, your primary responsibility is working with children with diverse and complex needs. In your work with students, think about the ways you will make a positive difference in their lives.

The following scene is from a classroom where the differences among learners are *not* being addressed in the best possible way. Tonya, the paraprofessional in this classroom, is *not* familiar with individual student needs. She's a beginner who hasn't learned yet how to recognize each student's needs and does not adjust her methods to meet those needs. As you read what happens in the classroom, think about how you would respond as a paraprofessional in Tonya's situation. Consider how you will support learning for your students.

Tonya: Boys and girls, it's time for the spelling competition! I will read a word, and then you'll be asked to spell the word to earn points for your team. It's your turn, Carlos. The first word is *photograph, photograph.*

Carlos: (Thinking aloud) Fotografía, fotografia.

Tonya: No Carlos, the word is pho . . . to . . . graph . . . (exaggerated). The English word is *photograph.*

Carlos: f-o-t-o-g-r-a-f-i-a.

Tonya: No that's wrong Carlos. The letter *f* is not in the word photograph. Next person. Karline, it's your turn. Please spell the word *photograph, photograph.*

Karline: (Karline can't be heard. She tries again but nobody can hear her, as she's facing away from the group).

Tonya: Karline I can't understand what you're saying. Will someone please move Karline's wheelchair away from the wall?

Tonya: Let's try another word, boys and girls. I don't think you've been studying. Next word. The word is *alphabet, alphabet.* Ian it's your turn.

Ian: *alphabet, alphabet* (thinking aloud). Let's see, a-l-h, . . . uhmm . . . a-l-h-p . . . No it's a-l-h-p-a-b-e-: *alphabet.*

Tonya: No Ian, you keep switching your letters in your words. Don't you remember that we've talked about this? You have to stop switching your letters when you're spelling words.

Tonya: Boys and girls, I can tell you're not studying your words. Let's try one last word. Ruby, it's your turn. Oh, sorry Ruby. I'll skip to the next person since we can't understand you very well.

As you read through the classroom scenario of this new paraprofessional, what are some of your questions about learner differences? How would you have acted if you were leading this lesson? Could Tonya have structured the lesson differently to better meet her students' needs? How did her instruction limit her students' success?

STUDENTS WITH EXCEPTIONALITIES

The stories of Carlos, Ian, Karline, and Ruby reflect the real worlds of many children in American schools. Their lives tell the stories of children learning English, those with learning differences, kids with different physical abilities, and students with differences in their hearing. Ian, Karline, and Ruby are students identified as having **exceptionalities** in their abilities. They make up about 12% of the student population in US schools (Heward, 2003). Since Carlos is learning English, his differences are not identified as exceptionalities. Differences in language require different strategies for instruction and plans for learning. As in the case with children with exceptionalities, students with language differences need extra resources to meet their full potential. For many students with exceptionalities, paraprofessionals are an important part of their educational experiences.

Classrooms for students with exceptionalities require educators with special training and practical experience. The special education teacher is licensed and has the professional training to work directly with children with many different needs. In the special education classroom, the special education teacher is the lead teacher, but depends on the hard work of the paraprofessional who is part of the education team. Paraprofessionals who work in special education classrooms have a number of jobs including:

1. Helping the classroom teacher with lessons, paperwork, and organization;
2. Monitoring student work inside and outside of class;
3. Tutoring and working with small groups of students;
4. Teaching teacher developed lessons;
5. Helping with classroom management; and
6. Sharing ideas and suggestions as part of the educational team (Boyle, 2002).

Each of these jobs is important and helps every child in a classroom. Let's look at the ways in which students' needs influence the kind of support they are given.

Ian, Karline, and Ruby are three children with exceptionalities. They require special accommodations in their classrooms. Ian has a **learning disability** which means he needs additional help, and his teacher must make changes in the materials he reads and writes. Learning disabilities may also include difficulties speaking, completing math assignments, or reasoning (National Joint Committee on Learning Disabilities, 1994). Ian's educational plan requires that his assignments are written. He writes his assignments through **computer assistive technology**. Assistive technology helps Ian with his writing. In our classroom scene, Ian's educational needs could have been met if the paraprofessional had allowed him to write his answers using a computer. Another option for Ian

---

exceptionalities
Differences present in children who need additional resources to meet their full potential. These children make up 12% of the US student population and are often served in either special education or mainstream classes.

excepcionalidades
Diferencias presentes en niños que necesitan recursos adicionales para lograr su mayor potencial. Estos niños componen el 12% de la población de estudiantes de los EE.UU. y asisten a menudo a clases de educación especial o clases regulares.

learning disability
An exceptionality that involves difficulties in acquiring and using information in areas such as listening, speaking, reading, and writing, and completing mathematical related assignments.

dificultades de aprendizaje
Excepcionalidades que implican problemas en obtener y usar información cuando se escucha, habla, lee o escribe, y para completar tareas de tipo matemático.

computer assistive technology
Technological support provided to students with special education needs.

tecnología de asistencia por computadoras
Apoyo tecnológico que se da a los estudiantes con necesidades especiales.

Today's classrooms are filled with students possessing unique needs and abilities.

Students with exceptionalities include those with special physical needs.

cerebral palsy
A condition that results in difficulty of movement. While cerebral palsy limits movement and muscle coordination, it doesn't necessarily affect other abilities such as intellectual capacity.

parálisis cerebral
Condición que resulta en problemas de movimiento. Si bien la parálisis cerebral limita el movimiento y la coordinación de los músculos no afecta necesariamente otras habilidades tales como la capacidad intelectual.

would have been to choose the correct answer from 2 or 3 options. Both of these adaptations would help Ian do his best work and provide him with the support he needs.

Karline is a child with **cerebral palsy**. Karline's cerebral palsy means she has difficulty controlling her movements, and she uses a wheelchair to move around more freely. While cerebral palsy limits movement and muscle coordination, other abilities such as intellectual capacity may not be affected (Cerebral Palsy Facts, 2007). Karline's educational goals reflect the need for additional time and accommodations when working on activities that require physical movements other than writing. Games and activities where Karline uses language are a great opportunity for participation. A verbal game is a good strategy for Karline, who uses an electronic keyboard. In the spelling competition Karline could have been given the chance to write her answer on her keyboard. Additional time to think about her answers is also important for Karline.

The differences among students in Tonya's classroom reflect only a few of the needs of learners in today's classrooms. Other differences include levels of **mental retardation**. People with mental retardation have an exceptionality that may include intellectual differences that affect reading, writing, listening, caring for themselves, and interacting with other people (Turnbull, Shank, & Turnbull, 2002). Educators must be aware that mental retardation exists at multiple levels. These levels determine whether the amount of support given to a child would be intermittent, limited, extensive, or all-around support (Turnbull, Turnbull, Shank, Smith, & Leal, 2004). Education goals might require that a student is given more time to complete assignments or that reading requirements are broken down in ways that make the content more accessible. Paraprofessionals who work with children with mental retardation understand that each child's needs are different.

Ruby is a student with a hearing impairment. Her abilities allow her to take part in a mainstream classroom where she participates in most lessons with the other students in her class. She has two hearing aids which help her understand others. Ruby receives support that helps with her language development. The requirements on Ruby's education plan state that she should be given both oral

mental retardation
An exceptionality that includes intellectual limitations that impact reading, writing, listening, self-care, and interacting with other people.

retraso mental
Excepcionalidad que incluye limitaciones intelectuales que afectan la lectura, la escritura, la audición, el cuidado de uno mismo, o la interacción con los demás.

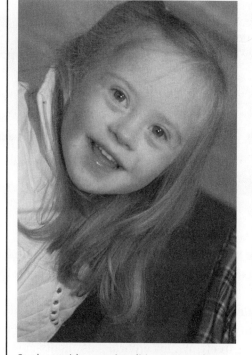

Students with exceptionalities are members of every school community throughout the country.

Computer assistive technology provides many students with the support they need to succeed in the classroom.

and written assignments with clear and brief directions. During the spelling competition, Ruby could have been given the opportunity to either write her response or choose the correct spelling from a series of options.

SPECIAL EDUCATION AND THE LAW

The children in this chapter represent the needs of many in today's classrooms. Table 4-1, Disability Categories, includes other exceptionalities of children attending public schools. As you can see from Table 4-1, Disability Categories, the needs of students with exceptionalities cover many different areas. Because special education spans such a wide range of services, laws have been created in response. In 1975, **Public-Law 94-142 (Education for All Handicapped Children)** was passed and required that all children with special needs receive a free and appropriate education.

The Americans with Disabilities Act, ADA, is a law that protects the civil rights of people with disabilities in schools *and* in the community. This law makes sure that people are given an equal chance to participate in different activities through accommodations they need at work, in transportation, through special services at school, and through extra support they might need when they communicate. ADA is important for paraprofessionals because they are often the people who make sure students are given support in classrooms and schools (Hardman, Drew, & Egan, 2006).

Another important law for educators is the Individuals with Disabilities Act (IDEA) that was passed in 1977, and was updated in 2004 to a version known as

Public Law 94-142
The Education of All Handicapped Children Act passed in 1975 specified state and local policies in protecting the rights and educational needs of students with disabilities.

Ley pública 94-142
Ley de educación de todos los niños discapacitados aprobada en 1975 que especifica políticas locales y estatales para proteger los derechos y las necesidades educativas de estudiantes con dificultades de aprendizaje.

TABLE 4-1 Disability Categories

DIFFERING NEEDS AMONG GROUPS OF STUDENTS WITH EXCEPTIONALITIES
Autism
Deaf-Blind
Developmental Delay
Emotional Disturbance
Hearing Impairments
Mental Retardation
Multiple Disabilities
Orthopedic
Other Health Impairments
Specific Learning Disabilities
Speech or Language Impairments
Traumatic Brain Injury
Visual Impairments including Blindness

Individuals with Disabilities Education Improvement Act (IDEIA)

The major special education legislation in the US adopted originally in the 1970s and reauthorized in 1990 and 2004. IDEIA primarily addresses the policies and procedures related to providing students with special needs with a "free and appropriate" education in the "least restrictive environment".

Ley federal de mejoras en la educación para niños con dificultades de aprendizaje (IDEIA por sus siglas en inglés)
La legislación de educación especial más importante de los EE.UU. fue adoptada originalmente en 1970 y reautorizada en 1990 y 2004. IDEIA trata de las políticas y procedimientos relacionados con proveer educación "gratuita y adecuada" en un "ambiente libre de restricciones" a los estudiantes con necesidades especiales.

special education
Educational services provided to students whose behavior or performance on various tests meets the standards that describe a specific disability.

educación especial
Servicios educativos para los estudiantes cuyo desempeño en varios exámenes coincide con los estándares que indican una dificultad de aprendizaje específica.

Individuals with Disabilities Education Improvement Act (IDEIA).

IDEIA helps people with disabilities. It's different from ADA because it focuses entirely on the rights of children at *school*. This law is also very important to paraprofessionals. It makes sure that preschool and school-aged children are given extra support in classrooms, often through the help of paraprofessionals.

ADA and IDEIA are laws that work together to provide support for students with special needs. Sometimes the help and services under IDEA may be limited. If this is the case, and students need even more support, they may receive extra services through the guidelines described under ADA.

Each of these laws has helped the education of millions of children with exceptionalities during the past 30 years. The laws make sure that each child's education is individualized and meets the legal requirement for students in the best ways possible.

IDEIA requires that children with disabilities are given an education that reflects their needs. The law also states that the services they receive must be clearly defined based on their needs. Students are eligible for **special education** services when their behavior or performance on different tests meets the standards for a specific disability. The services for children in special education classrooms must take place in **Least Restrictive Environments (LRE)**. LREs are classrooms where instruction and curriculum are planned specifically for students with exceptionalities. Least restrictive classrooms help keep all children within the regular education classroom and encourage **mainstreaming**.

Mainstreaming became a part of schools in the 1970s. Educators, parent groups, and community members made sure students receiving special education services were included in regular grade level classrooms as often as possible. The goal of including all children in mainstream classrooms is to encourage **inclusion**. Inclusive practices:

1. include students with special needs in regular classrooms;
2. make sure that students are in grade appropriate classrooms with additional support; and
3. provide necessary support in regular classrooms whenever possible (Kauchak & Eggen, 2005).

Inclusive classrooms rely heavily on the work of paraprofessionals. Paraprofessionals give students support and help classroom teachers adapt curriculum and instruction so that children with exceptionalities are contributing members in their classrooms. Often, the role of a paraprofessional is included in a student's education plan. These education plans are like "roadmaps" for a course of action. This "roadmap" includes goals for learning, a timeline for student progress, and ways of measuring student progress. An **Individualized Education Plan** or IEP spells out the long-term goals and the support services a student will need to reach those goals. These support services are delivered by the classroom teacher, paraprofessional, and other service providers working as team members. The contents of an IEP often include:

1. learning goals in content areas or in general skills such as reading or writing;

Least Restrictive Environment (LRE)
A requirement of IDEIA where instruction and curriculum are planned specifically for students with exceptionalities. Least restrictive environments are designed to keep all children within the regular education classroom as often as possible, and to encourage future mainstreaming into traditional classroom settings.

ambiente con menos restricciones (LRE)
Uno de los requisitos de IDEIA, por el cual la enseñanza y el currículo se planean específicamente para estudiantes con excepcionalidades. Los ambientes con menos restricciones están diseñados para mantener a todos los niños en un salón de clases común en la medida de lo posible, y para alentar su futuro ingreso a un salón de clases tradicional.

mainstreaming
A policy that became a part of school practices in the 1970s when educators, parent groups, and community members advocated for the movement of students from special education settings to traditional grade level classrooms.

con la mayoría
(mainstreaming)
Política que se convirtió en parte de las prácticas escolares en los años 70 cuando educadores, grupos de padres y miembros de la comunidad abogaron porque los estudiantes se trasladaran de las clases de educación especial a las clases regulares.

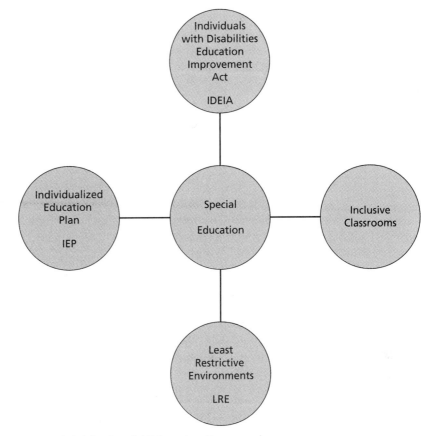

FIGURE 4-1 The Special Education Framework

2. goals for physical behaviors such as general movement, writing, or taking part in physical activities; and/or

3. social skills in areas such as getting along with students and teachers.

The exceptionalities of children help determine the direction of the services they receive. The policies and procedures in special education give educators guidelines for creating the best learning environments for their students. Figure 4-1, The Special Education Framework, provides an overview of each of the policies that support the education of children with exceptionalities.

DIVERSE EXCEPTIONALITIES

The majority of children receiving special education services have exceptionalities that are considered to be mild to moderate, such as many learning disabilities and **Attention Deficit Hyperactivity Disorders (ADHD)**. For children like Ian with learning disabilities, help from paraprofessionals may include working one-to-one with a student, reading to a student, assisting a student in a small group, or guiding a student's participation in the routines of a classroom.

Children with ADHD bring a unique set of needs to classrooms. Children with this exceptionality may show behaviors such as hyperactivity, impulsivity, and difficulties paying attention in class. While most children show these behaviors on some level at some point in time, children with ADHD display these behaviors more often and at high levels of intensity (Santrock 2006). Many children

inclusion
Participation of children with exceptionalities in the general education classrooms of their peers with appropriate support and services.

inclusión
Participación de los niños con excepcionalidades en los salones de clase de sus pares con el apoyo y los servicios apropiados.

Individualized Education Plan (IEP)
A requirement of IDEIA (see below) that lists the goals and services for a child identified as needing special education services. IEPs typically address the child's present level of performance; determines short and long-term goals; describes the extent to which a child will participate in mainstream classes; identifies dates for services to begin and end, and proposes plans for monitoring the child's growth.

Plan de educación individualizada (IEP por sus siglas en inglés)
Un requisito de IDEIA que enumera las metas y los servicios programados para un niño que requiere servicios de educación especial. Esos planes generalmente se refieren al nivel de desempeño actual del niño; determinan metas a corto y largo plazo; explican hasta qué grado el niño participará en las clases regulares; dan las fechas de comienzo y terminación de los servicios y proponen planes para controlar el desarrollo del estudiante.

with ADHD have difficulty paying attention. They may also be restless in class and they may find assignments difficult to complete. Medications and behavior modification may be recommended for children with ADHD in order to reduce many off-task behaviors. Support and medication allow many of these children to participate in most mainstream classrooms. Paraprofessionals working with children with ADHD help them focus during lessons, complete assignments, and provide one-to-one support. For children with more severe exceptionalities, the support provided by paraprofessionals is more intensive and is dispensed full time throughout the school day.

Under IDEIA, paraprofessionals are only allowed to work in areas for which they have been trained. The needs of children with severe exceptionalities require learning situations that meet their cognitive, social, or physical goals. As a result, the specific type of support provided by a paraprofessional must be clearly defined. In addition to appropriate training, paraprofessionals must be supervised in their teaching and professional responsibilities. For children whose exceptionalities are more severe, the support provided by paraprofessionals may include:

1. interpreting for students with communication disorders;
2. providing levels of physical therapy under the direction of a professional therapist;
3. assisting with feeding or hygiene needs; or
4. serving as a job coach for students ready to leave high school and enter the world of work (Ashbaker & Morgan, 2006).

TABLE 4-2 Special Education Vocabulary Worksheet

KEY TERM	FORMAL DEFINITION	YOUR WORDS
Computer Assistive Technology		
Exceptionalities		
Inclusion		
Individualized Education Plan (IEP)		
Individuals with Disabilities Education Improvement Act (IDEIA)		
Learning Disability		
Least Restrictive Environment		
Mainstreaming		
Mental Retardation		
PL 94-142		
Special Education		

*Attention Deficit
Hyperactivity Disorder
(ADHD)*
An exceptionality that often
includes behaviors such as
hyperactivity, impulsivity,
and difficulties paying
attention in class. These
behaviors occur at high
frequencies with high levels
of intensity.

*Desorden de hiperactividad
con déficit de atención
(ADHD por sus siglas en
inglés)*
Excepcionalidad que incluye a
menudo comportamientos
tales como hiperactividad,
impulsividad y dificultad para
prestar atención en clase.
Estos comportamientos
ocurren con gran frecuencia
y a un alto nivel de
intensidad.

In order to be an effective member of a special education team, paraprofessionals need to know the parts of special education programs. They must also understand their role as a member of educational teams. Table 4-2, Special Education Vocabulary Worksheet, gives a review of the content covered thus far in this chapter. The worksheet provides space to write down your notes and your own interpretation of key terms.

Successful special education programs result when educators, children and families, and service providers work together. Chapter 5 provides additional information on special education and legal issues. Chapter 7 includes a discussion on instructional and assessment tools for working with a wide range of students.

CHANGES AFFECTING CONTEMPORARY CLASSROOMS

Students with exceptionalities are among those who have not always been a part of mainstream classrooms. Today, their participation in regular education classrooms reflects a belief that all students have to be included. Today, like students with exceptionalities, children from many different parts of the world are also members of the US classrooms. Nationally, nearly 33% of school-age children are cultural minorities and 16% of the classroom teachers come from minority populations (Gay, Dingus, & Jackson, 2003; National Center for Education Statistics, 1996). Estimates for the next twenty years predict big changes in the people living in the US, with 61% of the population increases occurring among members of the Hispanic and Asian communities (Hodgkinson, 2002; Stanford, 1999). With these changes in the student population come changes in the education experiences provided to these students.

In a recent lunchroom discussion, Tracy and Maria shared their thoughts about working with students and families from multilingual and multicultural homes.

Maria: Did you have fun last night at the School-Community-Family night? This is the third year Dominguez Elementary and the district have sponsored this type of event.

Tracy: Yeah, I really had a good time. I didn't realize how many people are involved in our school community. It's neat how schools are inviting everyone to be a part of the school. When I first started as a paraprofessional seven years ago, we hardly knew anything about the families of our students.

Maria: I know what you mean, Tracy. It's also good for me to be a part of the family nights because this is the community where I live. The students are my neighbors. These events are a way for me to learn more about my students' lives. When I first arrived in the US twelve years ago, I didn't know how American schools worked at all. It was really hard for me to understand all the policies for my own children.

Talking with students and families about their needs helps me and improves communication. It's amazing what you can learn just by talking to someone! My classroom teacher is trying to figure out the best way to learn more about our students. She's using surveys, family nights, and anything community related. She says, the more we learn about our kids, the better.

ENGLISH LANGUAGE LEARNERS

Effective educators know that students bring their lives into classrooms. Effective educators know that students have unique needs, experiences, and abilities. Today educators understand that language *differences* are not the same as language *disabilities*. Students with language differences do not have the same exceptionalities as their classmates who receive special education services. In general, children learning English differ from other students because they speak a language other than English and not because of a disability. Students with language disabilities have limitations in their abilities to read, write, and/or produce their native language. Specially trained educators are the people who figure out whether students have language differences or language disabilities (Salend & Salinas, 2003).

Educators who test language differences study a lot of different information. They use many tests to get a good picture of a student's skills. For example, if they want to test a student's verbal ability they use a test that helps a student show how they actually use language. While a written test show parts of a language skill, it may not be the best tool. The problem with a written test is that it shows how well a student writes in English. An oral test may give a more accurate picture of a student's verbal ability. Neither test is better or worse than another; they only tell us different kinds of information.

Language differences among today's students provide a unique opportunity for learning about cultures from around the world.

English Language Learners (ELLs)
Children learning English for the first time.

Estudiantes del idioma inglés (ELLs por sus siglas en inglés)
Niños que comienzan a aprender inglés.

English as a Second Language (ESL)
Classrooms that are often set apart from mainstream classrooms and provide newcomers to American schools with the support they need to acquire the English language and to adapt to their new environment. Basics skills in reading, writing, and speaking are often very common in these settings.

Inglés como segundo idioma (ESL por sus siglas en inglés)
Salones de clase a menudo separados de los salones de clases regulares que proporcionan a los recién llegados a las escuelas de los EE.UU. la ayuda que necesitan con el idioma y la adaptación al nuevo ambiente. Habilidades básicas en lectura, escritura y lengua son usualmente muy comunes en estas clases.

Effective educators discuss differences between students' formal and in formal language skills.

People who work with **English Language Learners (ELLs)** also know that there are differences in how language develops over time. They understand that some types of language simply develop faster than others. These educators know that language development may be affected by many things such as exposure to the English language in a student's home country. If a student has had little or no contact with English, he or she will need a different level of instruction than a child who has had formal training in English before coming to the US (Salend & Salinas, 2003).

Finally, educators who work with English Language Learners study the differences between formal and informal language development. Think for a moment what we mean by differences between formal and informal language. When do you use formal language? When is your language more casual? When educators plan for their students they think about all the reasons why students produce language. For some students, the language used with friends at recess may be much stronger than the language they use in the classroom. Think about Carlos, from our spelling competition. How well did he do on his spelling test? Do you think his language skills affected how he did on his test? Carlos is a student who is a lot like many children across the country. He is relatively new to the US and the American school system. The primary language spoken in his home is Spanish. Like many of his peers who are learning English for the first time, Carlos spent his first two years in America in a classroom for English Language Learners (ELLs). These classrooms were formerly known as **English as a Second Language** or ESL classrooms. ELL or ESL classrooms are often set apart from mainstream classrooms and provide newcomers to American schools with the support they need to learn a new language. Basics skills in reading, writing, and speaking are often very common in these classrooms (Echevarria & Graves, 2007). The educators in ELL classrooms know that their lessons must help students learn not only the curriculum, but language as well. **Sheltered classrooms** try to teach both curriculum and language.

sheltered classrooms
Classrooms that are often set apart from mainstream classrooms and provide newcomers to American schools with the support they need to acquire the English language and to adapt to their new environment. Basic skills in reading, writing, and speaking are often very common in these settings.

salones de clase protegidos
Salones de clase separados de los salones regulares donde se proporciona a los estudiantes recién llegados al país el apoyo que necesitan para desempeñarse en inglés y adaptarse al nuevo ambiente. En estos salones se enseña por lo común destrezas básicas en lectura, escritura y lenguaje.

bilingual
Language programs designed to teach students English through the use of their native language.

Bilingüe
Programas de lengua destinados a enseñar inglés a través del uso de la lengua materna del estudiante.

transitional bilingual education
Language programs that link a student's knowledge of a new language with his or her native language using gradual progression from the native to the new language.

educación bilingüe transitoria
Programas de lengua que vinculan el conocimiento de un nuevo idioma a la lengua materna del estudiante basándose en una progresión gradual del idioma materno a la nueva lengua.

Classrooms for ELLs can be very different from one another. Some students who speak a language other than English may be placed in ESL classrooms while others are placed in sheltered classrooms. Sheltered classrooms include students who speak many languages and have general English language skills that allow them to communicate informally. Sheltered classroom lessons help students develop their English skills and their understanding of lessons. Instruction for ELLs includes language lessons about the routines and activities in classrooms as well as the language for subjects such as math, science, and language arts (Echevarria, Vogt, & Short, 2004). Students in sheltered classrooms spend a lot of time practicing reading, writing, listening, and speaking.

Bilingual classrooms are another type of classroom in which many English Language Learners begin their studies. Historically, bilingual classrooms in the US have been supported by the federal government. In 1968 Congress passed the Bilingual Education Act which was designed to educate students through a student's native language (Kauchak & Eggen, 2005). As with many topics in education, language programs are influenced by the country's political and social trends.

Today, bilingual classrooms are highly controversial in a number of communities across the US. Critics of bilingual education oppose these programs because one of their goals is to keep a student's native language while learning English. The critics believe that there are too many languages in the world and that it's impossible to give all students teachers who are fluent in each child's language. Bilingual critics think children won't interact with native English speakers if they use their native languages when learning English (Barrone, 2000). In addition to some educators and researchers, there are some politicians who don't think a student's native language should be used in their education. In fact, policies under the No Child Left Behind's English Acquisition documents state that US schools should only teach English and should not try to save students' native languages (No Child Left Behind, 2001). Some people believe the best way to learn a new language is to stop using a student's native language. Others believe that a student's native language serves as an important bridge to learning English.

Supporters of bilingual programs believe that one way to bridge a student's language development is through **transitional bilingual education**. Transitional programs help students learn English by making connections between their native and new language. Bilingual supporters rely on research that says students in bilingual programs perform better on standardized tests and learn English faster than students who are not in bilingual programs (Waggoner, 1995; Zehr, 2002). An in-depth look at the type of language programs for children in your community may help you understand the programs that will be most helpful for English Language Learners. Whether students are in sheltered, bilingual, or mainstream classrooms, the instruction they receive is important. Educators who understand each student's unique needs are educators who can help their students grow and develop. As a paraprofessional you may work in classrooms with children learning English. You may be asked to help them develop their language skills even further. The first step in helping the students' language development is to understand their existing skills and to create a plan to help them grow.

LANGUAGE DIVERSITY IN THE CLASSROOM

After two years in an ELS classroom for newcomers and then in a sheltered classroom, Carlos is now a member of a regular grade 5 classroom. His class includes twenty-three students who, like him, learn best from a standard curriculum and instruction. Carlos has made great progress as a student since arriving in the US. He works well with other students, participates in class discussions, listens to his teacher, and likes to share his ideas when working in small groups. With all of these accomplishments, Carlos still struggles on some of his assignments. Jan Harris, Carlos' teacher, likes having Carlos as a member of her grade 5 class, but knows that Carlos struggles with his reading comprehension and writing. Ms. Harris has been puzzled by the differences in Carlos' work. Carlos does well when he shares his ideas during class or when talking with his friends. The problem for Carlos is that he's not able to use the same conversation skills in his written work. Ms. Harris has worked with Maria in the past and knows Maria is a great resource to her school as a bilingual paraprofessional. Ms. Harris asked Maria for her advice on working with children learning English.

DAY-TO-DAY DILEMMA
HOW WOULD YOU HANDLE THIS SITUATION?

Ms. Harris: Maria, I could really use your help. You know that Carlos Hernandez is in my class. He is a great kid and works well with others. He adds to class discussions, asks great questions, and really participates. The trouble is, his written work and his reading comprehension are below grade level. I'm really confused because he can talk about the content of his classes and he shares great ideas during lessons, but his writing and reading are weak. Why is that?

Maria: I know what you mean about Carlos. He is a neat kid. I'm not surprised that he does so well in class, but he's struggling with reading and writing. This difference happens a lot with students who learn a new language. I remember when I arrived in the US. I did fine when talking with my friends or neighbors, but I had a lot of trouble with written work and writing my ideas. In my work with recent immigrant students I have to remind myself that just because a kid knows how to talk on the playground, it doesn't mean he or she has the language skills for the classroom. Have you heard of BICS and CALPS? BICS and CALPS are the types of language that people use both at school and in more informal places like home and on the playground. Knowing the difference between these two types of language helps understand students like Carlos. The district has developed a number of resources that share more information on these differences.

Basic Interpersonal Communication Skills (BICS)

The language skills people use in social settings. At school, BICS are put into effect in the conversations students have in the hallways, at recess, and in the lunchroom.

destrezas básicas de comunicación interpersonal (BICS por sus siglas en inglés)

Uso del idioma que se hace en un contexto social. En la escuela, este uso tiene lugar en las conversaciones que los estudiantes mantienen en los pasillos, durante el recreo y en la cafetería.

Cognitive Academic Language Proficiency Skills (CALPS)

Language used in more formal settings than BICS, like classrooms and the workplace. CALPS language development may take a number of years to acquire and requires that learners understand both the basic information in content areas such as math, science, history, or language arts as well as more complicated elements of the content.

proficiencia en el lenguaje académico de destrezas cognitivas (CALPS por sus siglas en inglés)

Lengua usada en situaciones más formales que las destrezas básicas de comunicación interpersonal (BICS). Su adquisición puede llevar años y requiere que los que la usan entiendan la información básica en áreas tales como matemáticas, ciencias, historia o artes del lenguaje, así también como elementos más complicados del contenido.

Basic Interpersonal Communication Skills (BICS)

The language we use varies depending on who we are with and the reason of our conversation. It is likely that the language you use at home or with your friends is much more informal than the language you use at work. In some places you feel more comfortable talking. In other places you like to listen and watch. The same is true for children learning English. We know that the language used in schools and other formal settings is much more complex and it usually requires a number of years for a person to learn. When people are in more informal settings, they use language that is more relaxed and casual. **Basic Interpersonal Communication Skills (BICS)** are the language skills that people use in social settings (Cummins, 1994). At school, BICS are used in the conversations students have in the hallways, at recess, and in the lunchroom. Educators know that it may take learners from one to three years to learn BICS. They also know that more complicated language in schools and classrooms takes a lot longer to learn, often from five to nine years (Cummins, 1994). Paraprofessionals who work with children learning English understand that a lot of the language in classrooms is more complicated than the language we use when we're talking with our friends. Let's take a look at the type of language used in classroom teaching.

Cognitive Academic Language Proficiency Skills (CALPS)

Cognitive Academic Language Proficiency Skills (CALPS) include the language used in more formal settings like classrooms and the workplace (Cummins, 1994). Learning BICS usually takes place faster because we talk informally with friends and family as part of our everyday lives. CALPS language abilities take much longer to develop. CALPS include the parts of language in content areas such as math, science, history, or language arts. Other kinds of "school" language include knowing how to follow directions, complete assignments, and apply knowledge in new ways (Cummins, 1994).

CALPS include very complicated skills. Native English speakers sometimes forget that learning a new language is hard work. In fact, researchers know that many different factors influence language development, including how comfortable a student feels in school. Students feel welcome when their native language is accepted and when they are taught using many different methods of instruction (Echevarria & Graves, 2007). If a student feels welcome and his or her native language is seen positively, the student is better able to learn English. What will you do to make new students feel accepted? How will students practice their language skills in your classroom?

Different types of language programs give students chances to build their conversational and academic language. Table 4-3, Language Programs, lists the language programs we have discussed in this chapter. Complete the worksheet and list the advantages and disadvantages of each program. Discuss your ideas with your classroom teacher and other paraprofessionals. In which type of classroom do you believe children will learn best? Why?

TABLE 4-3 Language Programs Worksheet

LANGUAGE PROGRAM	ADVANTAGES	DISADVANTAGES
English as a Second Language		
Sheltered Content		
Bilingual		
Transitional Bilingual		
BICS		
CALPS		

SUMMARY

As you learn more about the different needs of the students in your classroom, remember that even when students have things in common there is still a great deal of diversity across people (Olmedo, 1997). Educators know that each child must be treated as an individual with unique needs. This chapter discussed areas that educators should think about when working with students in today's classrooms. Programs for students with exceptionalities give children the academic, emotional, social, and physical support they need. For those learning English, differences in their language development and experiences influence the way they learn and how quickly they do it. Educators of students learning English know the differences between informal and formal language development. These educators teach and test their students in many ways. They make their lessons interesting and use different kinds of assessments. These educators respect the roles of parents and families in meeting students' needs and they make the classroom a special place for learning. After all, everyone wants to feel welcome in the classroom!

CHECKING FOR UNDERSTANDING

1. Each child is a unique person in your classroom. How are you going to learn about the strengths each child brings to the classroom? Together with your classroom teacher, figure out a system for keeping track of your students' abilities and interests. Your system might include portfolios, card catalogs, or scrapbooks.

2. What are the unique differences of students with exceptionalities discussed in this chapter? How do learner differences affect how they respond to their lessons?

3. How do different types of classroom setups help children learning English for the first time?

4. Least restrictive environments give students the support they need to contribute to their classrooms. As a paraprofessional, how will you provide support for children while accommodating their differences?

POINTS OF VIEW

Here are some ideas that will help you learn more about learner diversity in the classroom and at school.

- As a classroom paraprofessional, it is important to learn as much as possible about your students' learning needs. With the help of your classroom teacher, create a checklist of the areas that will help you learn more about your students. Sample questions might include students' preferences to read a story, listen to a story being read, or to create a drawing of their favorite story. The checklist below provides an example.

I learn best when I read.	Agree	Disagree
I learn best when I write.	Agree	Disagree
I learn best when I listen to others.	Agree	Disagree
I learn best when I work with others.	Agree	Disagree
I learn best when I work by myself.	Agree	Disagree

- What are some of the other questions you might ask your students in order to learn more about their learning preferences and abilities? To prepare, complete the checklist for yourself. What type of learner are you?
- There are many people who assist students with special learning needs. In addition to classroom teachers and paraprofessionals, school psychologists, counselors, reading specialists, speech therapists, and special educators contribute to the school experiences of a wide range of learners. When time allows, visit the classrooms or offices of some of these people to learn more about the services they offer students in your classroom and at your school.
- If you are working as a paraprofessional in a special education classroom, you have likely seen an IEP. If not, see the special educator at your school to learn more about the IEP process.
- How might educators help students learning English for the first time feel welcome in classrooms? What are some of the ways you will use classmates to help new students understand the English language?
- BICS and CALPS are not unique to ELLs. How does the language you use when visiting with friends compare with the language you use at work as a paraprofessional? Is your language with family members less formal? Before you meet with a parent or coworker, do you think about the language you will use in your conversations? Explain.
- Many children use reading or math skills in their homes every day. For example, they use reading when playing, and use reading and math when cooking or interacting in their community. The "funds of knowledge" or experiences (Moll & Gonzales, 1997) students bring to schools should be used in ways that help them succeed. How might you use students' knowledge about language and math in your classroom? Are there reading and math activities that students use in their daily lives that could be used to teach students English in your classroom?

PORTFOLIO CORNER

As we noted previously, you will be asked to gather a number of artifacts, or sample products, that show your work as a paraprofessional. This chapter focused on the ways in which paraprofessionals can assist students with learning differences. The suggestions given included strategies for understanding the unique needs of diverse learners, and the role that paraprofessionals have in working as members of an instructional team for diverse learners.

The artifacts, or lines of evidence, from this chapter address Standards I, III, and IV. Sample artifacts include: strategies for adapting curriculum and instruction; surveys you will use with parents and students; documents that describe your knowledge of student differences; and sample IEPs, or work samples that show how you interact with diverse groups of students in the classroom. Our friends Maria and Tracy share their ideas on how to put together your portfolio.

With the help of your classroom teacher, make a checklist and describe the kind of language that students use in their conversations at lunch or at recess. Then, make a list of the language they use in the classroom. Do you notice any difference in the BICS and CALPS of students in your classroom who are learning English? Your list should include examples of the BICS you have noticed in your students. What are some of the CALPS required in your classroom? Choose a specific content area such as mathematics, science, or reading and identify the CALPS. Examples in mathematics might include the content language used to learn math concepts (e.g., addition, subtraction, division, multiplication).

Use Table 4-4, Sample Portfolio Framework, and list sample artifacts that meet Standards I, III, and IV based upon our discussions in Chapter 4.

TABLE 4-4 Sample Portfolio Framework

STANDARD I—SUPPORTING INSTRUCTIONAL OPPORTUNITIES	STANDARD II—DEMONSTRATING PROFESSIONALISM AND ETHICAL PRACTICE
Sample artifacts might include: • Types of computer assistive technology available to students • Lessons that demonstrate your knowledge of the ways in which adaptations can be used with multiple learners • Your ideas	See Chapter 5
STANDARD III—SUPPORTING A POSITIVE LEARNING ENVIRONMENT	**STANDARD IV—COMMUNICATING EFFECTIVELY AND PARTICIPATING IN THE TEACHING PROCESSES**
Sample artifacts might include: • Learners' needs worksheet • A student survey • A parent/caregiver survey • BICS/CALPS content checklist • Funds of Knowledge worksheet • Your ideas	Sample artifacts might include: • Information from family community meetings • Participation in an IEP • Information about the IEP process • Information about specific exceptionalities • Your ideas

REFERENCES

Ashbaker, B., & Morgan, J. (2006). *Paraprofessionals in the classroom.* New York: Allyn & Bacon.

Boyle, M. (2002). *The paraprofessional's guide to the inclusive classroom: Working as a team* (2nd ed.). Baltimore: Paul Brookes Publishing.

Cerebral Palsy Facts (2006). Retrieved May 30, 2007 from http://www.cerebralpalsyfacts.com.

Cummins, J. (2001). *Negotiating identities: Education for empowerment in a diverse society* (2nd ed.). Los Angeles: California Association for Bilingual Education.

Echevarria, J., Vogt, M., & Short, D. (2004). *Making content comprehensible for English learners: The SIOP model* (2nd ed.). New York: Allyn & Bacon.

Echevarria, J., & Graves, A. (2007). *Sheltered content instruction: Teaching English learners with diverse abilities* (3rd ed.). New York: Allyn & Bacon.

Hardman, M, & Drew, C., & Egan, M. (2006). Human exceptionality: School, community, and family. New York: Allyn and Bacon.

Heward, W. (2003). *Exceptional children* (3rd ed.). Upper Saddle River, New Jersey: Merrill/ Prentice Hall.

Moll, L., & González, N. (1997). Teachers as social scientists: Learning about culture from household research in race, ethnicity and multiculturalism. P. M. Hall, (Ed.), *Missouri symposium on research and educational policy:* vol. 1 (pp. 89–114). New York: Garland Publishing.

National Joint Committee on Learning Disabilities (1994). *Learning disabilities: Issues on definition.* A position paper of the National Joint Committee in Learning Disabilities. In Collective perspectives on issues affecting learning disability: Position paper.

Olmedo, I. M. (1997). Challenging old assumptions: Preparing teachers for inner city schools. *Teaching and Teacher Education,* 17, 245–258.

Salend, S. J., & Salinas, A. G. (2003). Language difficulties or learning difficulties: The work of the multidisciplinary team. *Teaching Exceptional Children, March/April,* 36–43.

Santrock, J. (2006). *Educational psychology* (2nd ed.). New York: McGraw-Hill.

Turnbull, A., Turnbull, R., Shank, M., Smith, S., & Leal, D. (2004). *Exceptional lives: Special education in today's schools* (4th ed.). Upper Saddle River, New Jersey: Merrill/ Prentice Hall.

Additional selected readings and Paraprofessional electronic resources are available as part of the student Online Companion web site: www.earlychilded.delmar.com.

EN ESPAÑOL

OBJETIVOS DEL APRENDIZAJE

Después de leer y reflexionar sobre este capítulo podrá comprender mejor:

- El concepto de la diversidad de los educandos
- Las necesidades de los estudiantes que reciben servicios de **educación especial**
- Las necesidades de los estudiantes que comienzan a aprender inglés

A medida que lea este capítulo, hágase las siguientes preguntas:

1. ¿Qué es lo que quieren decir los maestros cuando hablan de la diversidad de la clase?
2. ¿Qué significa **inclusión**?
3. ¿Cuáles son algunas de las necesidades únicas que tienen los estudiantes en las clases de educación especial?
4. ¿Que es un plan individualizado de educación (IEP por sus siglas en inglés)?
5. ¿Cuáles son algunas de las necesidades únicas de los estudiantes cuyo idioma nativo no es el inglés?
6. ¿Cómo varía el lenguaje de los estudiantes según estén en la clase o en el recreo? ¿Cómo se diferencia una conversación formal de una informal? ¿Cómo afectan esas diferencias a los principiantes que comienzan a estudiar inglés?
7. ¿Qué documentos incluirá en su carpeta para demostrar su conocimiento de las necesidades educativas de los estudiantes que reciben servicios de educación especial y de aquellos que comienzan a estudiar inglés?

PARA VERIFICAR LA COMPRENSIÓN

1. Cada niño(a) es una persona única en el salón de clase. ¿Cómo va a saber la contribución que cada niño puede hacer a la clase? Junto con el maestro de clase elabore un sistema para seguir de cerca las habilidades y los intereses de sus estudiantes. Su sistema puede incluir carpetas, fichas, o libros de recortes.
2. ¿Cuáles son las diferencias únicas de los estudiantes con las **excepcionalidades** mencionadas en este capítulo? ¿Cómo afectan las diferencias de los educandos la forma en que reaccionan a la enseñanza?
3. ¿Cómo ayuda la disposición de **salones de clase** a los niños que comienzan a aprender inglés?
4. Un ambiente menos restrictivo da a los estudiantes el apoyo que necesitan para contribuir en la clase. Como paraprofesional, ¿Cómo puede apoyar a los niños al mismo tiempo que da cabida a sus diferencias?

---

educación especial
Servicios educativos para los estudiantes cuyo desempeño en varios exámenes coincide con los estándares que indican una dificultad de aprendizaje específica.

special education
Educational services provided to students whose behavior or performance on various tests meets the standards that describe a specific disability.

---

inclusión
Participación de los niños con excepcionalidades en los salones de clase de sus pares con el apoyo y los servicios apropiados.

inclusion
Participation of children with exceptionalities in the general education classrooms of their peers with appropriate support and services.

---

excepcionalidades
Diferencias presentes en niños que necesitan recursos adicionales para lograr su mayor potencial. Estos niños componen el 12% de la población de estudiantes de los EE.UU. y asisten a menudo a clases de educación especial o clases regulares.

exceptionalities
Differences present in children who need additional resources to meet their full potential. These children make up 12% of the US student population and are often served in either special education or mainstream classes.

salones de clase protegidos
Salones de clase separados de los salones regulares donde se proporciona a los estudiantes recién llegados al país el apoyo que necesitan para desempeñarse en inglés y adaptarse al nuevo ambiente. En estos salones se enseña por lo común destrezas básicas en lectura, escritura y lenguaje.

sheltered classrooms
Classrooms that are often set apart from mainstream classrooms and provide newcomers to American schools with the support they need to acquire the English language and to adapt to their new environment. Basic skills in reading, writing, and speaking are often very common in these settings.

PUNTOS DE VISTA

Le ofrecemos algunas ideas que lo o la ayudarán a aprender más sobre la diversidad de los estudiantes en el salón de clases y en la escuela.

- Como paraprofesional del aula, es importante aprender lo más posible sobre las necesidades de aprendizaje de sus estudiantes. Con la ayuda de su maestro de clase, haga una lista de las áreas que lo o la ayudarán a saber más sobre sus estudiantes. En la lista puede incluir las preferencias de cada estudiante: si prefiere leer un cuento, escuchar mientras se lo leen, o hacer una ilustración de su cuento favorito. La lista de abajo proporciona un ejemplo.

Aprendo mejor cuando leo.	SÍ	NO
Aprendo mejor cuando escribo.	SÍ	NO
Aprendo mejor cuando escucho a otros.	SÍ	NO
Aprendo mejor cuando trabajo con otros.	SÍ	NO
Aprendo mejor cuando trabajo por mi cuenta.	SÍ	NO

- ¿Qué otras preguntas puede hacerles a sus estudiantes para aprender más sobre sus preferencias y capacidades de aprendizaje? Para prepararse, anote en la lista sus propias respuestas. ¿Qué tipo de estudiante es usted?

- Hay muchas personas que asisten a los estudiantes con necesidades especiales de aprendizaje. Además de profesores y de paraprofesionales del salón de clases, los psicólogos escolares, los consejeros, los especialistas en lectura, terapistas del lenguaje, y educadores especiales contribuyen a las experiencias escolares de una amplia gama de estudiantes. Si tiene oportunidad, visite las clases o vaya a las oficinas de algunas de estas personas en su escuela para aprender más sobre los servicios que ofrecen a los estudiantes de su salón de clases.

- Si usted trabaja como paraprofesional en una clase de educación especial, probablemente haya visto un plan individualizado de educación, o IEP (según sus siglas en inglés). Si no, vea al maestro de educación especial de su escuela para aprender más sobre estos planes.

- ¿Cómo pueden los educadores hacer que los estudiantes que comienzan a aprender inglés se sientan bienvenidos en el salón de clases? ¿De qué métodos se valdrá para que los demás compañeros ayuden a los nuevos estudiantes a entender el idioma inglés?

- Las habilidades interpersonales básicas de comunicación *(Basic Interpersonal Communication Skills* o BICS, según sus siglas en inglés), y la proficiencia en el lenguaje académico de destrezas cognitivas *(Cognitive Academic Language Proficiency Skills* o CALPS, según sus siglas en inglés) se aplican solamente al idioma inglés. ¿Cómo se compara el lenguaje que usted usa cuando visita a sus amigos al que usa en su trabajo como paraprofesional? Antes de encontrarse con el padre de algún estudiante o con un colega, ¿piensa en el lenguaje que va a emplear al hablar con ellos? Explique.

- En su casa muchos niños utilizan a diario sus destrezas de lectura o de matemáticas. Usan la lectura cuando juegan y la lectura y las matemáticas cuando cocinan o interactúan en su comunidad. Los "fundamentos del conocimiento" (Moll y Gonzales, 1997) o la experiencia que traen consigo a la escuela deben usarse de un modo tal que les sirva para tener éxito. ¿Cómo puede utilizar el conocimiento de los estudiantes sobre lenguaje y matemáticas en su salón de clases? ¿Hay actividades de lectura y matemáticas que ellos usan en forma cotidiana que usted pueda utilizar para enseñarles inglés?

Para la carpeta

Como observamos antes, le pedirán que reúna algunos documentos que demuestren su trabajo como paraprofesional. Este capítulo enfocó las formas en que los paraprofesionales pueden asistir a los estudiantes con diferencias de aprendizaje. Las sugerencias de este capítulo incluyen estrategias para comprender las necesidades únicas de educandos diversos y el papel que los paraprofesionales desempeñan al trabajar como miembros de un equipo educacional para una diversidad de educandos.

Los documentos o líneas de evidencia de este capítulo se refieren a los estándares I, III y IV. Incluyen: estrategias para adaptar el currículo y la enseñanza, encuestas dirigidas a los padres y a los estudiantes; documentos relacionados con su conocimiento acerca de las diferencias entre los estudiantes,

TABLA 4-4 Estructura modelo de carpeta

ESTÁNDAR I—APOYO A TODA OPORTUNIDAD EDUCATIVA	ESTÁNDAR II—DEMOSTRAR UNA CONDUCTA PROFESIONAL Y ÉTICA
Los objetos de muestra pueden incluir: • Tipos de tecnología de asistencia por computadoras disponibles para los estudiantes • Lecciones que demuestren su conocimiento de cómo se pueden hacer adaptaciones para educandos diversos • Sus ideas	Vea el Capítulo 5
ESTÁNDAR III—OFRECER UN AMBIENTE CONDUCENTE AL APRENDIZAJE	**ESTÁNDAR IV—COMUNICARSE EFICAZMENTE Y PARTICIPAR EN EL PROCESO DE EQUIPO**
Los objetos de muestra pueden incluir: • Lista de las necesidades de los estudiantes • Encuesta a los estudiantes • Encuesta a los padres/guardianes • Lista de comprobación de BICS/CALPS • Hoja de trabajo de los "fundamentos del conocimiento" • Sus ideas	Los objetos de muestra pueden incluir: • Participación en el IEP • Información sobre las reuniones de familias de la comunidad • Información sobre el proceso de IEP • Información sobre excepcionalidades específicas • Sus ideas

o muestras de trabajo de clase que demuestren su interacción con diversos grupos de estudiantes. Nuestras amigas Maria y Tracy comparten sus ideas en cuanto a la carpeta.

Con la ayuda del maestro de su clase haga una lista en que describa el tipo de lenguaje que los estudiantes usan en sus conversaciones en el almuerzo o el recreo. Después, haga una lista del lenguaje que usan en el salón de clases. ¿Nota alguna diferencia en el BICS y el CALPS de los estudiantes de su clase que están aprendiendo inglés? Su lista debe incluir los ejemplos de BICS que usted ha notado en sus estudiantes. ¿Cuáles son algunas de las CALPS requeridas en su clase? Elija un área específica como matemáticas, ciencias o lectura e identifique las CALPS. Los ejemplos de matemáticas pueden incluir el lenguaje usado para aprender los conceptos matemáticos (por ejemplo: suma, resta, multiplicación, división).

Use la tabla 4-1, Estructura modelo de carpeta, y haga una lista de los documentos que están relacionados con los estándares I, III y IV basándose en las ideas presentadas en el Capítulo 4.

The Legal Rights and Responsibilities of Those Working in Schools

Learning Objectives

After reading and reflecting on this chapter you will understand:

- The rights and responsibilities of students, teachers, and families

- The laws and ethical considerations for educators

- Legal issues related to privacy, due process procedures, religion, and safety

As you read the following chapter, ask yourself these questions:

1. What are the legal responsibilities of paraprofessionals?

2. What is the Family Education Rights and Privacy Act?

3. What are the policies for reporting suspected child abuse?

4. What kinds of questions are appropriate to ask of students?

5. What kind of artifacts will you include in your portfolio to reflect your knowledge of the legal policies affecting the work of paraprofessionals?

KEY TERMS

Buckley Amendment

disclosure statements

due process of the law

The Family Education Rights and Privacy Act (FERPA)

freedom of speech

in loco parentis

indoctrinate

National Education Association (NEA)

negligence

privacy

professional ethics

reporting child abuse

The Americans with Disabilities Act (ADA)

INTRODUCTION

Answering machine: "I'm sorry I can't take your call. Please leave a message."

Tracy: Hi Maria. I was hoping you'd be home. It's me, Tracy. I just have to talk with you about what I heard in the lunchroom. I guess there's something going on in the district with one of the paraprofessionals at another school. You know how I hate to gossip, but I had to find out if you knew any of the details about what's going on. Call me back as soon as you can. Bye.

Maria: Hi Tracy, it's me Maria. What's going on? Your phone message sounded mysterious.

Tracy: Oh, good! I've been waiting for your call. Do you know what's going on at Pine View Elementary? I heard through a friend that one of the paraprofessionals got in trouble because of some information that was shared about a student. I heard it was something about talking with a parent about another student's test scores. Did you hear anything?

Maria: Hmm. I hadn't heard anything about the paraprofessional at Pine View. I know schools are getting really strict about making sure the staff follows all the rules and regulations—especially not talking about students and their records. Tracy, you know more than I do about all the laws in special education and kids with exceptionalities. I've heard there are other laws that we have to follow about the rights of kids, teachers, and other people who work in schools.

Tracy: Wow! I guess I really hadn't thought about the legal stuff besides what I know about the kids in my classroom. I know rules for helping kids with IEPs, but it sounds like there are a lot of other laws I need to make sure I know.

Maria: I guess we don't really think about the rules since things work pretty well most of the time. I don't think at all about the laws until something happens. My classroom teacher is taking classes on legal issues and has shared a lot of tips with me. She told me that because schools belong to the public, there are all kinds of policies and procedures to make sure they run the right way and everybody's rights are protected. There are laws about contact with students, sharing student work, testing students, and talking about private information.

Tracy: I guess I have a lot to learn Maria. I'm going to check the handbook at our school and talk with my classroom teacher. Maybe your classroom teacher could give us some suggestions on extra information we need to know. Do you know if the district offers workshops on legal issues? Maybe I should go to one.

Maria: It sounds like a good plan. You know, it's easy to get caught up in the drama that's going on in a school. I admit I'm guilty of gossiping. Sometimes it's exciting to guess what's going to happen when something big happens at school. I have to keep reminding myself that it's not professional to get distracted by all the drama. I have to remember that we're here for the kids and not the gossip. It is hard sometimes, but I have to keep myself focused on doing what's best for the kids and for our profession. Anyway, I'll find out how we can learn more about legal issues. I'll call you if I get information on a workshop we might be able to take. Bye

LAW AND ETHICS IN EDUCATION

As you learned from other chapters in this book, the American school system was built on the views of different people at national, state, and local levels. Curriculum decisions, policies for operating schools, and professional standards for educators are developed by many people. The same applies to legal policies and standards for professional behavior. Like teachers, paraprofessionals are also responsible for knowing the laws and regulations related to their work in schools. If you're updated on the policies and procedures at your school, you'll be able to provide students with the best education possible. This chapter covers information on many of the laws influencing the work of paraprofessionals in today's schools. Figure 5-1, Law and Policy in Education, lists important topics related to education and the law. Let's start with a discussion of the ethical aspects of teaching.

The Ethical Responsibilities of Educators

In Maria and Tracy's phone conversation we heard about the kind of issues that happen in schools. Schools house a lot of different people, and daily events are action packed and always changing. Because schools are so active, it is easy to get drawn into whatever happens to catch our attention. While it makes sense to

professional ethics
Set of moral standards for acceptable professional behavior.

ética profesional
Conjunto de estándares morales adecuados a una conducta profesional aceptable.

National Education Association (NEA)
Organization that created a code of ethics focused on students and the teaching profession for people who work as educators.

Asociación nacional de educación (NEA según sus siglas en inglés)
Organización que creó un código de ética enfocado en los estudiantes y la profesión docente para los que se desempeñan como educadores.

privacy
Policies that describe the type of information that may be shared about a student's personal life or academic records.

privacidad
Regulaciones que indican el tipo de información que puede divulgarse sobre los asuntos personales o académicos de un estudiante.

due process of the law
Process, under the law, that requires adequate notice to be given in advance, an explanation of evidence offered, and the participants having an opportunity to respond.

procedimiento de ley debida
Proceso de acuerdo a la ley que requiere que se dé previo aviso, se ofrezca justificación de la evidencia y se brinde oportunidad de respuesta a los participantes.

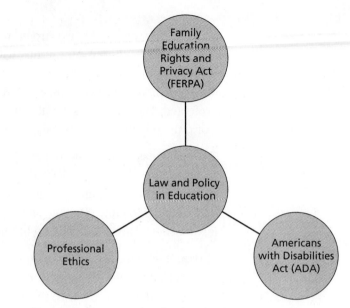

FIGURE 5-1 Law and Policy in Education

talk about what goes on in our schools, educators must remember that they are professionals who must respect the people they work with and the profession in general. **Professional ethics** include the set of moral standards for acceptable, professional behavior (Corey, Corety, & Callahan, 1993). As with laws, codes of ethics describe basic standards for behavior. A national professional organization for educators that helps educators understand professional ethics is the **National Education Association (NEA)**. The NEA is the nation's largest professional employee organization for education. There are 3.2 million members—from pre-school to university graduate programs. NEA has partners in every state and in more than 14,000 communities. The NEA sets up a code of ethics for educators that focuses on students and the teaching profession.

Ethics standards are policies that make sure students receive an education from professionals who value students (National Education Association, 2006). Educators who show professional ethics in their work are people who respect their profession and understand that they work for the public. While it's easy to get caught up in the events at our schools, educators must keep students at the top of their priority lists. For additional information on the NEA's code of ethics, visit their web site: www.nea.org. More formal policies for educators are in the form of laws. There are a series of laws that guide activities in schools.

Legal Policies

In addition to the ethical responsibilities of educators, certain laws affect the work of teachers and paraprofessionals. These laws stem from the United States Constitution and include **privacy**, **due process of the law** or due process, and **freedom of speech**. Each of these topics has direct connections to schools and the work of educators. Privacy issues in education have to do with the rules about sharing personal or academic information. Due process includes the steps for giving advance notice of what is expected on school-related issues.

freedom of speech
Rights related to the expression of ideas, values, and perspectives.

libertad de expresión
Derechos relacionados con la expresión de ideas, valores y puntos de vista personales.

The Family Education Rights and Privacy Act (FERPA)
Federal act that makes school records open and accessible to students and parents. The law also limits the kind of information that can be shared about a student.

Ley de derechos de educación familiar y privacidad (FERPA según sus siglas en inglés)
Ley federal que hace que los expedientes escolares sean accesibles a los estudiantes y sus padres. La ley también limita el tipo de información que se puede divulgar sobre un estudiante determinado.

Buckley Amendment
A term used interchangeably with FERPA regulations. See FERPA.

Enmienda Buckley
Término que se usa también para referirse a la Ley de los derechos de educación y privacidad de la familia.

Due process also requires that school personnel explain their policies and make sure that students and families have the right to respond to any claims made against them. Freedom of speech includes rights related to the expression of ideas, values, and perspectives. Privacy, due process, and freedom of speech are complicated issues in schools. Let's look at each one of these topics in more detail.

Privacy

Privacy in public schools generally includes rights related to physical property such as backpacks, lockers, or purses. Other types of "property" include test scores, teacher comments, or letters of recommendation. For the most part each of these forms of "property" is protected under the Fourth Amendment. The Fourth Amendment is a part of the US Constitution and it says that authorities can't go against a student's right to privacy. School authorities can't conduct a search without clear reasons for their actions. A teacher can't look in a student's backpack for no reason. There must be suspicion as to *why* a search is necessary (Kauchak & Eggen, 2005). Privacy laws also apply to testing, written communication, or personnel issues. In each of these examples, specific laws protect people in the school system. **The Family Education Rights and Privacy Act (FERPA)** is a specific law that affects the work of all educators in schools today. FERPA sets very clear standards about privacy and parental permission. In 1974 the US Congress passed the Family Education Rights and Privacy Act (FERPA), also known as the **Buckley Amendment**. FERPA gives parents the right to review their child's official records, to decide if the records are correct, and to decide if their child's record can be shared with others. In their phone conversation, Maria and Tracy talked about a paraprofessional at another school who had shared test information with someone else at the school. Sharing student information with unauthorized individuals is in clear violation of FERPA policies. Directory information like names and home addresses can be accessed by anyone. Directory information can be shared since it is already available and is not considered harmful if shared. However, more confidential information about a student may not be shared without parental consent.

In addition to the rules related to sharing student records, there are federal and state laws that make it illegal to ask students to talk about their beliefs on some very important topics. Topics that require parental consent include discussions of:

1. political affiliation and philosophies;
2. mental or psychological problems;
3. sexual behavior, orientation, and attitudes;
4. illegal, antisocial, self-incriminating, or demeaning behavior;
5. practical appraisals of close family members; religious affiliation or beliefs;
6. legally recognized privileged relationships (clergy or doctors);
7. income, unless required by law.

Under the law, educators are required to keep students' educational records private.

Each of these areas is considered privileged information and educators are forbidden from asking students to reveal any of this information without proper notification of parents (Title 53A-53A-13-101.1 Chapter 13—Curriculum in the Public Schools, 2006). It might seem obvious that these topics are off limits for discussion in schools. However, there are other times when educators may violate the law even if they don't intend to go against policies. Let's look at a few examples from Maria's and Tracy's classrooms.

DAY-TO-DAY DILEMMA
HOW WOULD YOU HANDLE THIS SITUATION?

Maria's classroom teacher wanted her to get involved in a project that would help them learn more about the students in their class. The teacher thought it would be a good idea to conduct a survey and asked Maria for her ideas. Maria remembered a book she had read that used surveys to learn about students, including their likes and dislikes, as well as their experiences. She thought they should ask the children to share information about their families, for example where they went to church, who they lived with, and if they had been in gangs or knew people who were involved in gang activity. When her teacher reviewed the questions Maria had written, she was concerned about some of them.

How would you feel if you were asked to answer the questions on the survey? Have some of Maria's questions violated privacy policies? If you answered yes, you are correct. The questions Maria asked regarding church attendance, family makeup, and whether students have gang contacts are all questions that violate privacy policies. Surveys are a useful way of learning about the students in your classroom. Questions about the curriculum and instruction, and students' interests in the classroom are very important. The answers to these questions help teachers plan and write interesting lessons. The key to writing a survey is to make sure the questions ask about *teaching* and *learning*. You may also include other questions about students' hobbies and interests, but educators must make sure they respect students' privacy rights at all times.

How would you respond if you were in this classroom?

Tracy's classroom teacher is in the middle of a class discussion on communication styles. During the discussion, one of the students *volunteers* that his mother and her boyfriend fight a lot and that their fights are loud and involve screaming, yelling, and sometimes slapping. When Tracy heard about the student's story, she wondered if her teacher's questions *had made* the student disclose private information.

Did the teacher in Tracy's classroom go against a privacy law? If you answered no, you are correct. Because the student *volunteered* the information, the teacher did not purposely try to find out information about the student's home life. The best advice in this situation would be for the teacher to redirect the discussion back to the curriculum and the topic of effective communication. The real concern for a teacher in this classroom is finding out if the student is in any sort of danger within his home. Let's take a look at the more serious issue of **child abuse** and **reporting** it.

Reporting Child Abuse

A teacher notices a set of drawings from one of the students in her classroom. The drawings show very violent actions. In the drawings a young child is often being hit by a larger, adult figure. This same student has come to school with bruises on her arms. The teacher is unsure of what to do. How should the educator respond to the student's drawing and her bruises? How would you respond if you suspected that a child might be in a position where he or she was being abused? Educators are in a unique position because they work very closely with students on a regular basis. They see students each day and are often the first people to know when a child is in distress. Under federal and state laws, the educator has a legal responsibility to report the information on the drawings and the child's bruises as there is "a reason to believe" that a child has been subjected to some sort of harm (Fisher, Schimmel, & Kelly, 2003). When you report information, make sure you follow the policies in your district and state to make sure you report the information to the right people. In some states, it may be allright to report the information to your school counselor or administrator. In other states, the law may require that *you* report suspected child abuse directly to

reporting child abuse
School district employees have a legal responsibility to report to legal authorities, within the regulations of each state, and within the specific contexts of schools, those situations where there is "reason to believe" that a child has been abused or is in danger.

Denuncia de abuso a menores
Dentro de las regulaciones de cada estado, y dentro del contexto específico de las escuelas, los empleados del distrito escolar tienen la responsabilidad legal de informar a las autoridades legales sobre situaciones donde haya "razón para creer" que existe abuso de menores o que un niño corre riesgo de abuso.

your local division of child and family services. Whether your state requires direct reporting of abuse to a division of protective services or reporting to your school district representative, everyone involved needs to understand the requirements for reporting suspected abuse. Check with your school, classroom teacher, and state office of education about the reporting policies in your community. Make no mistake, suspected abuse or neglect must be addressed and cannot be ignored. Failing to report suspected abuse is a violation of the law and is dealt with by local legal authorities.

Due Process of the Law

Due process of the law, or due process, in education, is a constitutional right that makes sure parents are made aware of what takes place in their child's education. Due process means parents should be told ahead of time of the policies, procedures, and outcomes related to their child's education. For example, when children receive special education services, parents have the right to decide if it is allright for their child to be tested. They have the right to ask for more testing if they are not satisfied with the testing conducted by a school. They have the right to be involved in the placement of their child in special education settings, and if they are in need of language assistance they must be given an interpreter. Due process rights are summarized into three specific areas:

1. written notice of policies and procedures;
2. the right for parents or students to respond to any actions made;
3. the right to appeal decisions (Kauchak & Eggen, 2005).

One way to make sure students and families know their rights and responsibilities is to communicate the policies, expectations, and standards to them. Parents need to know what to do if there are problems at school and they need to know where to go for additional help. Effective communication depends on making the information clear. School and district policy handbooks and websites are wonderful public resources. These resources include the school's and district's expectations for students. Class **disclosure statements** give students and parents or guardians information on behavior expectations, grading criteria, and the curriculum content that will be covered during a quarter, semester, or year. Disclosure statements are a lot like the syllabus that a teacher uses to describe plans for a class. Disclosure statements are not always required at every school, particularly at the elementary level, but some middle school, junior high and high school classes have a disclosure statement for each subject. Disclosures are like guides for the content and policies in a class.

As a member of an educational team, paraprofessionals are often in contact with families and notify parents of assignments and upcoming due dates. The information on a disclosure statement will help you share details with families. If you understand your classroom teacher's goals, you will be a partner in helping parents understand how their children's needs are met in the classroom. Disclosures are especially helpful for students who need extra support and planning time because requirements and assignments for a class are listed. Most disclosure statements also include a section that notifies students and parents of their

disclosure statements
Guides for the content and policies in a class that give students and parents or guardians information on behavior expectations, grading criteria, and curriculum content to be covered in a specific class. They are especially helpful for students who need extra support and planning time.

divulgación de propósitos
Lineamientos referentes al contenido y las regulaciones de una clase que dan a los estudiantes y a sus padres o tutores información sobre las expectativas de conducta, el criterio para adjudicar notas y el contenido del currículo a cubrirse. Beneficia sobre todo a los estudiantes que necesitan más apoyo y más tiempo de planificación.

Sharing information on educational policies and procedures with families protects their due process rights.

The Americans with Disabilities Act (ADA)
Federal civil rights legislation that protects individuals with disabilities from discrimination in all aspects of life.

Ley de personas discapacitadas (ADA según sus siglas en inglés)
Legislación federal de derechos civiles que protege a los individuos con discapacidades contra la discriminación en todos los aspectos de la vida.

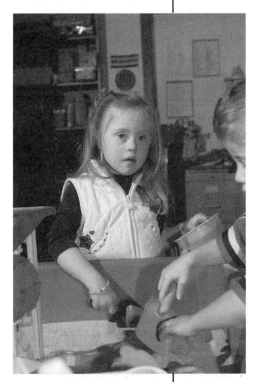

Individuals with exceptionalities must be provided with the necessary support for accessing opportunities in the school and the workplace.

rights for special accommodations in curriculum and instruction if a child receives special education services. Without the support of educators, many students in classrooms could be discriminated because of their disabilities. Let's take a look at an additional law that protects students with disabilities from discrimination.

Americans with Disabilities

FERPA and due process rights apply to the day-to-day activities within schools and the general population of students. Another law that followed FERPA is **The Americans with Disabilities Act (ADA)** which came about in 1990. ADA protects people with exceptionalities from discrimination based upon their disability. The law states that people with disabilities, when given appropriate support, must be allowed the chance to complete job or academic responsibilities in the same way as others. Employers and school officials must give students and employees support and cannot limit opportunities because of a person's disability. In Chapter 4 you learned about the differences among people with exceptionalities. Based on student needs, ADA requires that students must be given the support and accommodations they need to meet the same educational goals as other students. ADA is particularly important because paraprofessionals provide many children with disabilities with the support they need to be successful in the classroom (Ashbaker & Morgan, 2006). Without the support and expertise of paraprofessionals, many schools and districts would fail to meet the ADA regulations for necessary and appropriate accommodations.

Legal Issues and the Day-to-Day Work of Educators

FERPA and ADA offer guidelines on the policies and procedures for work in classrooms and schools. There are other important laws that affect the ways teachers create lessons and develop curriculum. As you learned in earlier chapters, the core curriculum gives educators an outline of the content in each grade level. The core curriculum gives guidelines, though teachers are allowed to make decisions about the way the curriculum is taught in their own classrooms. Educators use their professional judgment to make decisions about curriculum and instruction. However, there are also guidelines about how certain kinds of content may be taught. Religion in education is one of the most frequently debated topics.

Religion and the Law

As you learned in Chapter 1 religion has played an important role in America's history. Newcomers to the US often left their home countries in search of religious freedom. As a result of religion's role in American history it is nearly impossible to study any part of America's past, world history, art, or drama, without talking about the role of religion. Because religious freedoms are such an important part of American history, the people who created the US Constitution wanted to make sure different religions were accepted. They didn't want religion to get in the way of individual rights. In classrooms religious topics are common parts of the curriculum but there are limits to how religious discussions can take place in K-12 classrooms. Two areas that are talked about a lot are prayer and teaching about religion. Let's take a look at these issues in more depth as they are often part of discussions in many school communities.

DAY-TO-DAY DILEMMA
HOW WOULD YOU HANDLE THIS SITUATION?

Teaching about Religion

During a recent lunch period, Tracy sat with a group of teachers who were talking about religion as a part of the curriculum. One of the teachers said that religion should never be a part of classroom discussions. She claimed, "You're just opening yourself up to trouble if you start talking about religion." She said, "My policy is to simply avoid the topic of religion all together. When I teach about US history, I simply avoid any details related to religion. The topic of religion is just too controversial!" Another teacher at the table responded, "How can you teach American history, or many other content areas without talking about religion?" The bell rang and the teachers went back to their classrooms. Even though Tracy's lunch break was over, she kept thinking about the teachers' comments. What they said really bothered her. She knows it is important to separate religion from what goes on in the classroom. She also knows educators need to protect students' rights, but as someone who loves to study history she wondered how it would be possible *not* to talk about religion in some content areas. As usual Tracy made a list of questions to talk over with her classroom teacher.

After talking with her classroom teacher, Tracy understood how it's possible to talk about religion and stay within the law. A teacher's discussions about religion must be to *inform* about religious topics and not to **indoctrinate**, or share personal beliefs about religion or any other topic related to personal beliefs. A few suggestions from the US Department of Education on religion in schools (*Teachers' guide to religion in the public schools*, 1999) will guide your work and will reduce the chances of violating students' rights:

1. Advocating religion by educators should not exist in public schools. It is a violation of the US Constitution that establishes the separation between church and state.
2. Public schools should not interfere with a student's religious beliefs.
3. Students may pray during school hours only in private. The school may not support prayer by individuals or groups of students.
4. Public schools may teach about the history of religion, different religions, the Bible as literature, and the role of religion in the US.

Tracy was glad to learn that there are clear policies for talking about religion in public schools. The guidelines from the US Department of Education help educators understand how religion may be discussed in schools. As long as religion is directly linked to the core curriculum the rights of students and their families

indoctrinate
Promote a personal point of view.

indoctrinar
Promover un punto de vista personal.

Educators must be aware of the policies about the way religion must be addressed in the classroom.

in loco parentis
Latin expression meaning *in place of the parents.* A principle that requires teachers to use the same judgment and care as parents in protecting the children under their supervision.

In loco parentis
Expresión latina que significa *en lugar de los padres.* Principio que requiere que los maestros usen el mismo criterio y cuidado que usan los padres para proteger a los niños que están bajo su supervisión.

negligence
A teacher's or other school employee's failure to exercise sufficient care in protecting students from injury.

negligencia
Fracaso del maestro u otro empleado de la escuela en ejercer el cuidado debido para proteger a los estudiantes y evitar daños.

Monitoring student safety in the classroom and at recess is essential.

are recognized. Finally, while students may take part in their own prayer activities, those activities must not interfere with the basic practices within a school (Walsh, 1999). If you're like many educators, it's sometimes hard to know when the curriculum gets in the way of individual rights. Take Tracy's advice and talk with your classroom teacher or other educators if you have questions about the curriculum.

Safety in Schools

As a paraprofessional, you are part of an educational team that is legally responsible for educating students about their safety. It is hard to keep track of all that takes place in a classroom. Challenging or not, educators are legally responsible for the well being of their students while they are at school. The courts use the term **in loco parentis**, "in place of the parent", to describe the responsibilities of educators. *In loco parentis* means teachers must use the same level of judgment as parents and provide students with support and supervision. If it can be proved that an educator has not provided the necessary guidance and structure, the educator may be charged with **negligence** (Kauchak & Eggen, 2005). As a paraprofessional you may be wondering how educators avoid negligence. Consider how you would answer the following questions when working in the classroom:

1. Did I make a reasonable attempt to keep the children from harm?
2. Did I establish the proper rules and procedures to prevent problems from happening?
3. Were the children warned of potential dangers in a particular situation?
4. Did I provide the children with proper supervision?

If you are able to answer yes to each of these questions, you have acted in a responsible manner. If not, you may want to rethink your interactions with students.

TABLE 5-1 Legal Vocabulary Checklist

VOCABULARY TERMS	KEY POINTS TO REMEMBER	HOW DOES THIS TERM APPLY TO MY WORK IN A CLASSROOM?
Family Education Rights and Privacy Act (FERPA)		
Americans with Disabilities Act (ADA)		
Disclosure Statement		
Negligence		
Privacy		
Religion in Schools		
Ethics		
Indoctrination		
In loco parentis		

Educators are part of a system that is guided by laws and regulations. It's sometimes hard to keep track of all the policies related to working with children. The Legal Vocabulary Checklist, Table 5-1, provides space to write down new words from this chapter. Additionally, you may want to include notes on the areas where you have questions or need to do additional research.

SUMMARY

As with any other organization that involves a group of people, schools are complex institutions. With so many people working together, guidelines and policies help schools run smoothly. National, state, and local policies direct the daily work of educators. This chapter presented an overview of key laws related to privacy, due process of the law, the rights of individuals with exceptionalities, and laws related to religion in public schools. As a paraprofessional in today's classroom, you are responsible for knowing the legal policies that govern your classroom. This chapter provides the first step toward building your understanding of your legal responsibilities and provides a foundation for learning more about your role in an exciting system.

CHECKING FOR UNDERSTANDING

1. Describe the major laws that impact the work of educators in today's classrooms.
2. How do privacy policies impact the work of educators?
3. Why do educators need to be careful about the type of questions that they ask their students?

4. In what ways is it important to talk about religion as a part of the curriculum in schools? What must educators think about to make sure their discussions of topics are within the law?

5. When might an educator be considered liable or negligent?

POINTS OF VIEW

Maria and Tracy share the following suggestions on how to learn more about the legal issues that affect people working in classrooms.

1. Review your school handbooks for teachers and students. Pay close attention to the policies and procedures related to due process, students' rights, and teachers' rights. What are the policies about reporting child abuse in your school and district?

2. What policies does your school have about safety issues for students, transporting students, and providing general guidance? Are there times when students may be left alone in a classroom or on the playground? What can you do to help make your classroom and school safe for students?

3. With the help of your media specialist or local librarian, locate court cases that focus specifically on religion in schools and research two or three of them. The following list might be of help.

Lee vs. Weismann, 1992

Mozert vs. Hawkins County Public Schools, 1987, 1988

Smith vs. Board of School Commissioners of Mobile County, 1987

PORTFOLIO CORNER

The Praxis Standards for paraprofessional address four general areas regarding a paraprofessional ability to: 1) provide support for instructional opportunities within a classroom setting; 2) demonstrate professional and ethical practice; 3) provide a supportive learning environment; and 4) communicate effectively and participate in the team process. These standards are quite similar to the standards to which licensed teachers must submit.

The discussion topics in Chapter 5 addressed Standard II above. The artifacts, or lines of evidence, that you might share under Standard II include: a review and summary of the professional practices standards of your district and state, information gathered at your local teachers' association meetings related to law and ethics, a review and summary of the work standards for paraprofessionals at your school, handbooks from your school, and a list of appropriate topics for discussion. For additional artifacts, think about these ideas.

1. With the help of your classroom teacher, school administrator, or district human resource representative, find workshops or courses in your local community on legal issues related to working with students.

2. Many paraprofessionals work with students in special education classrooms. The National Resource Center for Paraprofessionals in Education and Related Services (NRCP) describes the work responsibilities of paraprofessionals in special education classrooms. Together with your classroom teacher, review the standards and job descriptions to decide if your

TABLE 5-2 Sample Portfolio Framework

STANDARD I—SUPPORTING INSTRUCTIONAL OPPORTUNITIES	STANDARD II—DEMONSTRATING PROFESSIONALISM AND ETHICAL PRACTICE
See Chapter 7	Sample artifacts might include: • Legal vocabulary checklist from this chapter • Key information from your school policy and handbook materials • Reviews and reactions to national and state policies • Review and evaluation of how your job responsibilities align with the NRCP standards • Your ideas
STANDARD III— SUPPORTING A POSITIVE LEARNING ENVIRONMENT	**STANDARD IV— COMMUNICATING EFFECTIVELY AND PARTICIPATING IN THE TEAM PROCESS**
See Chapters 4 and 7	See Chapter 6

work assignments match the regulations of your position. You can find information on NRCP at http://www.nrcpara.org that will provide ideas for additional portfolio artifacts.

Use Table 5-2, Sample Portfolio Framework, and list sample artifacts that will meet Standard II based upon our discussions in Chapter 5.

REFERENCES

Ashbaker, B., & Morgan, J. (2006). *Paraprofessionals in the classroom.* New York: Allyn & Bacon.

Corey, G., Corey, M., & Callahan, P. (1993). *Issues and ethics in the helping professions.* Pacific Grove, CA: Brooks/Cole.

Fisher, L., Schimmel, D., & Kelly, C., (2003). *Teacher and the law* (6th ed.). New York: Longman.

Kauchak, D., & Eggen, P. (2005). *Introduction to teaching: Becoming a professional* (2nd ed.). Upper Saddle River, New Jersey: Pearson, Merrill Prentice Hall.

National Education Association. (2006). *Code of Ethics of the Education Profession.* Washington, DC. Retrieved July 16, 2006 from http://www.nea.org/aboutnea/code.html

United States Department of Education (1999). *Teachers' guide to religion in the public schools.* Washington, DC.

Utah State Office of Education (2006). Title 53A—53A-13-101.1 *Chapter 13-Curriculum in the Public Schools.* Salt Lake City, Utah. Retrieved July 20, 2006 from http://www.usoe.k12.ut.us.

Walsh, M. (1999). Appeals court tosses out ruling in Alabama religious-expression case. *Education Week, 18,* 1, 10.

Additional selected readings and Paraprofessional electronic resources are available as part of the student Online Companion web site: www.earlychilded.delmar.com.

EN ESPAÑOL

OBJETIVOS DEL APRENDIZAJE

Después de leer y reflexionar sobre este capítulo usted podrá comprender mejor:

- Los derechos y responsabilidades de los estudiantes, maestros y familias
- Leyes y consideraciones éticas para los educadores
- Cuestiones legales relacionadas con la **privacidad**, los procedimientos de ley debida, la religión y la seguridad

A medida que lea este capítulo, hágase las siguientes preguntas:

1. ¿Cuáles son las responsabilidades legales de los paraprofesionales?
2. ¿Qué es la Ley de los derechos de educación y privacidad de la familia?
3. ¿Qué se debe hacer cuando se sospecha que un niño es víctima de abuso?
4. ¿Qué tipo de preguntas es apropiado hacerles a los estudiantes?
5. ¿Qué clase de documentos incluirá en su portafolio para demostrar su conocimiento de las disposiciones legales que afectan el trabajo de los paraprofesionales?

PARA VERIFICAR LA COMPRENSIÓN

1. Describa las principales leyes que afectan el trabajo de los educadores en las aulas de hoy en día.
2. ¿Cómo afectan las políticas de privacidad el trabajo de los educadores?
3. ¿Por qué deben los educadores tener cuidado con las preguntas que les hacen a los estudiantes?
4. ¿De qué manera se debe hablar de religión como parte del currículo en las escuelas? ¿En que deben pensar los educadores para asegurarse de que los temas que tratan no sean ilegales?
5. ¿Cuándo se puede considerar a un educador culpable o negligente?

PUNTOS DE VISTA

Maria y Tracy comparten las siguientes ideas para aprender más sobre las cuestiones legales que afectan a los que trabajan en el salón de clases.

1. Repase los manuales para profesores y estudiantes de su escuela. Preste mucha atención a las disposiciones y a los procedimientos de ley debida, los derechos de los alumnos y los de los maestros. ¿Cuáles son las regulaciones sobre la denuncia del abuso de menores en su escuela y distrito?
2. ¿Cuáles son las reglas de su escuela en cuanto a la seguridad de los estudiantes, el transporte de los mismos y el asesoramiento que se les brinda en general? ¿Hay momentos en los que se deja solos a los estudiantes en el salón de clases o en el patio? ¿Qué puede hacer para

---

privacidad
Regulaciones que indican el tipo de información que puede divulgarse sobre los asuntos personales o académicos de un estudiante.

privacy
Policies that describe the type of information that may be shared about a student's personal life or academic records.

ayudar a que el salón de clases y la escuela sean un lugar seguro para los estudiantes?

3. Con la ayuda del especialista en medios o el bibliotecario local, busque casos legales relacionados con la religión en las escuelas e investigue dos o tres. La siguiente lista puede ser de ayuda:

Lee v. Weismann, 1992

Mozert v. Escuelas públicas del condado Hawkins, 1987, 1988

Smith vs. Consejo de comisionados de las escuelas del condado Mobile, 1987

PARA LA CARPETA

Los estándares Praxis para paraprofesionales se refieren a cuatro áreas generales que tratan de la habilidad de los paraprofesionales para: 1) apoyar toda oportunidad educativa dentro del entorno del salón de clases; 2) demostrar una conducta profesional y ética; 3) ofrecer un ambiente conducente al aprendizaje; y 4) demostrar destreza para comunicarse eficazmente y participar en el proceso de equipo. Estos estándares son bastante similares a los estándares a los que deben ajustarse los maestros licenciados.

Los temas tratados en el Capítulo 5 se relacionan con el estándar II arriba mencionado. Los documentos o muestras que usted puede utilizar bajo el estándar II son: una reseña y resumen de los estándares de la práctica profesional de su distrito y estado, información recopilada en las reuniones de la asociación de maestros relacionada con leyes y ética, una reseña y resumen de los estándares

TABLA 5-2 Estructura modelo de carpeta

ESTÁNDAR I— APOYO DE TODA OPORTUNIDAD EDUCATIVA	ESTÁNDAR II— DEMOSTRAR UNA CONDUCTA PROFESIONAL Y ÉTICA
Vea el Capítulo 7	Los objetos de muestra pueden incluir: • Lista del vocabulario y los términos legales de este capítulo • Información clave sobre las regulaciones de su escuela y material del manual escolar • Comentarios y reacciones a disposiciones federales y estatales • Comentario y evaluación de la correspondencia entre las responsabilidades de su puesto y los estándares de NRCP • Sus ideas
ESTÁNDAR III— OFRECER UN AMBIENTE CONDUCENTE AL APRENDIZAJE	ESTÁNDAR IV—COMUNICARSE CON EFICAZMENTE Y PARTICIPAR EN EL PROCESO DEL EQUIPO
Vea los Capítulos 4 y 7	Vea el Capítulo 6

de trabajo para paraprofesionales, los manuales de su escuela y una lista de temas adecuados para discusión en clase. Para documentos adicionales, considere estas sugerencias:

1. Con la ayuda de su maestro de clase, el administrador de la escuela, o el representante de recursos humanos del distrito, busque talleres o cursos en su comunidad sobre cuestiones legales relacionadas con el trabajo con estudiantes.

2. Muchos paraprofesionales trabajan con estudiantes en las clases de educación especial. El Centro nacional de recursos para paraprofesionales de la educación y servicios relacionados (NRCP, según sus siglas en inglés) se ocupa de las responsabilidades del trabajo de los paraprofesionales en las clases de educación especial. Junto con su maestro de clase, repase los estándares y las descripciones de su puesto para saber si el trabajo que usted desempeña corresponde a lo que indican los reglamentos. La información sobre NRCP se encuentra en http://www.nrcpara.org y le proporcionará ideas adicionales de otros documentos para agregar a su carpeta.

Utilice la tabla 5-2, Estructura modelo de carpeta para hacer una lista de documentos que se relacionen con el estándar II, de acuerdo con lo tratado en el Capítulo 5.

EFFECTIVE COMMUNICATION AS AN EDUCATIONAL TEAM MEMBER

LEARNING OBJECTIVES

After reading and reflecting on this chapter you will
understand:

- Forms of communication
- Effective communication techniques
- Managing conflict
- Collaborating with families and community
  members

As you read this chapter, ask yourself these
questions:

1. What are some of the ways in which classroom teachers and paraprofessionals can
   communicate effectively?
2. How do educators send effective messages?
3. What should educators remember when they
   write notes and memos?
4. What kind of artifacts will you include in your
   portfolio to demonstrate your knowledge of
   effective communication?

KEY TERMS

academic learning time

allocated time

body language

electronic mail

engaged time

funds of knowledge

instructional time

I-statements

parent advocacy groups

restatements

shared governance

INTRODUCTION

Communication is one of the most important skills for educators. Communication tools help educators share their goals and plans with coworkers, students, and families. Communication takes place through daily conversations, formal memos, e-mail discussions, and feedback shared directly with students. As a paraprofessional you will work with many different people each day. You'll need to know how to ask for information from others, share your ideas, and show your abilities. The goal of this chapter is to learn more about effective communication between people working in your school and community.

A popular activity found at many childhood parties is the game *Telephone*. As a part of this game, players whisper a word or phrase to the next person in a circle. Each player then whispers what she heard to the next person until everyone in the group has heard the word or phrase. Even if you have never played this game, you may know that as words and phrases are passed from one person to the next the original word or phrase is often misunderstood, and in some cases completely misinterpreted. While players of the game *Telephone* often

Effective communication is an essential tool for every educator.

enjoy a good laugh as new words and phrases are created, communication in other settings is no laughing matter. Communication in classrooms and schools is no exception.

In a recent e-mail exchange Maria and Tracy talked about the need for effective communication. They share their ideas on how to learn as much as possible from the advice and experience of their teacher mentors.

Hi Maria,

Thanks for helping me figure out how to schedule time to talk with my classroom teacher. I know I can really learn a lot from her, because she has a lot of experience and knows about working with kids. I try to learn as much from her as I can, but the biggest problem I have is finding time to talk to her. I don't want to bug her. I know she has a lot to do every day, so I'm not always sure how to schedule a time to ask my questions and share some of my ideas. Your suggestions helped me organize my time. The first thing I did was learn more about the role of my classroom teacher as my mentor and my role in the classroom as a paraprofessional. Then I wrote down my ideas and questions before we met. When I put my ideas down on paper I am more focused when I talk with my teacher. Thanks again for your help.

In today's classrooms paraprofessionals are one piece in a large system that serves students. As team members, paraprofessionals work closely with their classroom teachers, other educators, and families. The relationship between classroom teachers and paraprofessionals means classroom teachers have one set of responsibilities and paraprofessionals have others. Paraprofessionals are usually responsible for clerical assignments and putting the plans of the classroom teacher into action. If you don't understand your job expectations, talk to your classroom teacher so you'll understand your responsibilities. In most settings the classroom teacher helps the paraprofessional understand their work assignments (Rueda & Monzo, 2000). To understand your role, follow these ideas:

1. plan a time to review your job expectations with your classroom teacher,
2. accept feedback from your mentor teacher to develop your skills,
3. set up a time to meet with your classroom teacher to set long-term goals.

Effective communication will help you understand your role in the classroom. After all, if we don't know what's expected in our jobs it's hard to know if we're serving students in the best way. Making the most of your time in the classroom is a great first step. Let's take a look at strategies that help educators use their time effectively.

allocated time
The official time that a state or district sets for teaching a specific content area.

tiempo asignado
Tiempo oficial que el estado o el distrito establece para enseñar un área específica de contenido.

instructional time
The time teachers are directly involved in instruction within a lesson.

tiempo educacional
Tiempo de la lección en que los maestros se dedican exclusivamente a enseñar.

engaged time
The time students are focused on their teacher's instruction during a lesson.

tiempo de concentración
Tiempo que los alumnos dedican a concentrarse en las enseñanzas del maestro durante una lección.

academic learning time
The amount of time students spend working on content through independent work or work with classmates.

tiempo de aprendizaje académico
Cantidad de tiempo que los estudiantes emplean para trabajar en un tema de forma independiente o con sus compañeros de clase.

USING TIME EFFECTIVELY

The roles of classroom teachers are very complex. Their days include work with students, administrators, families, and other school personnel. A closer look at the way teachers use time shows that the actual time spent teaching children is much less than you might expect. Two experts in education have developed a breakdown of the ways teachers use time in their classroom. Teachers use their time in four ways that include: **allocated time**, **instructional time**, **engaged time**, and **academic learning time** (Kauchak & Eggen, 2007). Table 6-1, Time Use in the Classroom, shows how time is used in schools. The key points to remember are:

a. allocated time is the official time that a state or district sets for teaching in specific content areas;

b. instructional time is the time teachers are directly involved in instruction during a lesson;

c. engaged time is when students are paying attention to instruction during a lesson; and

d. academic learning time is the amount of time students are working on projects, independent work or work with classmates (Kauchak & Eggen, 2007). Think about the different ways time is used in your classroom. Are there better ways to use time? Are there some kinds of assignments that would be helpful if students had more time to finish their work? Are there some activities where students only need a small amount of time to complete assignments? Most people agree that no matter how much time we have, we could always use more!

TABLE 6-1 Time Use in the Classroom

TYPES OF TIME	DEFINITION	WHAT HAPPENS IN YOUR CLASSROOM?
Allocated time	the official time that a state or district sets for teaching in specific content areas	What are the requirements in your state on the time that must be spent on specific content areas?
Instructional time	the time that educators use to teach content to their students	How much time do educators actually spend teaching students about each of the subjects in your classroom?
Engaged time	the amount of time students are paying attention to the educator's instruction	How do educators know when students are engaged?
Academic learning time	the amount of time students are successfully working with the content in the classroom	How much time do students spend on activities and projects in different content areas?

The ways time is used in classrooms show us how students and teachers spend their days. While the main responsibility of teachers is to work with students, they don't spend all of their time directly teaching. As a paraprofessional, be aware of the time demands on your classroom teacher. Talk openly with your teacher about the best times to plan and review your work. Once you've agreed on a time to meet, the next step is to plan for goals in your work with students.

SUGGESTIONS FOR BUILDING AN EFFECTIVE MENTORING RELATIONSHIP

In a study on relationships between paraprofessionals and classroom teachers, two researchers studied ideas for effective communication. These researchers found that the best classrooms are those where classroom teachers and paraprofessionals work as team members. Educators are most successful when they have open discussions and plan time to talk (Rueda & Monzo, 2000). Based on the suggestions of researchers and their knowledge and experience as paraprofessionals, Maria and Tracy share the following ideas for effective communication with classroom teachers:

shared governance
An approach to leadership in a classroom or organization that recognizes each individual as a team member who shares ideas, plans, and responsibilities.

autoridad compartida
Estilo de liderazgo de un salón de clases o de una organización que reconoce que cada individuo es un miembro del equipo que comparte ideas, planes, y responsabilidades.

1. Strong work relationships happen when a philosophy of **shared governance** is in place. Shared governance means the classroom teacher believes that paraprofessionals are a part of the education team. Team members share ideas, plans, and responsibilities. There is a feeling that each team member has much to offer students. Even if your classroom does not include a shared governance philosophy, ask your teacher about the best ways to share your ideas on how to work with the children in your classroom.

2. As a paraprofessional, practice your language and writing skills so that you can share your ideas and perspectives with your teacher. Keep a journal or complete the portfolio assignments in this book as a way of improving your writing skills.

3. Learn to observe your teacher. There are few substitutes for learning from others. Watching other teachers gives paraprofessionals the chance to improve their own skills.

4. Remain open to advice. Your classroom teacher is a wonderful resource and has a lot of information to share. As a paraprofessional you also bring important skills and talents that will add to the classroom environment. Ask your teacher for advice on how to develop your skills even further.

5. Understand that teachers are busy people with a lot of responsibilities. Make the most of meeting times with teachers by making a list of questions in advance. Strong speaking and writing abilities and a willingness to watch and learn from others are important skills for paraprofessionals.

The above suggestions will improve your talents and help you build mentoring relationships with your classroom teacher (Burbank, McCandless, & Bachman, 2006).

Effective educators learn from their experiences; they watch, think about what they've seen, and take action in the classroom. Think about the following questions as you improve your communication skills: Have you ever taken the time to watch your teacher working with groups of students? What did you learn from these observations? How does your classroom teacher communicate with other adults at your school? In what areas would you like to improve your communication skills? What are some of your strengths when you communicate with others? If your classroom teacher is not willing to communicate, are there other teachers or paraprofessionals at your school who might be good resources?

TOOLS FOR SHARING INFORMATION

The tools we use to communicate our messages are often as important, if not more important, than the information we share. Traditional forms of communication in schools include brief notes, formal letters, e-mail messages, and informal conversations. When educators communicate with others, they have a responsibility to share information that is clear, free from errors, and understandable. In addition to what we share, it's also important to think about the *way* we share. How we respond, including our tone of voice and our body language, are important factors when we communicate. In a recent e-mail exchange, Tracy mentioned her frustrations when the lines of communication were not as strong as they could have been at her school. Think about how you would have handled Tracy's situation as a part of her Day-to-Day Dilemma.

DAY-TO-DAY DILEMMA
HOW WOULD YOU HANDLE THIS SITUATION?

Re: I'm so frustrated. Help!
Hi Tracy,

I just got your e-mail. I was really surprised by how frustrated you were at the end of the day. It sounds like you had a really bad day. I wasn't sure what was going on with the media specialist in the library. She's always been really easy for me to work with whenever I need something. You said there was some kind of problem with the day and time you had scheduled the video equipment and that when you went to pick up the recorder it had already been checked out by someone else. What happened next?

Let me know,

Maria

Re: What happened next?
Hi Maria,

Yeah, the media specialist is really nice but I was so mad the other day when I went to get the video camera. You'll never believe what happened when I went to the library. Okay, so I followed the rules and reserved the camera a week in advance for a project we were doing with the kids. But when I went to the library, the camera was gone! What was I supposed to do? We needed the camera that day! You'd have been so proud of me Maria! I stayed calm. I remembered from that training in the district that we're supposed to stay calm, figure out the problem, and then think of two or three ways to solve it. Of course my first impulse was to run screaming from the school, but I thought, hmm . . . bad idea. So the media specialist and I came up with a couple of ideas on how to reschedule the camera for later in the day. The fact that we both stayed calm and tried to solve the problem together was a big help!

How would you have responded if you were in Tracy's position? Most of us have days when we feel frustrated at work. As educators, we all find ourselves in situations where we have to make quick decisions. The key for Tracy was staying calm and coming up with a way to solve her problem. In any stressful situation it is important to remember that *how* we respond to others affects whether or not we reach our goals. If we remain calm and work with others we're more likely to see success. If we respond with anger and frustration, it's less likely that others will be willing to work with us in problem solving. Educators who remain positive and proactive are more likely to see positive results in their work.

Communication experts agree that some ways of communicating are more effective than others. Our tone of voice, the language we use, our body language, and even how loud or soft we talk impact how our messages are received. In a book on effective classroom interaction, C.M. Charles (2006) says effective communication includes three parts: language that makes situations less stressful, a tone of voice that is calm, and body language that shows we are open and willing to listen to others.

LANGUAGE THAT HELPS REDUCE STRESSFUL SITUATIONS

Schools and classrooms are filled with people working together. Whenever people communicate, there is a chance they will not always agree. Researchers and teachers tell us that the language we use in stressful situations can help reduce tensions. Experts on effective communication suggest the following skills for effective communication: 1) "**I-statements**"; 2) **restatements** that summarize the comments of a person with whom you are speaking; 3) clarifying when you have a question; and 4) making a plan for following up on a conversation.

I-Statements

I-statements are words or phrases that describe how the person delivering the message is feeling at the time the message is delivered. I-statements are used to help others understand the point of view of the person sending the message. The advantage of I-statements is that they let the sender of a message tell what he or she thinks without criticizing or attacking the listener. For example, when Tracy arrived at the media center, she said "I felt frustrated when I arrived at the library." She used an I-statement. A less positive way of responding would have

---

I-statements
Words or phrases that describe how the person delivering a message is feeling when they deliver a message. I-statements are used to help others understand the perspective of the person delivering a message.

declaraciones en primera persona
Palabras o frases que describen cómo se siente una persona en el momento en que transmite un mensaje. Las declaraciones en primera persona se usan para ayudar a los demás a comprender el punto de vista de la persona que transmite el mensaje.

restatements
A way to tell a speaker what they heard in a conversation. Restatements let the listener tell what they heard using their own words and are important because they help both parties in a conversation make sure that the message was heard as intended.

reafirmaciones
Modo de informar al hablante de lo que se escuchó en una conversación. Las reafirmaciones permiten que el oyente diga lo que escuchó con sus propias palabras y son importantes porque ayudan a los participantes en una conversación a cerciorarse de que el mensaje fue recibido tal como era previsto.

been to blame the media specialist for the mistake. If she had said to the specialist, "You've made a mistake and now I don't have the video equipment I need. You've gotten me into trouble!", the outcome of the conversation could have been very different. I-statements help the speaker share information without blaming the other person.

Restatements

Restatements give the listener the chance to tell a speaker what they heard through their own words. Restatements are important because they help the listener and the sender make sure that the message was heard in the way the sender wanted. Through restatements, both the speaker and the listener make sure they understood. If speakers and listeners don't agree, they have the chance to make their points more clear. Have you ever been in a situation where you were misunderstood? As a paraprofessional you are in contact with many different people each day. Most conversations take place with no problems. At other times miscommunication happens. When miscommunications happen, think about how I-statements and restatements could make your conversations more effective. But what if these tools don't work? Let's take a look at how you might respond.

Tracy and Maria are good friends, but even good friends don't get along all the time. In a recent conversation, they tried to figure out the best way to put together their portfolios. Maria wanted to include video clips of her work with students in her portfolio. Tracy was more interested in including samples of students' work. Because they each had a different plan for gathering artifacts, they disagreed on the best way of making their portfolios. Let's take a look at how they worked through their disagreement. Pay close attention to the communication skills used in their conversation.

Tracy: I just don't know why you're going to make an electronic portfolio to show your work as a paraprofessional. It seems to me that you're going to spend a lot of time making an electronic version of the old-fashioned scrapbook. If you spend all that time on an electronic portfolio, you won't have any good artifacts to include. Wouldn't it just be better to collect some assignments from the students in the class? I don't think that an electronic portfolio is a very good idea. In fact, I think it's a waste of time.

Maria: Well Tracy, I don't think you even know how to use technology in your portfolio. I also think your paper portfolio is too simple. It's better to use an electronic portfolio because everybody is using technology these days. I think you're trying to take the easy way out and don't want to spend the time learning to make your portfolio the right way.

Tracy: Are you saying that I'm trying to take the easy way out because I'm not using technology? Why are you accusing me of being lazy?

Maria: Tracy, technology is important and calling an electronic portfolio a "waste of time" shows how little you know about what's going on in education today.

The discussion between Maria and Tracy describes how each person plans to show their work in a professional portfolio. Each person has an idea on the "best" way to create their portfolios. The problem with their discussion is the way their language is making each person defensive and critical of the other's ideas.

In addition to using I-statements, communication experts suggest restating and clarifying the comments of the person with whom you are speaking. Listen to Maria's and Tracy's discussion when they use I-statements, restatements, and clarifications. As you read their role play, think about how you would respond if you were in Tracy's or Maria's position.

Tracy: Maria, I'm putting together my portfolio and want to use artifacts that show my work with students. I know you're going to make an electronic presentation of your work in the classroom. I don't know a lot about the use of technology, but it seems like it takes a lot of time. Can you help me understand how I could use this type of portfolio? I want to include some assignments from the students in the class. What do you think?

Maria: Electronic portfolios are really cool. Once you get the hang of putting them together, they're actually kind of fun. Technology is new to a lot of people and I can understand why people are unsure of how it's used. I'd be happy to show you what I know about making electronic portfolios. I'd like to learn more about the artifacts you're going to use. You mentioned that you'll include samples of the notes and messages you've shared with students and families. I'm not sure I really know how these could be used in my portfolio. I'll bet I could learn more if we share our ideas.

Tracy: Thanks Maria. It would really help me if you'd share some of your ideas. After all, you're the technology expert! I'll share my ideas with you, if you want.

Maria: Thanks Tracy. I'll bet there other artifacts I haven't even thought of including. I'd like to see the artifacts you're going to use.

The second discussion between Maria and Tracy shows how they use I-statements and restatements. In the second conversation, Maria's and Tracy's individual ideas were acknowledged by the other, so they both felt important and valued. Their conversation showed they could learn from each other. These win-win opportunities serve everyone and reduce the chances for people to become frustrated with each other.

Body Language

body language
The nonverbal communication shared through eye contact, posture, gestures, and facial expressions.

lenguaje corporal
Comunicación no verbal efectuada a través del contacto visual, la postura, los gestos y las expresiones faciales.

Most of us have had days where good news from a friend or family member made us stand taller, even walk more quickly—maybe even skip! We have also had days where we received bad news. To an observer, our body language, facial gestures, posture, and/or overall demeanor may show that we have heard bad news. While many educational researchers and teachers know the importance of nonverbal communication, Frederick Jones was among the first people to talk about nonverbal communication in classrooms (Charles, 2002). He talked about the nonverbal messages we send through **body language** during conversations. Body language includes nonverbal communication through eye contact, posture, gestures, and facial expressions. Researchers think that as much as 90% of communication takes place through nonverbal behaviors and that these behaviors send clear messages regarding feelings, perspectives, and an overall approach to work (Charles, 2002; Mehrabian & Ferris, 1967). Common nonverbal behaviors used by educators include hand signals to remind students they need to listen, a smile or a frown to express approval or disapproval, or a thumbs-up showing that a job was well done. These forms of communication are common in many American schools. There are also body language and general communication styles that are unique to different cultures and communities. Educators must understand how communication differs across groups of people.

Body language is a nonverbal form of communication. The teacher and the paraprofessional in this picture show their willingness to listen to one another's points of view.

TABLE 6-2 Effective Communication Tools

COMMUNICATION TOOL	EXAMPLES
I-statements	"I get angry when I'm not clear in my explanations to others."
Rephrasing	"What I thought you said was that you'd like our meeting to take place on another day?"
Highlighting the strengths of others	"That's a great point." "I hadn't considered that before." "Nice work!" "I appreciate your ideas on this issue."
Body Language	Maintain eye contact. Smile, nod, shake hands when appropriate.

Paraprofessionals work with a wide range of students and their families. The range of difference is seen most often in classrooms for English Language Learners. Different backgrounds and life experiences may affect how messages are sent and received. Communication differences across groups of people influence how they interact, speak, and socialize (Grossman, 2004). Differences may exist in the following ways:

1. Responses to questions—in some cultures, it's inappropriate to share personal opinions in a classroom because the educator, or person in authority, is believed to hold knowledge;

2. Individual versus group rights—in some cultures, it's not appropriate for individual rights to rise above the rights of the entire community;

3. Social space, or the amount of distance between people, differs across communities—differences in how social space is used affects how physically close or distant people are when they communicate;

4. Formal versus informal communication styles differ across cultural groups and affect the type of language people use.

Students in today's schools come from diverse language and cultural backgrounds. We have discussed only a few of the ways these differences might affect communication in classrooms. As you work with students and families, think about how your messages are sent and received. What are some of the nonverbal messages you send to others? How do you respond when others show open and welcoming behaviors? What forms of nonverbal communication have you observed in others? Keep these suggestions in mind when communicating with others at your school. Table 6-2, Effective Communication Tools, includes examples of some of the most effective ways of sharing your messages with others.

EFFECTIVE COMMUNICATION WITH PARENTS AND CAREGIVERS

Paraprofessionals play unique roles in classrooms. They work closely with students and are in regular contact with parents. They provide direct support to students, share information with other educators, and keep parents updated on children's progress. As a paraprofessional you may be asked to review homework assignments with students or you may be asked to provide very specific support to students with special needs. You may even be asked to write progress reports showing the amount or quality of work a student has completed in a given day. These reports to parents are typically written. Whether you use a hand-written note or fill out a checklist on student work it's important that your note is written clearly and professionally.

A form of written communication that is more and more popular is **electronic-mail** or e-mail. E-mail is a quick way to send information and share documents with individuals and large groups. Limitations of electronic communication include the lack of direct contact with others and the tendency to send out information too quickly. E-mail may also cause senders and receivers to feel alone and disconnected. This isolation may make people feel like others don't really appreciate them as people (Kauchak & Eggen, 2005). Another weakness of e-mail is that a lot of people don't have computers at home or they don't have a lot of experience using technology. Even when families have access to electronic communication, either at home or through libraries, they still like face-to-face contacts through conferences and open house meetings at schools (Langdon, 1999). Whether you are sending home a brief note, sending an e-mail, or outlining an assignment for a student to complete, it is important to send a clear and well-written message.

TIPS FOR WRITTEN COMMUNICATION

The following suggestions will help you prepare written notes to families. While most formal contacts with parents are made through the classroom teacher or a principal, paraprofessionals also sign progress reports or send home general updates. Keep these tips in mind when sending information in writing:

1. plan in advance for what you are sending;
2. make sure your writing is professional in tone and in the way you present information;
3. think about the perspective of the person who will read or hear your message;
4. organize your thoughts;
5. make a draft or practice version of the formal letter or note you will send;
6. make sure your writing is clear, is accurate in presentation, and has been checked for spelling errors; and
7. communicate in ways that are easier for others to understand. (Reep & Sharp, 1999).

If a phone call is more effective than a note, place a call. If parents or caregivers are busy, a note may be the most effective form of communication. No matter who the audience is, it is always important to ask someone to read your work to make sure that your message is understood. Your classroom teacher is ultimately responsible for notes and letters shared with families. The teacher is also the person who should give you feedback on the notes and letters you share. Take advantage of the experts around you and get their advice on how to improve the messages you send to others.

electronic mail
An electronic form of communication using the Internet.

correo electrónico
Forma electrónica de comunicación por medio de Internet.

Correspondence with families may be sent through notes, e-mail, formal letters, or in person as seen in this picture.

Sharing Good News

If you are like most people, it is always nice to receive good news. When you communicate with families and other school personnel, start with a positive comment. The sample cards in Table 6-3, Sample Note Cards to Share with Parents/Guardians, give ideas on how to share notes that show students' progress or areas in need of improvement. Contacts with parents may include either a blank card where individualized notes are shared, or prepared cards that include a list of areas in need of attention. Many teachers also start out the school year with an introductory greeting. No matter what format you use, check with your school or district office to make sure the necessary translations are provided for families whose first language is not English. Remember, it's always important to find a way to share good news.

Working in Communities through Advocacy Programs

Effective communication with parents and caregivers is only one step in creating a positive relationship. Teachers and paraprofessionals are valuable parts of a student's success in schools. Parents and caregivers are another important part of a student's school experiences. Today, educators recognize the expertise, experiences, and concerns families bring to school communities. A number of communities around the nation know that when families, schools, and communities work together, children succeed. The United for Kids (UFK) project is an example of a program that links a school district, a university, and the educational community. Through this program parents and caregivers receive important information on success in school, access to higher education, and educational resources. Workshops provided in English and Spanish offer parents and caregivers information on topics such as child development, tips for success in schools, information on NCLB, and the legal rights and responsibilities of

TABLE 6-3 Sample Note Cards to Share with Parents/Guardians

SAMPLE GOOD NEWS NOTE
Dear (name of Parent or Guardian), Just a quick note to let you know some good news about (student's name). Your child has shown great effort during the past few weeks and is making good progress in her work. Thank you for your continued support. We appreciate the chance to work with you and your child. Sincerely,

SAMPLE NOTE FOR A STRUGGLING STUDENT
Dear (Name of Parent or Guardian), This note is sent because of my concerns over (name of student)'s school work or behavior. (Note these are sample areas you may want to highlight. You will likely have other areas you would like to report to parents and caregivers.) Homework Test Performance Classroom Behavior Please contact your child's classroom teacher so we can talk further. We want to work with you so that we can come up with a solution. If we work together we can make your child's classroom experience as productive as possible. Sincerely,

students, families, teachers, and community members (University Neighborhood Partners, 2006). Many UFK workshop presenters and participants work in their children's schools as paraprofessionals. Think about the ways you could help bring information to your community about public schools. For more information on United for Kids, go to http://www.partners.utah.edu.

Funds of Knowledge

The contributions of families and the life experiences of each child add to the school experiences of children in classrooms. The backgrounds and experiences of students are sometimes called the "**funds of knowledge**" that students bring to school. These "funds of knowledge" are strengths that should be celebrated and used in ways that help students succeed (Moll & Gonzales, 1997). "Funds of Knowledge" include the different ways that our backgrounds help us to understand and learn. Researchers know that people have different life experiences. They differ in how they approach work and learning. For example, many children use literacy or math skills in their homes and communities each day. They use reading and math in play and through print materials in activities such as cooking, playing games, and interacting in their community. While these activities may be not be the

funds of knowledge
The life experiences, ways of approaching work, and learning strategies all children have when entering classrooms.

banco de conocimientos
Experiencias de vida, formas de trabajar y estrategias de aprendizaje con el que llegan a la escuela todos los niños.

Students and families bring valuable forms of knowledge to schools and communities. The knowledge that educators and families share improves the education of children.

same as school-based activities that involve sitting down at a desk and reading a book, children are still engaged in literacy activities. The Moll and Gonzales (1997) research team suggests that teachers and those working in classrooms recognize that children bring valuable experiences and knowledge to classrooms even when these experiences are different from their peers. They suggest that teachers and school personnel take advantage of students' knowledge by linking school experiences to the knowledge children bring to classrooms. Educational teams who communicate with families understand students and teach in ways that build on students' strengths and life experiences. Think about the ways you'll learn more about the funds of knowledge children bring to your classroom and school.

Parent Advocacy Groups

Parent advocacy groups are another example of organizations that increase communication between families and schools. Historically, parent advocacy groups served students receiving special education services. These parent advocates help the family-school communication process. Today, advocate roles may include writing letters and attending meetings; sharing information with families on policies and the law, identifying ways to ask questions; and providing ideas for parents on how to prepare for school-based meetings where educational plans are identified (Special Education Advocacy—Getting Started—Wrightslaw, 2006). Advocates also help families whose children are affected by the recent policies of NCLB within Title I schools. Advocates assist families in learning more about current accountability issues; they provide parents with information on testing and the ways in which performance is measured; and they share information on how parents and caregivers can access tutoring and special education services. Who are the people in your school's community who

Effective communication with families involves valuing and respecting parents and caregivers. © *Karen Struthers*

parent advocacy groups
Groups who serve the needs of students, particularly those eligible for special education or English language services. Advocate roles may include writing letters and attending meetings, sharing information on policies and the law, putting forward strategies for asking questions, and providing ideas on how to prepare for school-based meetings where educational plans are identified.

grupos de defensa de los padres
Grupos que prestan atención a las necesidades de los estudiantes, particularmente los que requieren educación especial o aprendizaje del idioma inglés. Los defensores pueden ejercer muchas tareas como, por ejemplo, escribir cartas y atender reuniones, compartir información sobre leyes y regulaciones, elaborar estrategias para hacer preguntas y brindar ideas sobre cómo prepararse para las reuniones escolares que tratan de planes educativos.

help communicate information about your school? As a paraprofessional, how will you learn more about partners in you community? Parent advocacy programs are only one way of opening the lines of communication between home and school. Keep thinking about how you will encourage communication in your school community.

SUMMARY

Effective communication includes the skills for sending and receiving information. This chapter discussed effective ways to speak, write, and problem solve. We reviewed communication ideas to use in stressful situations and we listed tools for sharing information with parents and caregivers. In addition to the traditional tools used to communicate in schools, educators are aware that e-mail and home-school partnerships are new ways of sharing information. As communities become more diverse, educators respond in ways that recognize each child's background and life experience. The tools that improve communication help create open and productive discussions with students, coworkers, and families.

CHECKING FOR UNDERSTANDING

1. Communication is part of the daily work of paraprofessionals. What are some of the tools for effective communication? Develop a list of all the individuals with whom you communicate each day. Begin your list with the people you meet on your way to work. Include contacts at school before the first bell of the day, your contacts with students in your classroom, and contacts that take place on the playground. Don't forget to list any contacts with parents and family members. Describe two or three situations where you have used effective communication strategies. Have these situations been successful? In what ways might they be improved?

2. Body language differs from person to person. Some people communicate with their eyes or their body movements. Think about how you can use your body language to effectively communicate with others as a paraprofessional. For example, in what ways might your body language make people feel welcome? When is eye contact most effective? When might eye contact make a situation more stressful? What cultural differences should be considered with regard to body language such as eye contact or personal space?

3. The "funds of knowledge" children bring to classrooms include educational, family, and community experiences. What are some of the funds of knowledge you bring to a school as a paraprofessional? Describe the experiences in your life that help you understand American schools and the education of young people.

4. Writing is an important communication tool used by professionals. Describe how you use writing in your professional life. When do you enjoy writing and when is writing more difficult?

POINTS OF VIEW

Maria and Tracy share their ideas on how to learn more about effective communication strategies.

1. There are many ways to learn more about effective communication. During a meeting at your school, listen to and observe the conversations that take place. How does the language people use influence how others respond? In what ways does body language influence others' responses?

2. With a coworker, develop a list of terms or phrases that teachers use to highlight the good work of students. Examples might include "Good work," "Nice Answer," or "Great attention to detail in your answer!" Specific feedback to students gives them a better understanding of their strengths and the skills you want them to work on.

3. Effective writing is an important part of communication. Local community colleges and universities offer course work on how to become an effective writer or speaker. What are the resources within your community for learning more about becoming an effective writer?

4. Parent Advocacy programs have a long history in many school communities. Advocacy programs have been most common for parents of children receiving special education services. Find out how your school shares information with parents. How will you share your knowledge of advocacy programs with the parents of the children in your school or community? How could you serve as a community advocate at your school?

PORTFOLIO CORNER

This chapter focused on the ways paraprofessionals can become effective communicators. Effective communication strategies pay attention to the role of parents and families as a part of educational teams. The ideas and suggestions shared by Maria and Tracy are linked to Standard IV: Demonstrate an ability to communicate effectively and participate in the team process. The artifacts, or lines of evidence, that you might share under Standard IV include: formal letters or notes you have written to parents and students, an attendance log of the time spent in team meetings at your school, or work samples that show how you interact with students and coworkers.

1. With the help of your teacher, develop a classroom newsletter on events in your classroom that you will share with the students and parents. What kind of information will you share?

2. Use the sample note cards in this chapter to share information with parents/guardians of the students in your classroom. These short memos explain students' classroom performance, behavior, or upcoming events at the school. What are the key areas that you plan to share?

3. With the help of your teacher, create a checklist that includes the policies and procedures that will help families in your classroom to understand the American school system. Pick out the areas that parents should remember as they prepare to send their children to school.

TABLE 6-4 Sample Portfolio Framework

STANDARD I—SUPPORTING INSTRUCTIONAL OPPORTUNITIES	STANDARD II—DEMONSTRATING PROFESSIONALISM AND ETHICAL PRACTICE
See Chapters 4 and 7	See Chapters 2, 5, and 8
STANDARD III—SUPPORTING A POSITIVE LEARNING ENVIRONMENT	STANDARD IV—COMMUNICATING EFFECTIVELY AND PARTICIPATING IN THE TEACHING PROCESSES
See Chapters 3 and 4	Sample artifacts might include: <ul><li>Notes home to parents</li><li>A school newsletter</li><li>Note cards</li><li>Memos to colleagues</li><li>Your ideas</li></ul>

Use Table 6-4, Sample Portfolio Framework, and list sample artifacts that will meet Standard IV based upon our discussions in Chapter 6.

REFERENCES

Burbank, M.D., McCandless, R., & Bachman, M. (2006). *Collaborative networks and the role of site-based mentors in preparing paraprofessionals.* A paper presented at the Association of Teacher Education, Atlanta, Georgia.

Charles, C.M. (2002). *Building classroom discipline* (7th ed.). Boston: Allyn & Bacon.

Grossman, H. (2004). *Classroom management for diverse and inclusive schools.* Lanham, Maryland: Oxford, Rowman, & Littlefield.

Kauchak, D., & Eggen, P. (2007). Learning and Teaching: Research Based Methods (5th ed.). New York: Allyn & Bacon.

Langdon, C.A. (1999). The fifth Phi Delta Kappa poll of teacher's attitudes toward the public schools. Phi Delta Kappa, 80, 611–618.

Mehrabian, A., & Ferris, S. (1967). Inference of attitude from nonverbal behavior in two channels. *Journal of Consulting Psychology, 31,* 190–198.

Moll, L., & González, N. (1997). Teachers as social scientists: Learning about culture from household research in race, ethnicity and multiculturalism. In P.M. Hall, (Ed.), *Missouri Symposium on Research and Educational Policy:* Vol. 1 (pp. 89–114). New York: Garland Publishing.

Rueda, R., & Monzo, L. (2000). *Apprenticeship for teaching: Professional development issues surrounding the collaborative relationships between teachers and paraeducators.* Research Report # 8—Center for Research on Education, Diversity & Excellence (CREDE).

Special Education Advocacy—Getting Started, Wrightslaw—Retrieved February 2, 2006 2, 2006 from http://www.wrightslaw.com/advoc/articles/advocacy.intro.htm.

University Neighborhood Partners (2006). Retrieved June 30, 2006 from http://www.partners.utah.edu/boardroles.htm.

Additional selected readings and Paraprofessional electronic resources are available as part of the student Online Companion web site: www.earlychilded.delmar.com.

EN ESPAÑOL

OBJETIVOS DEL APRENDIZAJE

Después de leer y reflexionar sobre este capítulo podrá comprender mejor:

- Diversas formas de comunicarse
- Técnicas eficaces para comunicarse
- La resolución de conflictos
- La colaboración con las familias y los miembros de la comunidad

A medida que lea este capítulo, hágase las siguientes preguntas:

1. ¿Cómo pueden comunicarse eficazmente los maestros de clase y los paraprofesionales?
2. ¿Cómo pueden los educadores enviar mensajes efectivos?
3. ¿Qué deben recordar los educadores cuando envían notas y memorandos?
4. ¿Qué documentos incluirá en su carpeta para demostrar sus conocimientos sobre comunicación?

PARA VERIFICAR LA COMPRENSIÓN

1. La comunicación es parte del trabajo diario del paraprofesional. ¿De qué medios podemos valernos para una comunicación eficaz? Haga una lista con los nombres de todas las personas con quienes usted se comunica a diario. Comience con la gente que encuentra camino al trabajo. Incluya los contactos en la escuela antes de que suene el primer timbre del día, los contactos con sus estudiantes en el salón de clase, y los que tienen lugar durante los recreos. No olvide enumerar los contactos con los padres y los miembros de la familia. Describa dos o tres situaciones en las que haya utilizado estrategias eficaces para comunicarse. ¿Han tenido éxito estas situaciones? ¿Cómo podría mejorarlas?

2. El **lenguaje corporal** es diferente de una persona a otra. Hay personas que se comunican usando los ojos o los movimientos corporales. Piense cómo utiliza su lenguaje corporal para comunicarse efectivamente con los demás en su desempeño como paraprofesional. Por ejemplo, ¿de qué manera puede su lenguaje corporal hacer que la gente se sienta cómoda? ¿Cuándo es más efectivo establecer contacto visual? ¿Cuándo hace el contacto visual que una situación sea más estresante? ¿Qué diferencias culturales se deben considerar con respecto al lenguaje corporal, como por ejemplo el contacto visual o la distancia de persona a persona?

3. El **"banco de conocimientos"** que los niños aportan a la clase incluye experiencias educativas, de la familia y de la comunidad. ¿Cuál es el banco de conocimientos que usted aporta como paraprofesional? Describa las experiencias de su vida que lo o la ayudan a entender las escuelas de los EE.UU. y la educación de los jóvenes.

4. La escritura es un importante medio de comunicación que usan los profesionales. Describa cómo usa la escritura en su vida profesional. ¿Cuándo disfruta escribiendo y cuándo le da más trabajo hacerlo?

---

lenguaje corporal
Comunicación no verbal efectuada a través del contacto visual, la postura, los gestos y las expresiones faciales.

body language
The nonverbal communication shared through eye contact, posture, gestures, and facial expressions.

---

banco de conocimientos
Experiencias de vida, formas de trabajar y estrategias de aprendizaje con el que llegan a la escuela todos los niños.

funds of knowledge
The life experiences, ways of approaching work, and learning strategies all children have when entering classrooms.

Puntos de Vista

Maria y Tracy comparten sus ideas sobre cómo aprender más sobre estrategias para comunicarse eficazmente.

1. Hay muchas maneras de aprender más sobre cómo comunicarse eficazmente. Durante una reunión de su escuela, escuche y observe las conversaciones que tienen lugar. ¿Cómo el lenguaje que usan unos influye en la forma en que responden los demás? ¿De qué manera influye en esas reacciones el lenguaje corporal usado?

2. Con un compañero de trabajo, haga una lista con los términos o frases que los profesores usan para alentar el buen trabajo de los estudiantes. Los ejemplos pueden incluir: "¡Buen trabajo!", "¡Excelente respuesta!" o "¡Esa es una respuesta bien detallada!"

3. La escritura eficaz es una parte importante de la comunicación. Los colegios y las universidades locales ofrecen cursos para aprender a escribir y a hablar bien. ¿Qué recursos hay en su comunidad para aprender a ser un escritor eficaz?

4. Hace mucho tiempo que existen programas de apoyo a los padres en muchas comunidades. Estos programas han estado dirigidos especialmente a los padres de los niños que requieren educación especial. Averigüe cómo su escuela hace llegar la información a los padres. ¿Cómo compartirá usted lo que sabe sobre los programas de apoyo con los padres de los niños de su escuela o de su comunidad? ¿Cómo puede usted hacer de abogado de la comunidad en su escuela?

Para la carpeta

Este capítulo trata de las distintas maneras en que los paraprofesionales pueden llegar a comunicarse eficazmente. Las estrategias eficaces de la comunicación tienen en cuenta el papel de los padres y las familias como parte del equipo educativo. Las ideas y las sugerencias compartidas por Maria y Tracy están vinculadas al estándar IV: Demostrar habilidad para comunicarse eficazmente y trabajar como miembros del equipo educativo. Los documentos o muestras que usted puede presentar de acuerdo a ese estándar incluyen: cartas formales o notas que haya escrito a los padres y a los estudiantes, un registro de su asistencia a reuniones de equipo en su escuela, o muestras de trabajo que demuestren su interacción con los estudiantes y con sus compañeros de trabajo.

1. Con la ayuda de su profesor, cree un periódico informativo sobre lo que pasa en la clase para compartir con los alumnos y sus padres. ¿Qué información podrá incluir?

2. Utilice las esquelas de muestra de este capítulo para compartir información con padres y guardianes de los alumnos. Estas esquelas sirven para describir el rendimiento de los alumnos y su conducta, así también como para anunciar futuros acontecimientos escolares. ¿Sobre qué áreas clave podrá informar?

3. Con la ayuda del maestro de su clase, cree una lista de comprobación que incluya regulaciones y procedimientos que ayuden a los padres de sus

TABLA 6-4 Estructura modelo de carpeta

ESTÁNDAR I—APOYO DE TODA OPORTUNIDAD EDUCATIVA	ESTÁNDAR II—DEMOSTRAR UNA CONDUCTA PROFESIONAL Y ÉTICA
Vea los Capítulos 4 y 7	Vea los Capítulos 2, 5 y 8

ESTÁNDAR III—OFRECER UN AMBIENTE CONDUCENTE AL APRENDIZAJE	ESTÁNDAR IV—COMUNICARSE EFICAZMENTE Y PARTICIPAR EN EL PROCESO DE EQUIPO
Vea los Capítulos 3 y 4	Los documentos de muestra pueden incluir: ● Notas a los padres ● Boletín informativo de la clase ● Tarjetas de notas ● Memorandos de los colegas

alumnos a comprender el sistema escolar de los EE.UU. Escoja las áreas que los padres deben tener en cuenta cuando se preparan para enviar a los niños a la escuela.

Use la Tabla 6-4, Estructura modelo de carpeta, y haga una lista de documentos que se refieran al estándar IV según lo tratado en el Capítulo 6.

EFFECTIVE INSTRUCTIONAL STRATEGIES FOR WORKING WITH ALL STUDENTS

CHAPTER OUTLINE

LEARNING OBJECTIVES

After reading and reflecting on this chapter you will understand:

- Components of effective instruction and assessment
- Learner development and effective instruction
- Different types of instruction
- Different types of assessment
- Developing instruction for diverse learners

As you read this chapter, ask yourself these questions:

1. What do educators mean by effective classroom instruction?
2. What are the ingredients for effective lessons?
3. How do educators meet the needs of learners at different grade levels?
4. What are some of the advantages and disadvantages of different kinds of testing for students?
5. How do educators adjust their instruction according to the needs of different learners?
6. What kind of artifacts will you include in your portfolio to reflect your knowledge of different types of instruction and assessment in the classroom?

KEY TERMS

advisory periods

alternative forms of assessment

assessing

assessment plans

classroom schedules

cognition

cooperative learning

developmental differences

developmental programs

differentiated instruction

discovery-based lesson

early childhood education

expert groups

goal setting

grade level teaming

instructional strategies

jigsaw

lesson planning

multiple intelligences

National Association for the Education of Young Children (NAEYC)

National Middle School Association (NMSA)

performance assessment

portfolio assessment

process

sheltered content instruction

teacher-centered instruction

INTRODUCTION

If you ask most people who work in classrooms to describe a typical day, they might describe a teacher or paraprofessional leading a lesson. They might tell you about children working on their own or in groups. Most visitors to classrooms would describe the tools in classrooms as books, learning centers, and technology. Each of these parts of a classroom lets visitors know that different ways to learn are in place. The parts of classrooms that might not be as obvious from a first visit include lesson plans, or the guides that help educators deliver their lessons. You might also be unaware of the ways that educators assess, or test, their students. Teachers' plans for teaching and testing might not be obvious to a visitor, but are the backbone of classroom teaching.

In today's classrooms effective educators have a plan for sharing the curriculum with their students and know how to adjust their plans as they go. Educators who adapt their plans understand that it is important to teach and test in ways that give students many ways to succeed. These goals mean that educators must think about their work in new and exciting ways. Tracy and Maria are paraprofessionals who understand that working with young people involves planning and having the ability to change plans when necessary. They are the kind of educators who take advantage of opportunities to learn more about teaching. During a recent professional development day at their school, Maria and Tracy attended a workshop for educators interested in learning about new ways of teaching and testing their students.

Maria: Hi Tracy! I thought you weren't coming today. To be honest, I wasn't even sure if I was going to be able to make it, but I figured since we're out of school today I'd come downtown and see what the conference is all about.

Tracy: Sorry I'm late. I had to catch a later train. I've got so much going on right now I hardly know what I'm doing some days! With my work at school, my family, and getting my kids where they need to be, I'm amazed I make it out of the door on time! I am glad I'm in time for the sessions on ways to work with different kinds of learners. My classroom teacher said the educators' conference will give us all kind of ideas on different ways to teach. She said the special meetings they have for paraprofessionals and new teachers are really interesting.

Maria: It seems like I can barely keep up with everything these days, but I really need some new ideas for my work. Let's make the most of these meetings and then we can go to lunch! If we each go to two or three different sessions, we can share later any of the stuff we learn. I hate to admit it, but I tend to get stuck in the pattern of doing things the way I've always done them. Maybe these workshop sessions will give us new ideas. Let's meet back here at noon.

LIFE IN CLASSROOMS

Like Maria and Tracy, we all depend on the routines that make up our days. Knowing what will happen in advance helps us plan and gives general order to our lives. Life in classrooms is no different. Many educators are comfortable with routines and patterns of teaching lessons, working with children, and sharing information with students, families, and coworkers. While routines are helpful and provide students and educators with consistency, it is also important to remember that there are different ways to meet educational goals. When educators do not adjust and adapt their teaching, they may limit opportunities for news ways of teaching and testing their students. When we're too busy or too comfortable we sometimes rely on strategies that aren't always the best for our students.

Effective educators are people who think about different ways of teaching and testing their students. They try new strategies for meeting their goals. At times, though, educators struggle with knowing exactly how to adjust their teaching and testing. When we get into habits in our teaching, it's sometimes difficult to think of new ways of doing things. How would you handle this situation when working in today's classrooms?

DAY-TO-DAY DILEMMA
HOW WOULD YOU HANDLE THIS SITUATION?

Tracy: I just had a meeting with my classroom teacher. She's great to work with, but I'm just not sure of how to meet the needs of all the students in our classroom. We try new teaching styles so that more students will understand the content. Now she tells me we need to try and think of even more lessons that meet the interests and abilities of the kids. I'm not sure I know what she means. Let's face it, there are only so many ways you can teach some of this content!

Maria: So, what made her bring all this up now? I thought she was happy with how the kids are doing in your class.

Tracy: The school got back some results from the No Child Left Behind tests and the kids aren't learning as much as they need to in some areas. My classroom teacher wants us to start testing the kids in a bunch of different ways so we can get a better picture of what they know and figure out where they need more help. If you ask me, it seems like there are a few basic ways to teach lessons and as far as testing goes, the district's tests ought to tell us if the kids get the information or not.

What would you do if you were in Tracy's place? Does it really matter if we teach students differently? What about variety in testing? Are some ways of testing better than others? Let's find out!

THE INGREDIENTS OF SUCCESSFUL CLASSROOMS

Successful classrooms are made up of key ingredients. **Classrooms schedules**, **lesson planning**, and **assessment plans** help educators teach and students learn.

Classroom schedules provide an outline for the day's events. Schedules remind the students of what will take place when they enter the classroom. Routines help students understand how they should complete assignments, how they should ask for help, and what is expected from the teacher and from them. If students know that some assignments are completed individually and that some may be completed in a group, then they have a better understanding of their roles as learners.

Lesson planning provides educators and students with a roadmap of goals for student learning, a description of the directions during lessons, and a plan for testing. Assessment plans help educators decide if their lessons are effective and if students have met the goals teachers planned for them. These are just some of the "ingredients" that help make sure that lesson content is shared in the best way possible.

Let's take a look at some of the additional classroom "ingredients" that make teaching and learning more effective. After talking about effective instruction, we'll review testing tools that help educators decide whether or not their lessons worked as they had planned. Then we'll see the ways learner differences

---

classroom schedules
An outline for a day's events.

horario de clases
Guía de lo que se hace durante el día escolar.

lesson planning
A roadmap of goals for student learning, a description of the directions during lessons, and a plan for testing student learning.

planes de clase
Plan de los objetivos de aprendizaje del estudiante, descripción de las indicaciones a impartir durante las lecciones y plan para evaluar el aprendizaje.

assessment plans
Tools that help educators decide if their lessons are effective and if students have met the goals teachers planned for them.

planes de evaluación
Instrumentos que ayudan a los educadores para saber si su enseñanza es eficaz y si los estudiantes han alcanzado los objetivos previstos.

impact curriculum and instruction. Listen to our friends Maria and Tracy as they talk about their experiences as learners. Many of the students in your classroom might share Maria's feelings.

Maria: (Sighing) I've had it, Tracy. I just want to give up!

Tracy: What's the matter, Maria? I thought you liked the creative writing classes you're taking at the community college. All you talk about is how much fun you're having and how you can't wait to get to class each week. What's wrong now?

Maria: Well, I like one of my classes, but I just can't seem to get interested in the other class. I know this sounds completely crazy, but my grammar class is so interesting. I just love going to class each week. Can you believe that a person could actually like something as boring as learning about grammar? I think that what I like the most about the class is the fact that the teacher really makes the content connect to my life. The teacher's excitement and the way she teaches make it really interesting.

The other class, on modern literature, is just terrible. I just can't seem to get through all of the work we're supposed to do each week. I know that the literature class should be more interesting because it's all about stories about real people and their lives, but I'm just not that motivated.

Tracy: You're kidding? I can't believe a grammar class could be more fun than a literature class! How is that possible? That's too weird.

Maria: I know it's weird but I'm interested in the grammar class for a couple of reasons. My teacher makes me want to learn. She gives interesting lessons, we do all sorts of activities, and we use real-life examples so we can understand what we're studying. I can tell the teacher likes working with us. In my literature class we read fragments of the stories out loud and then we spend the rest of the class writing answers to questions about what we've read. While I really like the stories, I get tired of doing the same thing every week. It's so boring! And you know, I don't really think the teacher seems that interested in how any of us do in the class. She still doesn't know some of our names after three weeks!

Tracy: I guess your classes aren't that different from the classrooms we work in. Maybe what you're going through will help you have a better idea of why some of our students get bored and don't seem interested. Maybe we can talk with your classroom teacher about lesson ideas that keep the kids interested. Your classroom teacher really knows how to keep the students involved, and I know she cares about the success of the kids. Anyone who spends that much time thinking about lesson plans must want the kids to have fun and learn.

If your own learning experiences are like Maria's, you may have been in a class where the subject you were studying *should have been* interesting. Like Maria, you may have found yourself disappointed, bored, or uninterested because of the way the information from the class was presented. You may have even felt the teacher didn't care about your success in the class. On the other hand, you may have also been in a class or completed professional development activities in your district that seemed like they were going to be boring or uninteresting. But, on the contrary, you were surprised because of the type of instruction used, or the ways you were asked to share what you knew about the subject. In the classes that were more interesting, you probably were motivated to learn and participate. Let's take a look at each of the key areas related to effective instruction and assessment. These areas of effective teaching include: planning, understanding learner development, and meeting the needs of diverse learners.

PLANNING

Effective lesson planning includes: **goal setting**, identifying the **instructional strategies** necessary for meeting learning goals, **assessing** student learning, and thinking about how individualized instruction will meet the needs of many different learners. Each of these lesson parts provides educators with a roadmap for effective lessons. Table 7-1, Sample Lesson Plan, includes the different components of typical lesson plans used in many classrooms. The plan includes goals, activities, and plans for measuring student learning.

Goal Setting

Goal setting helps educators decide what they want to teach within each lesson. Setting goals gives an outline for the content to be covered in a lesson and helps an educator decide what the students should learn during the lesson. Research tells us that teachers who are thoughtful planners have better

goal setting
An outline for the content to be covered, and the specific learning outcomes a teacher is planning to meet within the lesson.

establecimiento de objetivos
Guía del contenido a cubrirse y de resultados determinados de aprendizaje que el educador planea lograr en una lección.

instructional strategies
The tools teachers use to teach content to their students.

estrategias educacionales
Medios que los profesores usan para enseñar contenido a los estudiantes.

assessing
The process of gathering information on a learner's understanding of content.

evaluar
el proceso de reunir información sobre la comprensión de contenido que tiene un educando.

TABLE 7-1 Sample Lesson Plan

LESSON PLAN COMPONENTS
1. Lesson goal—What is the content of your lesson, broadly speaking?
2. Performance objective—Students will . . .
3. Rationale—Why is this lesson important?
4. Content (e.g., concepts, facts, vocabulary)—What is being taught?
5. Instructional procedures
a. Focusing event—How will the lesson begin?
b. Teaching procedures—What will you do within the lesson?
c. Student participation—What will students do?
d. Closure—How will the lesson end?
6. Evaluation (e.g., formal and informal)
7. Plans that describe how you will accommodate diverse learners (e.g., ability, language)
8. Materials and aids

student learning outcomes (Eggen, 1998). Educators who set clear goals and testing plans are better able to deliver information that is important for student learning.

In addition to teaching the content, educators must decide how well their students understand what is taught. Researchers have long studied the different ways of learning topics in school. For example, if you want to learn about the United States, you might learn the names of each state. Next, you might figure out where each state is located on a map. If you learned the name of each state and found out where it fit on a map, you would be able to show that you have a basic understanding of the location of each state within the US. If you wanted to show that you know even more about the states, you might also talk about the parts of states that are the same or different. You might also discuss the advantages and disadvantages of living in different areas of the country, based upon their geography. Your knowledge about states now includes basic facts about state names, locations, and special features.

As people learn more about a topic, they understand that the content is more than just basic facts. Teachers who set learning goals that go beyond the facts try to help their students learn the content in deeper ways. **Cognition** includes the ways we think about information. Researchers who study teaching and learning tell us that good educators create lessons that help their students think about more than just the facts. These educators plan lessons that reach multiple cognitive levels. For example, in addition to teaching the facts related to a topic, teachers must also teach their students to *apply* what they know, to *analyze* the subject, and to *judge* the content. Teachers who include multiple teaching strategies help their students learn about content in different ways. Let's take a look at some of the teaching strategies used by classroom educators to strengthen their students' background knowledge.

Instructional Strategies

Instructional strategies are the tools teachers use to share content with their students. Specific instructional strategies might include: lectures, group work, or activities where students go on field trips or create projects. Each of these instructional tools helps students learn about the curriculum in different ways. Let's visit Tracy's classroom on three different days. Which method of instruction do you find most useful?

Tracy's classroom teacher asked her to guide a science lesson on planting. For the first lesson Tracy read students a short story about how farmers plant and harvest their crops. The story described the ways farmers prepare their soil and choose the plants they will grow during a season. The story also described the ways farmers harvest, or gather, their crops. In this lesson Tracy used a **teacher-centered instruction** while students listened to the information presented.

cognition
The ways we think about information.

cognición
Las formas en que pensamos sobre la información.

teacher-centered instruction
Instruction where the teacher carefully specifies goals, presents the content to be learned, and actively directs learning activities. In these formats the teacher directs the lesson in the form of a lecture or class discussion. Students in a teacher-centered classroom are usually passive, waiting for the teacher to directly guide their learning.

instrucción centrada en el profesor
Enseñanza en que el profesor fija con cuidado metas, presenta el contenido a ser aprendido y dirige activamente el aprendizaje. En este tipo de formato el profesor dirige la lección en forma de conferencia o discusión. Los estudiantes en una clase centrada en el profesor son generalmente pasivos y esperan que el profesor dirija el aprendizaje directamente.

discovery-based lesson
Lessons where educators support students and help them explore content in depth.

lección basada en el descubrimiento
Lecciones en que los educadores apoyan a los estudiantes y los ayudan a explorar el contenido en profundidad.

expert groups
A type of cooperative learning group where students learn about content and get the chance to share what they know, so that everybody in the group learns the same information.

grupos expertos
Tipo de aprendizaje cooperativo en grupo en que los estudiantes aprenden sobre contenido y tienen la oportunidad de compartir su conocimiento de modo que todos los integrantes del grupo obtienen la misma información.

For the second lesson, Tracy took her students on a walking tour to a nearby community garden. In order to prepare for their tour, Tracy asked her students to write down the questions they had about farming. She also asked them to describe what they already knew about farming. Finally, Tracy asked her students to make predictions, or guesses, about the stages involved in farming—from planting to harvesting crops. In this lesson Tracy used a **discovery-based lesson** plan.

In the third lesson, Tracy divided her students into groups of three. Each

Discovery-based methods of instruction help students learn through investigation and discovery using objects from the real world.

member of the group was responsible for learning about one part of gardening. Tracy gave each student books and brochures on farming. She also gave her students packages of seeds and directions on how to plant crops. Using the materials Tracy shared with her students, one group member was responsible for learning about how to prepare soil; another one read about the ways of planting seeds; and the third one learned about when and how to harvest crops. In this lesson Tracy used **expert groups**.

In each one of Tracy's lessons, students learned about farming in different ways. Her lessons took very different formats because she used different teaching strategies. Even though Tracy used different strategies, her goal was the same—to teach students how farmers plant and harvest their crops. Let's look at each lesson more carefully.

Lesson 1: Tracy used teacher-centered instruction; students listened to her as she read about the process of farming. Students then had to answer questions about farming based on the story she had read.

Lesson 2: Tracy used a discovery-based lesson; students visited a garden and were later asked to share what they had learned about farming in their trip. Tracy asked her students to predict or guess what would happen to the seeds and plants in the garden. Tracy also asked the children to list their questions

Lessons that allow students to use real world objects in the classroom to help them understand content in more meaningful ways. Tracy's farming lesson let her students experience planting and harvesting using a hands-on format.

about farming, and to describe how they would measure changes in plant life from planting to harvesting.

Lesson 3: Tracy used expert groups where students learned as much as possible about an area related to farming. In the expert group lesson, students learned specific information about farming and then shared what they knew with their classmates so that all students understood the process of farming.

Similar to what happened in Tracy's classroom, many educators help their students learn content in different ways. Let's look at each of Tracy's instructional strategies and figure out their strengths and weaknesses.

Teacher-Centered Lessons

Teacher-centered lessons are led by the teacher. In these classrooms, the teacher often guides the lesson through a lecture or class discussion. Students in a teacher-centered classroom are more passive, waiting fo the teacher to directly guide their learning (Shuell, 1996). One of the advantages of teacher-centered lessons is that they allow the teacher to share large amounts of information with students in a short time period. Teachers often model what they expect from students, explain key ideas, and provide students with time to complete work by themselves.

Discovery-Based Lessons

cooperative learning
A lesson format where students work together for the purpose of learning content within the context of a group.

aprendizaje cooperativo
Formato de lección en que los estudiantes trabajan juntos para aprender contenido en un contexto de grupo.

In discovery-based lessons and in expert groups students are active during the lesson (Kauchak & Eggen, 2005). Discovery lessons let the teacher guide students toward lesson goals. With the help of the teacher and paraprofessionals, students explore lesson content in many different ways. Expert groups are a type of student-centered learning that was part of Tracy's third lesson on farming. Expert groups are a type of **cooperative learning** where students work together in groups. Working in groups gives students the chance to share what

TABLE 7-2 Strengths and Weaknesses of Instructional Strategies

LESSON TYPE	ADVANTAGES	DISADVANTAGES	WHEN WOULD YOU USE THIS TYPE OF LESSON?
Teacher-Centered Instruction	Allows an educator to cover a large amount of information	Students are not very involved in the lesson	Sharing new information with students. Sharing information that is more complicated and needs direct teacher guidance.
Cooperative Learning			
Discovery-Based Lessons			
Expert Groups			

jigsaw
A type of cooperative learning where students investigate and explore a specific type of information and then share their information with peers.

rompecabezas
Tipo de aprendizaje cooperativo en que los estudiantes investigan y exploran un tipo específico de información para luego compartir la información con sus compañeros.

they know so that everybody in the group learns the same information. The specific type of lesson used in Tracy's expert group is called a **jigsaw** (Slavin, 1996). A jigsaw lesson is a special learning tool where students work like investigators who explore information and then share what they learned with their friends. The advantage of this type of lesson is that every student gets the chance to be an expert. The weakness of many cooperative activities is the large amount of work required from the teacher, who has to make sure all the participants benefit form the activity. For some students who work in groups, there are too many opportunities to talk about topics other than the content. The teacher must plan group work carefully, so that students get the most from the activity.

Based on your experiences in classrooms and schools, what are some of the advantages and disadvantages of each different type of lesson format? Table 7-2, Strengths and Weaknesses of Instructional Strategies, provides a review of the ways in which these lesson types might be used and describes some of the possible weaknesses. The first example has been completed for you. Complete the remaining sections of the worksheet with your classroom teacher or another paraprofessional. Remember that different kinds of instruction help all learners in a classroom.

ASSESSING STUDENT LEARNING

The type of assessment or testing used in classrooms is perhaps among the most frequently debated topics in education. As you learned in Chapter 2, educators and the general population have very different opinions when it comes to the topic of testing students. In the age of accountability, educators and policy makers look for ways of measuring students' success in the classroom. Today, testing is a common part of the daily practices in classrooms and schools. In fact, some schools use standardized tests to evaluate student learning more than they ever have in the past. Strengths of standardized tests include their capability to:

1. measure many students' abilities at one time;
2. provide a picture of student performance over time;
3. create a fast way to compare how students perform.

Some researchers and educators believe standardized tests are weak because they only measure a small part of a student's ability (Cuban, 1996; Kauchak & Eggen, 2005). Critics think standardized tests only measure information related to school in math, language arts, and science. It's not that it's a bad idea to measure these areas, but students differ in their experiences with these subjects. Other people believe that standardized tests may be limited because they don't reflect the backgrounds of many different students and their school experiences (Gutiérrez, 2002). The critics of standardized tests also believe that a test score can't give a full picture of a student's abilities. What do you think? What are some of the strengths and limitations of standardized tests? Figure 7-1, Strengths and Limitations of Standardized Testing, describes some of these strengths and limitations and gives you room to include your ideas about your experiences with assessment.

Students are not the only people required to take standardized tests. Paraprofessionals are also required to take standardized tests that measure school-related knowledge. In Chapter 2 we discussed the Praxis Parapro Test, the exam published by the Educational Testing Service (ETS). Under the rules and regulations of NCLB, highly qualified paraprofessionals show their professional abilities through their scores on this test. In addition, paraprofessionals in many communities are also asked to show their professional abilities through **alternative forms of assessment** such as portfolios. Let's look at the topic of alternative assessment in more detail.

Alternative Assessment

What are the ways you might show others what you know about education? Are there certain types of tests where you feel you do your best work? Are there other types of tests where your skills and abilities are not shown? It is important to keep your own feelings about testing in mind when working with students in classrooms. Alternative assessment tools give students the opportunity to show their abilities in many ways. Supporters of alternative assessments believe that the use of many different types of tests gives a bigger picture of a person's abilities and potential.

Types of Alternative Assessments

Alternative forms of assessment help educators develop a picture of a student's understanding of the curriculum in different ways. Many alternative assessment tools measure student performance through "real life" tasks (Wiggins, 1997). Examples of alternative forms of assessment might include:

1. writing a story for a language arts class;
2. creating a restaurant menu in a foreign language classroom;
3. completing a lab experiment in a science classroom, or
4. developing assignments using assistive technology for a student in a special education classroom.

alternative forms of assessment
Tests that measure student performance through "real life" tasks.

formas alternativas de evaluación
Pruebas que evalúan el desempeño de un estudiante por medio de tareas "de la vida real".

FIGURE 7-1 Strengths and Limitations of Standardized Testing

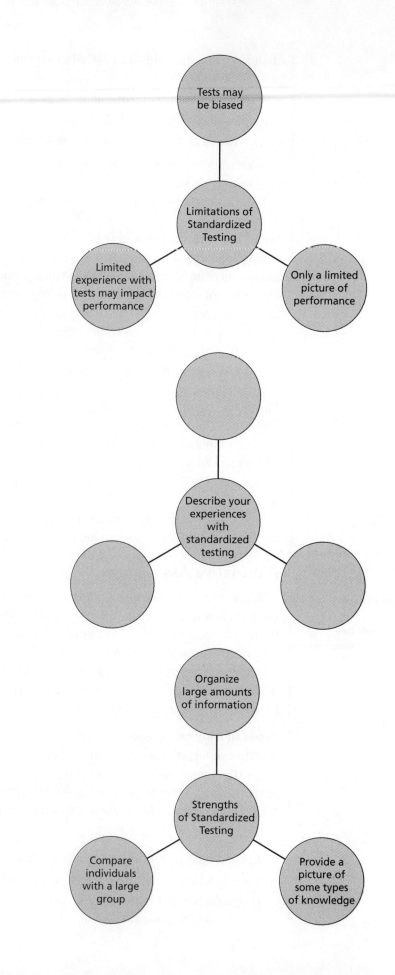

process
The way the student completes a particular assignment or skill.

proceso
Modo en que el estudiante desarrolla una tarea particular o una destreza.

performance assessment
A test of the ways that students show their knowledge in a lifelike situation.

evaluación de desempeño
Prueba en que los estudiantes demuestran su conocimiento por medio de su actuación en una situación de la vida real.

portfolio assessment
A form of testing that gives a picture of performance through a collection of products or "artifacts".

evaluación de la carpeta
Tipo de examen que da una imagen del rendimiento a través de una colección de productos u objetos.

Each of these activities lets a student show what he or she knows about a specific topic. In addition to grading the actual work product created by a student, educators can grade the **process** used by the student to create the work product. This is a type of what is called performance assessment.

When educators use **performance assessments** in their teaching, they look at how a student shows what they know in a lifelike situation. If a teacher wanted to grade how well a student can apply his or her knowledge of a topic, the student would show it through an activity. For example, to show knowledge of public speaking, the student would give a speech. A student in a special education classroom might show knowledge of social skills interacting with co-workers or with a supervisor at a job site. Performance assessments provide educators with the chance to test student work in applied or "real world" ways.

A common alternative assessment tool used by teachers with their students undergoing professional development is through **portfolio assessment**. As you learned in Chapter 1, portfolio assessments give a picture of performance through a collection of products or "artifacts". Portfolios have many advantages including the freedom to make them on your own. Educators bring a personal touch to portfolios when they include work samples that show their abilities, interests, and professional goals. For educators, portfolios also keep track of workshops, college credits, or college degrees.

In today's world, assessment may take many forms. We have discussed standardized assessments and performance assessments. Portfolios are another type of assessment. While many educators and members of the public talk about the role of standardized testing in their schools, there are many other types of assessment in classrooms. As you work with students, and prepare professionally, consider the types of assessment that best show your abilities. What are some of the artifacts you might include in your portfolio? How will you share with others what you have accomplished as an educator?

In Maria's and Tracy's school district, classroom teachers and paraprofessionals must create a professional portfolio. Tracy recently spent time putting together her portfolio and asked Maria for her opinion on its content. During a teacher professional workday where teachers in their school were involved in meetings, Maria and Tracy met to share ideas on developing their portfolios. Let's listen to their conversation.

Maria: Wow Tracy, your portfolio really looks good! How much time have you spent on this? Where did you get all these ideas?

Tracy: Well, I've been collecting stuff for a while. My plan is to gather enough samples to make sure that I meet each of the categories for the Praxis standards, but I also want to show off my best work. I've done a lot within my school over the past few years. I've taken a few classes and workshops, so I'd like to put all my hard work into a booklet. It's actually been kind of fun to put this together, since it's like putting together a story of all my work. I know that you've been thinking about going back to school to get a teaching license at some point. Making a portfolio is a great first step in organizing your work.

Maria: Yeah, it's taken me a while to figure out if I should go back to school to get a teaching license, but I really think the time is right for me. Putting together my portfolio has helped me organize all the work I've been involved in as a paraprofessional over the past few years. I tell you though, my portfolio doesn't look anywhere near as good as yours. I never thought of including all of the stuff you have here. I do know that creating a portfolio shows off more of me and who I am than a test score will show!

I never thought about including the certificates from the professional development trainings of the district. That's a good idea. I've also shared ideas for lesson activities with my classroom teacher, and I'm responsible for all the bulletin boards in our classroom. I love the way you've included photographs and video clips of your work in creating classroom decorations and bulletin boards. I'm impressed!

---

developmental differences
Changes in the students' learning process over the course of their lives.

diferencias del desarrollo
Cambio en el proceso de aprendizaje de los estudiantes durante el transcurso de su vida.

---

developmental programs
Classrooms where instruction and curriculum choices are geared toward the cognitive, social, and emotional needs of the students.

programas de desarrollo
Clases en que las opciones de enseñanza y currículo se dirigen a las necesidades cognitivas, sociales y emocionales de los estudiantes.

---

early childhood education
Education programs for children usually between 3 and 5 years old. These programs provide children with the chance to explore their environment through touch, sight, sound, taste, and feel.

educación de la primera infancia
Programas de educación para niños entre 3 y 5 años de edad. Estos programas les brindan a los niños la oportunidad de explorar el medio ambiente a través del tacto, la vista, el sonido y el gusto.

If you're like Tracy and Maria, you know that sharing your professional goals with others is not as simple as showing a test score. As you build your professional portfolio, think about how you can share your professional goals in ways that show others who you are as an individual. The sample portfolio artifacts found in Table 7-1, Sample Portfolio Framework, give examples of the items you may want to include in your portfolio.

THE IMPACT OF LEARNER DEVELOPMENT ON INSTRUCTION AND ASSESSMENT

In Chapter 4 we talked about the importance of learners' language and ability differences. Educators also need to be aware of **developmental differences** among their students. A student's developmental ability affects how he or she responds to individual lessons and influences how well the material is learned. If an educator understands the developmental abilities of the learner, lesson plans help make the information better understood by different kinds of learners. The first step in matching lessons with the needs of learners is figuring out how the developmental needs of children change across the grade levels in our schools.

DEVELOPMENTAL DIFFERENCES AMONG LEARNERS

Many educators and researchers have shared their ideas on the differences and similarities in learners across their life spans. Young children, for example, often experience their worlds through their senses. They want to see, touch, and even taste their worlds in very real ways. A famous researcher who studied the development of his own young children came up with a system of categories that describes learner differences. Jean Piaget was a psychologist who studied how people learn from the time they are born through adolescence. He studied the ways in which children interact with others and how they develop physically over the course of their lives. His work helps educators understand how developmental differences influence school experiences. Let's review how developmental differences affect teaching and learning in the classroom.

Early Childhood Education

Children's developmental needs, learning abilities, and strengths change over the course of their lives. As you remember from Chapter 1 we talked about the layout of schools in the United States and how different grade levels include children from different age groups. The organization of schools in the US reflects developmental needs of students at different points in time. Today most schools are divided into early childhood, elementary, and secondary schools. For the most part, these schools are based upon the age and developmental needs of students. **Developmental programs** provide classroom educational experiences and curriculum choices that are geared toward the cognitive, social, and emotional needs of the students.

Children in **early childhood education** programs are typically between 3 and 5 years old. However, some programs include services for infants and young children.

Early childhood education usually provides children with the chance to explore their environment through touch, sight, sound, taste, and feel. Learning experiences help children develop their motor, cognitive, and social skills. Developmentally appropriate classrooms allow children to explore their environment through activities such as comparing the heights of structures using building blocks or comparing how different objects float by filling a tub of water with different sized objects (Gelstwicki, 2007; Kauchak & Eggen, 2005). In each of these examples, students are involved in hands-on activities where they learn about ideas such as measurement and size in ways that correspond to their developmental abilities. The **National Association for the Education of Young Children (NAEYC)** is the largest professional association for early childhood education. For more information, check their website: http://www.naeyc.org.

Children in early elementary school programs learn about content through work with objects that allow them to measure, stack, and build.

National Association for the Education of Young Children (NAEYC)
The largest professional association for early childhood education.

Asociación Nacional para la Educación de Niños Jóvenes (NAEYC por sus siglas en inglés)
La asociación profesional más importante para la educación de la primera infancia.

Elementary Education

The elementary grades of most public schools in the United States include grades kindergarten through grades 5 or 6. Children in these classrooms are typically from 5 to 11 years old. Students study basic information related to social studies, math, science, reading, and the arts. The curriculum often includes hands-on learning activities where learners are actively involved in lessons such as organizing different types of information including animals, plants, and numbers. Students in elementary grades also begin to think about the different ways objects can exist. For example, in a science class students look at what might happen to water when it is heated up or made cold. In social studies classes students might write about what they know about explorers from the past. Next, these students might write about how those explorers are the same as or different from modern day explorers. For elementary students, what they learn becomes more abstract but still links ideas from real life to situations that

Students in Early Childhood programs enjoy learning activities where they play, explore and use real-world objects in the classroom. The children in this lesson are learning about health care through pretend play as doctors and nurses.

might exist in the future. Students in elementary classrooms learn about cause and effect relationships in the world and they learn how to work both in large and small groups. Activities for children in the elementary grades might include: making guesses or predictions in science classrooms or deciding what will happen to story characters based upon information learned from a story.

Secondary Education

Children who attend secondary schools are most often between the ages of 12 and 18. Their schools typically include grades 7-12 or in some communities grades 6-12. In addition to studying basic skills in reading, math and science, students in secondary schools begin to focus in more depth on their areas of study. Courses in high school might include physics, chemistry, government, and literature. Because of the developmental changes among adolescents, the secondary curriculum asks students to think about ideas in more complicated and involved ways. Students in a high school might debate topics related to democracy. They might also study how events from history are the same as or different from the events they experience in their own worlds. A curriculum for adolescent learners moves their thinking from hands-on activities to thinking and reasoning in more abstract ways of viewing the world. Let's look at an example that shows how adolescents view their subject matters.

grade level teaming
In middle schools groups of teachers from across content areas such as language arts, history, math, and science work together. Team members plan lessons that connect the content of different areas.

equipos por nivel de grado
Grupos de maestros de enseñanza secundaria en los que profesores de diversas áreas de contenido como artes del lenguaje, historia, matemáticas y ciencias trabajan juntos. Los miembros del equipo planean las lecciones que conectan el contenido de sus áreas respectivas.

Students in middle school science classrooms learn about the parts of the water cycle by learning key vocabulary words such as rain, evaporation, surface water, and runoff. The teacher in their classroom includes lessons where students memorize definitions or label the parts of a picture showing how the water cycle works. These lessons

advisory periods
A period in the daily schedules of many junior high and high schools. Students meet with teachers so that they don't feel lost in a large secondary school. Advisory periods give students regular contact with an adult during each school day.

período de asesoramiento
Período durante el día escolar de muchas escuelas medias y secundarias en que los estudiantes se reúnen con profesores para evitar sentirse perdidos en una de las enormes escuelas secundarias de la actualidad. Los períodos de asesoramiento ponen a los estudiantes en contacto con un adulto durante cada día escolar.

National Middle School Association (NMSA)
A professional association for middle school education.

Asociación Nacional de Escuelas Secundarias Medias (NMSA por sus siglas en inglés)
Asociación profesional para la educación en las escuelas secundarias medias.

Students in middle and high schools depend on support from friends. Secondary educators often provide adolescent learners with lessons where they get to work with peers in small groups.

give students basic factual information on the ways in which water moves throughout the earth. Students who are more abstract thinkers get to understand the basic parts of the water cycle and are able to go farther. They begin to think about how water movement fits into discussions about the water cycle, pollution, and the breakdown of land due to flooding. These learners are able to move beyond basic facts and can show an ability to think about content in many different ways.

In addition to preparing lessons that meet students' cognitive needs, educators of middle, junior high, and high school students focus on the unique social and physical needs of students. Many junior high and high schools include in their extracurricular offerings competitive sports, social activities such as dances, and community service. Middle schools are specifically focused on meeting the social and emotional needs of students through the support provided by their teachers. Many middle schools create support systems for students through **grade level teaming**. Grade level teaming means groups of teachers from across content areas such as language arts, history, math, and science work together. Team members plan lessons that connect the content of different areas. Teaming allows teachers to focus on smaller groups of students through **advisory periods** where one teacher meets with groups of students each day (Gallagher, 1999). Many junior high and high schools include formal advisory periods so that students don't feel lost in today's large secondary schools. Advisory periods are important because they provide students with an adult who is a regular contact person during each school day. The **National Middle School Association (NMSA)** is a professional association for middle school education. For more information, visit their website: http://www.nmsa.org.

multiple intelligences
An idea that people have skills and abilities related to schoolwork as well as other skills and talents in music, interacting with others, or playing sports.

inteligencias múltiples
concepto de que las personas tienen destrezas y capacidades relacionadas con el trabajo escolar así como también con otras destrezas y talentos en música, la interacción con los demás o la práctica de deportes.

differentiated instruction
Lessons that meet students' needs in many different ways through different activities and ways of testing.

instrucción diferenciada
enseñanza que tiene en cuenta las necesidades de los estudiantes de diversas maneras a través de distintas actividades y formas de evaluación diferentes.

sheltered content instruction
Classrooms that, through changes in curriculum and instruction, include multilingual students who are developing their English skills. The instruction addresses language development in routines and activities of classrooms as well as the actual content of subjects such as math, science, and language arts.

enseñanza de contenido bajo protección
La instrucción que se imparte, a través de cambios en el currículo y en la enseñanza, a estudiantes multilingües que están comenzando a aprender inglés. Las lecciones incluyen el desarrollo del lenguaje relacionado con la rutina y las actividades del salón de clases así como el contenido de materias tales como matemáticas, ciencias y artes del lenguaje.

MEETING THE NEEDS OF DIVERSE LEARNERS

The developmental needs of learners are very important. You have learned about the needs of children with different social, academic, and physical needs. Teachers respond to their students by creating lessons that include reading and writing. Some classrooms also pay attention to other types of talents at school. The first step in helping all students is seeing the different strengths children bring to classrooms. Let's take a look at a few examples of how educators can pay attention to their students' talents.

Multiple Intelligences

Most of us have known people who are very good in school subjects such as math, science, or language arts. Some of us have also known talented artists, singers, or athletes. We may also know people who get along with their friends in supportive ways and always know the right thing to say in a difficult moment. A famous researcher believed that each of these abilities and talents is a form of intelligence. Howard Gardner, a psychologist from Harvard University, developed a theory called **multiple intelligences** (1999). Gardner believed that people may have special abilities in different areas. Gardner suggested that in addition to the skills and abilities related to schoolwork, people may also have other skills. He believed that some people are especially talented in areas such as music, interacting with others, or playing sports. Gardner challenged educators to recognize that many students bring different abilities and talents to classrooms. Unfortunately, schools don't always include teaching and learning experiences that meet the needs of a variety of students (Viadero, 2003). One of the ways educators can respond to many different students is with **differentiated instruction**, that is to say curriculum and instruction that are more personalized. Differentiated instruction means that educators create classrooms where lessons meet students' needs in many different ways. These classrooms include multiple ways of teaching students, using different activities, and testing learners (Gregory, 2003). Tracy's farming lessons from earlier in the chapter are examples of differentiated lessons. She taught and tested her students in different ways.

In addition to differentiating lessons, today's educators respond to the needs of children learning English for the first time. Lessons for children learning English require a focus on both content and language goals. For children learning English, educators identify language through **sheltered content instruction** (Echevarria & Graves, 2007). Let's take a look at the specific ways in which educators might adapt their lessons for English Language Learners.

Instructional Adaptations for Language Learners

As you learned in Chapter 4 sheltered classrooms include instruction that addresses learners' ability to learn both content and the English language. The students in sheltered classrooms are often multilingual and are developing their English skills through carefully planned lessons in the curriculum and instruction already in place within a classroom. For example, students in a mathematics classroom learn the concepts of mathematics, but they also learn specific vocabulary related to mathematics. The same is true for students across content areas such as science and language arts (Echevarria, Vogt, & Short, 2004). Other ideas for educators who want their students to understand English more easily include:

1. understanding the difference between social and school-based language;

2. using books and pictures in the classroom that celebrate many languages;

3. assigning reading buddies for students who are developing their reading skills;

4. labeling classroom objects so students can learn the names of the items in the classroom;

5. teaching students school vocabulary including directions, how to complete assignments, and the rules that may be unfamiliar to those new to schools in the US (Nance, 2007).

These are only a few of the suggestions for those learning English in the classroom. For additional ideas, visit the classrooms of teachers who work with children new to the US.

SUMMARY

Educators in today's classrooms know that their students bring different abilities and talents to classrooms. Success in school depends on the ways the curriculum, instruction, and assessment meet the needs of students. Through multiple types of instruction, a culturally relevant curriculum, and varied assessment strategies, today's educators meet the needs of a wide range of learners. If you want to try new ideas in your work in classrooms, follow the advice of Maria and Tracy. Think about how you'll take advantage of the routines and patterns that help make your classroom run smoothly. When appropriate, try new routes to make learning interesting and exciting for your students. Your students will benefit and you just might enjoy the ride yourself!

CHECKING FOR UNDERSTANDING

1. Effective teachers and paraprofessionals plan their lesson goals, change their instructional strategies, and use different kinds of tests or assessments. Together with your classroom teacher, make a list of the different types of lesson plans you use with your students. Do your lessons change much from day to day? What about the testing tools used in your classroom? Does your classroom include different types of tests?

2. Children's needs change depending upon their grade level. In what ways do the needs of children in early childhood programs differ from the needs of children in elementary programs? How do the needs of adolescents affect the ways teachers teach?

3. Howard Gardner is a famous psychologist who studied the different talents of learners. He called these different talents multiple intelligences. Gardner believes that people have talents that include their ability to read, write, move, talk, and work with others. Based upon your experiences in classrooms, what are some of the different talents you have observed in your students? What about your own talents? In what areas are you most talented?

4. With your classroom teacher, create a list of all the language (words and phrases) used in your classroom that might be confusing to students learning English for the first time. In addition to the language used to teach content, do teachers use special language when they ask students to complete assignments or tests? For example, teachers sometimes ask their students to compare and contrast ideas. Teachers might also ask their students to organize objects from smallest to largest. Do you think some of this language could be confusing to students new to the US? How will you explain these terms to students?

POINTS OF VIEW

Maria and Tracy share the following suggestions on how to learn more about effective instruction and assessment.

1. As a classroom paraprofessional, it is important to learn as much as possible about the different ways the curriculum can be shared with students. With the help of your classroom teacher, create a list of the ways you might teach students the same content using a different lesson plan. Keep Tracy's farming activity in mind as you create your list. For example, if your students are learning how to add or subtract, what are some of the different ways that you might teach them to learn about the concepts of addition or subtraction in a teacher-centered classroom? How might the same content be taught using an inquiry approach?

2. What are some of the ways that classroom teachers and paraprofessionals can assess student learning? What do certain types of tests tell educators about students' knowledge? Take a look at these examples:

   a. When can educators use pencil and paper tests to find out what a learner understands?

   b. What do portfolios tell us about learners?

   c. When can a teacher ask students to share what they know using a performance test?

   d. If the children in your classroom create portfolios of their work in school, what kind of artifacts should they include? In some classrooms, portfolios include writing samples, artwork, lab experiments, or video or audio clips of a song or dance.

3. Many educators learn from the professional organizations that are connected to the grade levels they teach. With your classroom teacher, learn more about the professional organizations that relate to your work. If you work with children in early childhood education, visit the National Association for the Education of Young Children (NAEYC) web site: http://www. naeyc.org. Review the resources available for early childhood educators.

PORTFOLIO CORNER

The suggestions in this chapter addressed strategies for adjusting instruction and assessment in your classroom. We also studied the effects of grade levels and language differences on teaching and learning. The artifacts, or lines of evidence, that you might share under Standards I, III, and IV include strategies for adapting curriculum and instruction, surveys you will use with parents and students; documents that describe your knowledge of student differences, sample Individualized Education Plans (IEPs), and samples of work that show how you interact with diverse groups of students. The thoughts and suggestions shared by Maria and Tracy provide general ideas as you begin to put together your portfolio.

1. With the help of your teacher, find electronic resources that help educators change their curriculum and instruction according to their students' needs. For example, think about how video and audio resources could be used in the curriculum. Describe how you might use web-based resources to teach students. Visit the media specialist at your school for more information about how teachers use electronic lessons and grading databases.

2. With the help of your classroom teacher, read the state core curriculum for children in your classroom and/or grade level. Study the key concepts that must be taught in the grade level of your students. With your classroom teacher, or with other paraprofessionals, develop a list of different lesson activities that meet the core standards for your students.

Use Table 7-3, Sample Portfolio Framework, to list the artifacts that will meet Standards I, III, and IV based on our discussions in Chapter 7.

TABLE 7-3 Sample Portfolio Framework

STANDARD I— SUPPORTING INSTRUCTIONAL OPPORTUNITIES	STANDARD II—DEMONSTRATING PROFESSIONALISM AND ETHICAL PRACTICE
Sample artifacts might include: • Lesson plans using computer assistive technology available to students with special needs. • Lesson plans that demonstrate your knowledge of the ways in which adaptations can be used with multiple learners • Your ideas	See Chapter 8
STANDARD III— SUPPORTING A POSITIVE LEARNING ENVIRONMENT	**STANDARD IV— COMMUNICATING EFFECTIVELY AND PARTICIPATING IN THE TEACHING PROCESSES**
Sample artifacts might include: • Knowledge of learners' needs • A student survey • A parent/caregiver survey • Your ideas	Sample artifacts might include: • Participation in an IEP • Information from family/ community meetings • Information about the IEP process • Information about specific exceptionalities • Your ideas

REFERENCES

Cuban, L. (1996). Curriculum stability and change. In P. Jackson (Ed.), *Handbook of research on curriculum* (pp. 216–247). New York: Macmillan.

Echevarria, J., Graves, A. (2007). *Sheltered content instruction: Teaching English learners with diverse abilities* (3rd ed.). New York: Allyn & Bacon.

Eggen, P. (1998). *A comparison of inner-city middle school teachers' classroom practices and their expressed beliefs about learning and effective instruction.* Paper presented at the annual meeting of the American Educational Research Association, San Diego, California.

Gallagher, J. (1999) Wuz Up? In *Affirming middle grades education*, C. Walley & W. Gerrick (eds.). Boston: Allyn & Bacon.

Gardener, H. (1999). The understanding pathway. *Educational Leadership, 57,* 12–17.

Gestwicki, C. (2007). *Developmentally appropriate practice: curriculum and development in early childhood education,* (3rd ed.). United States: Thomson Delmar Learning.

Gregory, G. (2003). *Differentiated instructional strategies in practice: Training, implementation, and supervision.* Thousand Oaks, California: Corwin Press Inc.

Gutiérrez, R. (2002). Beyond essentialism: The complexity in teaching mathematics to Latinos. *American Educational Research Journal, 39,* 1047–1088.

Kauchak, D., & Eggen, P. (2005). *Introduction to Teaching: Becoming a professional* (2nd ed.). Upper Saddle River, New Jersey: Pearson, Merrill Prentice Hall.

Nance, R. (2007). *Workshop for Sheltered Content Instruction.* The Salt Lake City School District.

National Association for the Education of Young Children (NAEYC). (2006). Retrieved October 8, 2006 from http://www.naeyc.org.

National Middle School Association, (2006). Retrieved October 8, 2006 from http://www.nmsa.org.

Shuell, T. (1996). Teaching and learning in a classroom context. In D. Berliner & R. Calfee (Eds.), *Handbook of educational psychology* (pp. 726–764). New York: Macmillan.

Slavin, R. (1986). *Using student team learning* (3rd ed.). Baltimore, Maryland: The Johns Hopkins University, Center for Research on Elementary and Middle School.

Viadero, D. (2003) Staying power. *Education Week, 22,* 24–27.

Wiggins, G. (1996/1997). Practicing what we preach in designing authentic assessment. *Educational Leadership, 54,* 18–24.

Additional selected readings and Paraprofessional electronic resources are available as part of the student Online Companion web site: www.earlychilded.delmar.com.

En español

Objetivos del aprendizaje

Despúes de leer y reflexionar sobre este capítulo podrá comprender mejor:

- Los componentes de la enseñanza y la evaluación eficaces
- El progreso del estudiante y la enseñanza eficaz
- Diferentes tipos de enseñanza
- Diferentes tipos de evaluación
- El planeamiento de la enseñanza para estudiantes diversos

A medida que lea este capítulo, hágase las siguientes preguntas:

1. ¿Qué quieren decir los educadores cuando hablan de una enseñanza eficaz en el salón de clases?
2. ¿Cuáles son los ingredientes de una lección eficaz?
3. ¿Qué hacen los educadores para satisfacer las necesidades de los educandos de diferentes grados?
4. ¿Cuáles son algunas de las ventajas y desventajas que los diferentes tipos de exámenes tienen para los estudiantes?
5. ¿Cómo adaptan los educadores la enseñanza a las necesidades de distintos estudiantes?
6. ¿Qué tipo de objetos incluirá en su portafolio para demostrar su conocimiento de los diferentes tipos de instrucción y evaluación?

Para verificar la comprensión

1. Los profesores y paraprofesionales eficaces planean los objetivos de la lección, cambian sus **estrategias educacionales** y utilizan diferentes clases de pruebas o evaluaciones. Junto con el maestro de su clase, haga una lista de los diversos tipos de **planes de clase** que usa con los estudiantes. ¿Cambian mucho sus lecciones de un día al otro? ¿Y el tipo de pruebas o evaluaciones que usa? ¿Utiliza diferentes tipos de pruebas?
2. Las necesidades de los niños cambian según el grado en el que estén. ¿De qué modo difieren las necesidades de los niños en programas preescolares de las necesidades de los niños en la escuela primaria? ¿Cómo afectan las necesidades de los adolescentes la forma en que enseñan los profesores?
3. Howard Gardner es un psicólogo famoso que estudió los diversos talentos de los educandos. Él llamó a esos diversos talentos "**inteligencias múltiples**". Gardner sostiene que la gente tiene talentos que incluyen la habilidad para leer, escribir, moverse, hablar y trabajar con otras personas. Según sus experiencias en el salón de clases, ¿cuáles son algunos de los diferentes talentos que usted ha observado en sus estudiantes? ¿Y sus propios talentos? ¿En qué áreas tiene usted más talento?
4. Con el maestro de su clase, haga una lista del lenguaje que se usa en su clase (palabras y frases) que puede confundir a los estudiantes que están comenzando a aprender inglés. Además del lenguaje usado para enseñar un tema, ¿usan los profesores un lenguaje especial cuando les piden a los estudiantes que hagan las tareas o rindan una prueba? Por ejemplo, se

---

estrategias educacionales
Medios que los profesores usan para enseñar contenido a los estudiantes.

instructional strategies
The tools teachers use to teach content to their students.

planes de clase
Plan de los objetivos de aprendizaje del estudiante, descripción de las indicaciones a impartir durante las lecciones y plan para evaluar el aprendizaje.

lesson planning
A roadmap of goals for student learning, a description of the directions during lessons, and a plan for testing student learning.

inteligencias múltiples
concepto de que las personas tienen destrezas y capacidades relacionadas con el trabajo escolar así como también con otras destrezas y talentos en música, la interacción con los demás o la práctica de deportes.

multiple intelligences
An idea that people have skills and abilities related to schoolwork as well as other skills and talents in music, interacting with others, or playing sports.

les pide a veces a los estudiantes que comparen y contrasten ideas. También se les puede pedir que agrupen objetos de menor a mayor. ¿Piensa usted que ese lenguaje podría confundir a los estudiantes recién llegados a los EE.UU.? ¿Cómo explicaría esos términos a los estudiantes?

PUNTOS DE VISTA

Maria y Tracy comparten las siguientes ideas sobre cómo aprender más sobre la enseñanza y la evaluación eficaz.

1. Como paraprofesional del salón de clases, es importante aprender lo más posible sobre las formas en que se puede enseñar el currículo a los estudiantes. Con la ayuda del maestro de su clase haga una lista de las distintas formas en las que puede enseñar a los estudiantes el mismo contenido con un plan de clase diferente. Tenga en mente la actividad del cultivo que organizó Tracy al hacer su lista. Por ejemplo, si sus estudiantes están aprendiendo a sumar o restar, ¿de qué diferentes maneras les puede enseñar el concepto de la suma o de la resta? ¿Cómo podría enseñar el mismo contenido usando un enfoque de investigación?

2. ¿De qué modo pueden los maestros de clase y los paraprofesionales evaluar el aprendizaje de los estudiantes? ¿Qué indican acerca de lo que saben los estudiantes ciertos tipos de pruebas? Observe estos ejemplos:

   a. ¿Cuándo pueden los educadores hacer una prueba de papel y lápiz para saber lo que comprende un educando?

   b. ¿Qué nos indican las carpetas acerca de los educandos?

   c. ¿Cuándo puede un profesor pedir a los estudiantes que compartan lo que saben mediante una prueba de desempeño?

   d. Si los niños de su clase hacen una carpeta de su trabajo escolar, ¿qué tipo de documentos deben incluir? En algunas clases, las carpetas incluyen muestras de escritura, trabajos de arte, experimentos de laboratorio, o videos y audios de una canción o baile.

3. Muchos educadores obtienen información de las organizaciones profesionales relacionadas con los grados que ellos enseñan. Con el maestro de su clase, infórmese más sobre las organizaciones profesionales que se relacionan con su trabajo. Si trabaja con la primera infancia, visite la Asociación Nacional para la Educación de Niños Jóvenes (NAEYC por sus siglas en inglés): http://www.naeyc.org. Averigüe cuáles son los recursos disponibles para educadores de párvulos.

PARA LA CARPETA

Las sugerencias de este capítulo se refieren a las estrategias para adaptar la enseñanza y la evaluación a su salón de clases. También estudiamos los efectos que los distintos grados y las diferencias de lenguaje tienen en la enseñanza y el aprendizaje. Los documentos, o líneas de evidencia, que puede presentar de acuerdo a los estándares I, III, y IV incluyen estrategias para adaptar currículo y enseñanza, encuestas para utilizar con los padres y los estudiantes, documentos que describan su conocimiento de las diferencias entre los estudiantes, muestras de planes de educación individualizada (IEPs según sus siglas en inglés), o muestras de su trabajo que demuestren su interacción con diversos

Tabla 7-3 Estructura modelo de carpeta

Estándar I— Apoyo a toda oportunidad educativa	Estándar II— Demostrar una conducta profesional y ética
Los objetos de muestra pueden incluir: ● Planes de lección por medio de tecnología de asistencia de computadoras disponible para los estudiantes con necesidades especiales. ● Planes de lección que demuestren su conocimiento de la forma en que se pueden usar adaptaciones para una variedad de educandos. ● Sus ideas	Vea el Capítulo 8
Estándar III— Ofrecer un ambiente conducente al aprendizaje	**Estándar IV— Comunicarse eficazmente y participar en el proceso de equipo**
Los objetos de muestra pueden incluir: ● Conocimiento de las necesidades de los estudiantes ● Encuesta para estudiantes ● Encuesta para padres o guardianes ● Sus ideas	Los objetos de muestra pueden incluir: ● Participación en un Plan de educación individualizada (IEP) ● Información de reuniones de la familia y la comunidad ● Información acerca del **proceso** del IEP ● Información sobre excepcionalidades específicas ● Sus ideas

proceso
Modo en que el estudiante desarrolla una tarea particular o una destreza.

process
The way the student completes a particular assignment or skill.

grupos de estudiantes. Las ideas y las sugerencias compartidas por Maria y Tracy le dan una idea general para comenzar a organizar su carpeta.

1. Con la ayuda del maestro de su clase, busque recursos electrónicos que sirvan de ayuda a los educadores para modificar el currículo y la enseñanza de acuerdo a las necesidades de los estudiantes. Por ejemplo, piense cómo puede usar los recursos de video y audio en su currículo. Describa cómo puede usar recursos de Internet en la enseñanza. Visite al especialista de medios de su escuela para obtener más información sobre cómo los profesores usan lecciones electrónicas y bases de datos para las clasificaciones.

2. Con la ayuda del maestro de su clase, lea el currículo básico de su estado para los niños de su clase o grado. Estudie los conceptos clave que se deben enseñar en ese nivel. Con el maestro de su clase, o con otros paraprofesionales, desarrolle una lista de diferentes actividades de clase que se ajusten a los estándares básicos para sus estudiantes.

Use la Tabla 7-3, Estructura modelo de carpeta, para hacer una lista de los documentos que se ajustan a los estándares I, III, y IV de acuerdo a lo tratado en el Capítulo 7.

PROFESSIONAL DEVELOPMENT OPPORTUNITIES FOR PARAPROFESSIONALS

LEARNING OBJECTIVES

After reading and reflecting on this chapter you will understand:

- How to complete your professional portfolio

KEY TERMS

alternative routes to licensure

anecdotal feedback

checklists

- Types of educator evaluations
- Types of teacher licensure programs
- Professional development experiences for paraprofessionals

As you read this chapter, ask yourself these questions:

1. How do educators use professional portfolios?
2. What types of teaching licensure programs are available in your community?
3. How does a paraprofessional go about applying to a licensure program?
4. How will you continue to grow professionally as a paraprofessional?
5. What type of artifacts will you include in your portfolio to reflect your knowledge of professional development for educators?

community colleges

self-reflection

teacher preparation programs

Reflections on Professional Development

We all experience new beginnings in our lives. Sometimes new beginnings take place within our families. Sometimes new beginnings relate to our work. It's important to remember that changes in our lives help us learn and grow. Like Maria and Tracy, you will experience a number of opportunities in your work and professional lives. Let's take a look at how they respond.

Maria: Hi Tracy, I'm glad you could meet for coffee this afternoon. I know it's a Saturday, but I figured this was the only time I could share my news. Well, here it goes. I've finally made a decision about what I'm going to do with the rest of my life!

Tracy: Oh, let me guess . . . You're going to take another class at the community college? Maria, you take more classes than anyone I've ever known! What's it going to be this time, skydiving? No, wait, you want start your own business. Pass the sugar . . .

Maria: Hmm, I hadn't thought about skydiving . . . I'll have to give it some thought . . . But seriously, you know I've loved being a paraprofessional. But I've been at my school for the past 12 years, and it's time for me to think about what I want to do for the next 20. I've talked with my classroom teacher about some of my ideas and she's really helped me figure out what to do next.

Tracy: So what are you thinking?

Maria: Well . . . I think I want to go back to school and get a teaching license. I want my own classroom.

Tracy: Wow! Really? Aren't you happy with your work? I thought you loved working with your classroom teacher? Do you really want to leave all the support you have from her? How much does it cost to go back to school? And more important, what will I do without you here?!

Maria: You know I love my work as a paraprofessional. My teacher and I are such a great team! And I also love my school. But I think there are new possibilities for me. I haven't thought through everything just yet. I'm going to have to talk to people at the community college where I got my associate's degree first. I know a great teacher there who really helped me when I was a student. My classroom teacher said she also thinks there are different kinds of grants or loans and financial aid for people who want to be teachers. So I think I'm going to go for it!

Tracy: I remember you said you learned a lot at the educators' conference from the sessions for paraprofessionals and new teachers, but I didn't think you were serious about getting a teaching license. This sounds so great for you, Maria! Your plan sounds like the perfect move, but I have to admit I'm feeling a little selfish. I'd miss seeing you every day if you left our school.

Maria: H-e-l-l-o . . . Tracy . . . I'm *thinking* about going back to school to get a teaching license . . . to work here . . . on earth . . . Not on the moon! Don't think you'll get rid of me that easily! We've been friends and coworkers too long to let anything get in the way of our friendship. Who knows? . . . We may end up at the same school!

Like many paraprofessionals, Maria wonders what it would be like to have her own classroom. She has enjoyed her years working with her classroom teacher and knows she is a valued member of her classroom's education team. She is aware she's made a difference in the lives of hundreds of children and families during her 12 years as a paraprofessional. She is also at a time in her life when she is ready to go back to college. Her own children are grown and she's enjoyed classes through her district and the community college. Maria's plan to go back to school is not an easy decision. She has a lot to think about including:

1. deciding where she wants to go to get a teaching license,
2. figuring out how to apply,
3. finding out how much it costs to go to school, and
4. setting up a support system of family and friends as she prepares to go back to college.

With so much to do, Maria is not quite sure of where to start. The thoughts of getting a teaching license seem overwhelming. The first step she has to take is to organize her portfolio adequately to best show her professional development experiences in the past few years. Whether you decide to get a teaching license at some point in your career, or whether you want to grow professionally in your current position as a paraprofessional, organizing your portfolio is a first step in presenting all that you have accomplished.

MOVING FROM PLANS INTO ACTION—COMPLETING A PROFESSIONAL PORTFOLIO

Throughout this book you have learned about professional portfolios. We have discussed the ways different portfolio artifacts show what educators know about teaching and learning. The portfolio guidelines used in this book include four sections based upon the Praxis Standards for Paraprofessionals. Under each of the four standards you have added artifacts to your portfolio through different activities and assignments; now it's time to pull together all the parts into a final document to be shared with others. Remember that there may be many different reasons for preparing a portfolio. You may create a portfolio in response to your district's requirements for meeting the highly qualified standards for paraprofessionals under the No Child Left Behind Act. You may also develop a portfolio as part of a college course or professional development requirement in your district. You may also be the type of person who likes to keep track of your

Take some time to share your portfolio ideas with your classroom teacher or fellow paraprofessional. They will have great ideas to share and can give you invaluable feedback on your document.

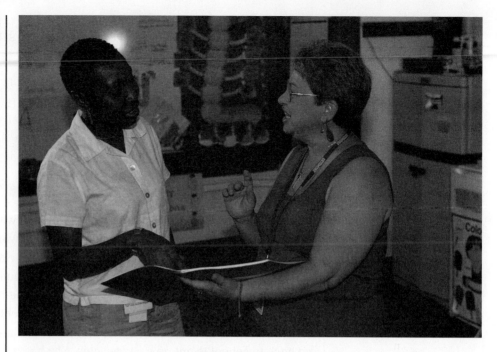

professional accomplishments for your own records. A portfolio is a great way to organize your professional experiences.

Preparing your portfolio means you must think about the best way to show your work as a paraprofessional. As you prepare your document, think about these questions:

1. What are my goals for creating a portfolio?
2. How will the artifacts I've collected meet my goals?
3. Are there other artifacts that I haven't collected that I want to include in my final portfolio?
4. What will my portfolio actually look like? How will I organize the content?
5. Who might be interested in reading my portfolio?

As you've learned from this book, common portfolio artifacts for paraprofessionals include work products you've created as a partner in your education team. Lessons you've led, notes or letters that you've sent to parents and guardians, or videotapes of your work with children are among the artifacts you might include. Many people use a paper-based portfolio, but more often educators use electronic portfolios to showcase their work (Kilbane & Milman, 2003). To create an electronic portfolio you'll need the technology to create and store the kind of information you want to include. For example, if you plan to use video clips of your work with students, make sure you have both the technology to allow video streaming and parental and school permission to use images of students. Check with the technology specialist in your school, the district Human Resource Director, and your building principal to make sure that the contents of your portfolio don't violate students' privacy rights. In addition to your portfolio artifacts, you might also want to include evaluations from your mentor teacher or supervisor. Your evaluations may come in many different forms. Let's take a look at a few examples.

EVALUATING EDUCATORS

Just like students in classrooms, educators must show how well they do their jobs. As members of educational teams, the work of paraprofessionals is evaluated by on-the-job supervisors; typically a classroom teacher or administrator. Evaluation is a part of life at work, and includes many different types of information. Evaluation feedback gives a picture of how well employees meet their job responsibilities. Evaluation reports may show a person's strengths and identify areas for improvement. Feedback also helps mentors set goals for ongoing professional development. The kind of information shared with educators can take different forms. Feedback types include **anecdotal feedback**, descriptions of how well a paraprofessional meets standards on **checklists**, and information that is shared more informally.

Anecdotal feedback includes the thoughts that an evaluator shares from observations during a lesson led by a paraprofessional. Oftentimes, anecdotal notes include a description of what an evaluator observed in the classroom, with special notes on strengths and areas in need of development (Borich, 2004). An evaluator's anecdotal notes might include the following type of feedback:

"Today during my observation you worked with a group of five students on a reading assignment. You led the group and reviewed the content students learned during an earlier lesson. You modeled the way students should complete their assignment. Next you helped students while they worked by themselves.

Strengths: You worked well with individual students. Your work with the kids was positive and caring. You answered students' questions and helped them complete their assignments.

Suggestions: Make sure that students' have your attention when you are giving directions. When a student makes a mistake, help the student find the right answer before you give the correct answer".

In this scenario, the evaluator shared her notes with the paraprofessional and offered ideas on ways that she could improve. One of the advantages of anecdotal reporting is that it gives a description of what an observer might see in a classroom. One of the disadvantages of anecdotal evaluations is that they may be too subjective. This means they may reflect only the opinion of the observer. There are a couple of ways to make sure the opinions of the observers give an accurate picture. First, it's important to know that most evaluators are trained in their work as observers, so they have had plenty of experience watching educators in many different classrooms. Usually observers also have to complete many observations on different days (Borich, 2004), which helps them see patterns in an educator's work with students over time.

A second type of evaluation tool is a checklist. Checklists are like scales that include questions or areas about behaviors that an observer looks for when watching a teacher or paraprofessional. Today's evaluation checklists include performance standards related to NCLB. If an evaluator at your school were to use a checklist, he or she might base the questions on the professional standards checklist your district uses to evaluate highly qualified paraprofessionals. If you were to use the portfolio framework from this book, the checklist might look like the sample in Table 8-1, Sample Paraprofessional Performance Checklist.

anecdotal feedback
The thoughts that an evaluator shares based on what he or she saw during a lesson led by a paraprofessional. Oftentimes the notes from the evaluator include a description of what they observed in the classroom, with special notes on the strengths and areas for further development.

crítica anecdótica
Las ideas que un evaluador comparte basándose en lo que vio durante la lección conducida por un paraprofesional. A menudo las notas del evaluador incluyen una descripción de lo observado en el salón de clases con notas especiales sobre los puntos más fuertes y los que requieren reforzarse más.

checklists
A kind of rating scale that include a set number of questions or areas that an observer looks for when watching a teacher or paraprofessional. Today, many checklists include areas of teaching that link to different types of external standards for evaluating the performance of educators.

lista de control
Similar a una escala de clasificaciones, incluye un número determinado de preguntas o áreas en que un observador se concentra al observar a un profesor o un paraprofesional. En la actualidad muchas listas de control incluyen áreas de enseñanza relacionadas con distintos tipos de estándares externos para evaluar el desempeño de educadores.

TABLE 8-1 Sample Paraprofessional Performance Checklist

STANDARD	ALWAYS PRESENT	SOMETIMES PRESENT	NEVER PRESENT	NO CHANCE TO OBSERVE
Supporting instructional opportunities:				
a. is prepared when working with students.				
b. keeps students on task during lessons.				
c. uses praise when working with students.				
d. records student performance using the record keeping system in the classroom.				

Feedback helps educators improve their teaching. Suggestions may be shared using anecdotal notes or through feedback from a checklist.

This checklist shows key areas that match the job responsibilities of many paraprofessionals. The rating scale used on the checklist describes whether or not the observer saw the paraprofessional use the skills related to a particular standard during a classroom visit.

Checklists and rating scales can be very complex. Researchers spend a lot of time preparing checklists that evaluate educators' performances. They study ways to make sure they have the best type of questions and rating scales, and they spend time developing evaluators' skills. What type of tool will show an evaluator your best work?

Some educators report that informal conversations and discussions are the best way to share their ideas and descriptions of their work. These educators believe more informal evaluations give a better picture of an educators' work from the viewpoint of the person being evaluated. While not always objective, an individual's views of his or her own work are important. The evaluations in your portfolio are one part of your professional story. When you create a portfolio you get to decide what and how you'll share information about yourself. The artifacts of your work show the ways that you work with children. If you plan to stay in your current position or if you are thinking about new opportunities, your portfolio is a useful resource. In fact, many university teacher education programs require portfolios as part of their programs.

NEXT STEPS IN PROFESSIONAL DEVELOPMENT— CHARACTERISTICS OF COLLEGES AND UNIVERSITIES

Once you have made the decision to enter a professional licensure program, you will need to think about the type of program you want to enter. There are a lot of reasons people choose to further their education and get a teaching license. For many people a college degree and teaching license bring both professional and personal satisfaction. For others, a college degree and a teaching license bring possibilities for greater pay and new job opportunities. As you make plans for the kind of program you want to enter, think about these questions:

1. What types of teacher licensure programs are available in my community?
2. What type of teaching position do I hope to have some day?
3. Are there other jobs in education that I might want to think about even if I don't complete a teacher licensure program?
4. What are the resources available in my community for going to a college or university?

Today there are a lot of teacher education programs for people who want to become teachers. Traditional four-year **teacher preparation programs** and **alternative routes to licensure** are most common. Traditional four-year programs at colleges or universities include one to two years of general education requirements followed by specialty courses in education. The final year of many four-year programs includes an extended student teaching experience. In these programs a person completes a college degree and a teaching license within four years in a specific area of study, such as elementary or early childhood education. In other types of programs a person completes a bachelor's degree followed by a fifth-year licensure program.

If you're feeling a bit overwhelmed by attending a large college or university, you're not alone. For many people in the United States, the first step toward a four-year college or university is to begin at a **community college**. In fact, at one western US university the majority of the students in their teacher licensure program attend a local community college before moving on to the four-year university.

Community colleges, or junior colleges, are two-year institutions where students complete an associate's degree in a specialized area of study. Just like many of the topics we've studied in this book, community colleges were influenced by

---

teacher preparation programs
Programs whose goal is to prepare future teachers in general and special education. These preparation programs work closely with state offices of education to make sure the education they provide meets state and national standards. The coursework in these programs covers many subject areas and requires extensive time working with students in schools and communities. Most programs take between four and five years to complete.

programas de preparación de maestros
Programas cuya meta es preparar a futuros maestros de educación general y educación especial. Estos programas trabajan en conjunto con las oficinas de educación estatales para asegurarse de que la educación que proveen se ajuste a los estándares nacionales y estatales. El trabajo de curso en estos programas cubre muchas materias y requiere un extenso tiempo de trabajo con estudiantes en la escuela y la comunidad. La mayoría de los programas son de cuatro a cinco años de duración.

different social and economic movements in America's history. For example, the need for different types of laborers throughout the history of the US influenced how the curriculum of many community colleges prepares workers. Coursework at community colleges is often specialized, and has focused on training for job skills at different points in history. Today, the emphasis on technology is one area of specialized training for many people who attend community colleges. The classes at community colleges often lead to a two-year associate's degree and many courses transfer to four-year colleges or universities. In the field of education, many community colleges offer courses in early childhood education, child care, and pre-education for those who go on to attend colleges and universities (Community Colleges, 2006). For people who complete an education-related degree at the community college, the next step is to enroll in a teacher preparation program at a college or university.

Teacher Preparation Programs

Teacher preparation programs in colleges and universities have a focused mission. The goal of teacher education programs is to prepare future teachers in general and special education. These preparation programs work closely with state offices of education to make sure the education they provide meets the state and national standards. Like many other groups, teacher preparation programs are affected by the policies of the NCLB. Just like school districts, colleges and universities need to show they are preparing teachers in the best manner possible. In addition to making sure new teachers understand schools and the work of teachers, teacher preparation programs must also include coursework in the following general areas:

a. multicultural education
b. technology
c. child development
d. content areas such as math and reading
e. special education
f. classroom management
g. curriculum and assessment

Specialized coursework in each of these areas is just a small portion of the topics studied by future teachers. Teacher preparation programs also require that their students work directly with students and families in classrooms, day care centers, and other community organizations as a part of their preparation. Students in these programs are often required to keep professional portfolios as part of their training. As a paraprofessional, you will bring valuable experience of your work with children to a teacher preparation program. Your experience with portfolio development is another advantage that sets you apart from many others seeking a teaching license. Traditional teacher education programs offer content and school-based experiences that give new teachers valuable skills, support, and mentoring. However, these programs do take time. For those who want a quicker way to teaching, there are other options.

Teacher education programs require students to work with children across many different settings. Time spent with children is an important part of any preparation program.

Alternative Routes to Licensure

In many communities across the US there are shortages of qualified teachers across different content areas. Teachers in mathematics and science are in especially high demand in many districts. Because of the great need for highly qualified educators, state offices of education have created a number of alternative routes to licensure. These alternative routes are often shorter than traditional teacher education programs and allow people with college degrees to begin teaching without a formal license. In some states alternative programs are guided by state offices of education. The students in these programs must take coursework while teaching so that they can earn a teaching license. People who support alternative programs believe they are the answer to the teacher shortage in many communities. Critics argue these teachers are placed in classrooms without any prior training in education, child development, multicultural education, or knowledge of how to pass on their content knowledge to students (Darling-Hammond, Chung, & Frelow, 2002). Many people in alternative programs have worked in other fields such as business or science, but lack experience working directly with children. They have the content knowledge but are not adequately trained on how to transfer their knowledge to students. In addition, many critics believe alternative programs do not provide the levels of mentoring new teachers often require (Ansell & McCabe, 2003).

After you read the sections on types of teacher education programs, think about the advantages of attending one of these programs. Use Table 8-2, Educator Training Programs, to help you decide the type of program you might consider. Write down the advantages and disadvantages of these different programs.

Like Maria, if you decide you want to further your education and enter a teacher preparation program, you'll have plenty to think about. It takes a lot of

TABLE 8-2 Educator Training Programs

TYPES OF EDUCATOR TRAINING PROGRAMS	ADVANTAGES	DISADVANTAGES	AVAILABLE PROGRAMS IN YOUR AREA
Community Colleges			
4-Year Colleges or Universities			
Alternative Routes to Licensure			

effort and planning to apply to programs, complete all of the paperwork, and find resources to attend college. The first step in finding out more about your options is to meet with representatives from programs in your area. Your local state office of education is a great place to start your search for teacher education programs in your area. Once you've learned more about two- and four-year programs, go ahead and review the application materials.

Applications

If you've ever been in a situation where you had to complete what seems like endless numbers of forms, the paperwork could leave you feeling overwhelmed. Let's take a look at the steps Maria followed as she prepared to apply to a teacher education program. She began the process of applying to college by meeting her classroom teacher, Sherry Willy.

DAY-TO-DAY DILEMMA
HOW WOULD YOU HANDLE THIS SITUATION?

Maria: Thanks for meeting with me, Sherry. I have to admit I'm feeling totally overwhelmed by all the work I need to do to apply to State University. I didn't think it would involve so much.

Sherry: Well, it's a lot of work, but with the help of the guidance counselor at SU, the process could be made easier. It sounds like you got a lot of good information from your professor at the community college too.

Maria: Yeah. I did. She helped me get copies of my transcripts and test scores, so that I can begin to apply to the teacher education program at SU. There's just so much paperwork!

Sherry: I know a person who works at the admissions office at SU and she sent me a helpful checklist with a timeline and a list of everything you need to plan ahead. She said a lot of universities use these checklists to help students plan in advance. Take a look at the list and we'll make sure you're on track.

Maria: Thanks, Sherry. This checklist is great! It breaks down all the information I need into small amounts of work for each month. Between the two of us and the advisors at SU, I think I'm going to make it through all this paperwork!

As you prepare your materials for college admissions, use Table 8-3, College Preparation Checklist, to gather the information you'll need to get your application ready. The timeline will remind you of the jobs you'll need to complete the year before you attend a college or university. A successful application depends on planning ahead and making sure you meet the deadlines. A good rule of thumb is to begin your college application about a year in advance. Most applications ask you to fill out general information questions on your background and your educational history. You may also be asked to take an entrance test and write an essay. Keep the College Preparation Checklist in a location where you can review it each month to make sure you're on track for applying.

A plan of action makes the process of applying to college easier. Work closely with the admissions and financial aid counselors at your college or university. Their help is invaluable. Whether or not you attend a college or university, professional development is an important part of the work of paraprofessionals and also includes a plan. Let's take a look at the ways in which Tracy plans to continue her professional development training through her district and community.

DEVELOPING AS A PARAPROFESSIONAL

Tracy is a paraprofessional who loves working with students with exceptionalities. She has worked in the same school for seven years and can't imagine any other type of job. She's happy that her good friend Maria is making new decisions in her life, but Tracy is not interested in going to college or becoming a full-time classroom teacher. She finds her work fulfilling and knows she's making a difference in the lives of her students. As a professional, Tracy thinks about ways to continue her own professional development, as she is committed to excellence in all that she does. Tracy is a lifelong learner and is always looking for new professional development opportunities. Her district offers different workshops for paraprofessionals that encourage **self-reflection** and continued professional growth.

Self-Reflection

Self-reflection in education is how educators think about their work in classrooms. Reflective educators are people who teach, study the results of their teaching, and think about how they'll teach in the future (Zeichner & Liston, 1996). Researchers who study effective teachers know that the strongest educators are those who think about their work all the time and then make changes in their teaching. Reflection is an important part for any educator, and is just one way professionals develop. Let's look at other forms of professional development among paraprofessionals.

---

self-reflection
In education, self-reflection is how educators think about their work in classrooms. Reflective educators are people who teach, study the results of their teaching, and think about how they'll teach in the future.

autorreflexión
En educación, la autorreflexión se refiere a la actitud de los educadores al reflexionar sobre su trabajo en la clase. Los educadores reflexivos son personas que enseñan, analizan los resultados de su enseñanza y piensan sobre su enseñanza en el futuro.

TABLE 8-3 College Preparation Checklist

August

___ Complete rough drafts of college applications.

___ Practice writing the essay portion of your application.

___ Ask family, friends, teachers, and advisors to look at the organization, content, and grammar of your practice essay. Ask yourself whether the essay represents your ideas.

September

___ Decide if you want to apply for "early admission" by submitting your application in October/November of this year to receive a decision by January 1 of next year.

___ Send for information from schools that you want to attend and send back their reply cards.

October

___ Narrow your list of colleges to the ones you really want to apply to.

___ Check your transcripts to be sure you will have all the credits and required classes for admission.

___ Give recommendation forms to the people who have agreed to write letters of recommendation for you (include a stamped envelope addressed to the college). Make sure your portion of the recommendations is completely and accurately filled out.

___ Gather your high school diploma or college transcripts.

___ Have your official test scores sent to the colleges you want to attend. Send off all "early admission" applications before the deadlines marked on your application.

___ Create the final, well-written version of your application essay.

November

___ Submit all other college applications before the deadlines.

December

___ Schedule any remaining interviews with campus admissions officers.

___ Call colleges to be sure your test scores have arrived for admission application.

January

___ Check the mail for "early admission" acceptance replies in the mail.

___ Get a copy of the Free Application for Student Financial Aid (FASFA) form.

___ Complete and send in all college financial aid applications, especially the FAFSA form, between January 1 and February 15. Remember the FAFSA is needed in order for you to be considered for any form of financial aid.

February

___ 4 weeks after turning in your FAFSA you should receive your Student Aid Report (SAR).

___ Make any corrections needed on your SAR and return it to the FAFSA office at your college/university.

___ Complete all scholarship applications.

___ Check with the college financial aid office to be sure they have received all needed information.

March and April

___ Plan to hear from the colleges to which you applied on their decision to admit you to their programs.

___ Compare acceptance letters, financial aid, and scholarships.

___ Note that when you decide on a college that has accepted you, a nonrefundable fee to hold your place in the freshman class may be required.

___ Choose a college by April 30 and notify them immediately.

June

___ Decide if you will need student health insurance.

Summer

___ Participate in any summer orientation program for incoming freshmen.

___ Check on costs of tuition, books, room and board, etc.

Professional Development Opportunities

A group of researchers were interested in finding out what type of topics paraprofessionals like to study. They asked about 300 paraprofessionals why they took certain workshops or training classes. For the group of paraprofessionals in this study, the researchers found that the majority of paraprofessionals took classes to improve their job skills or to help in their work with specific groups of children. The next most common reason paraprofessionals took part in trainings was to gain professional qualifications, followed by personal interests and encouragement by a teacher or administrator (Ashbaker & Morgan, 2006). There are many reasons why paraprofessionals want to develop professionally. Professional development training benefits paraprofessionals themselves, and most important, the children in their classrooms. What are some of the reasons you have taken different classes as a paraprofessional? Were there certain classes you enjoyed more than others?

SUMMARY

Maria and Tracy are paraprofessionals who enjoy and take great pride in their work in classrooms. They are committed to the students in their classrooms and work to improve professionally. As paraprofessionals for many years, their time in classrooms has helped them decide the next steps in their careers. Maria plans to continue her education and hopes to enter a teacher preparation program. This chapter described some of the programs available to Maria and the process she will follow to apply to her local university. While the application process is time consuming, Maria has a plan for meeting the application deadline and admissions requirements.

Tracy also has a plan for her future. She is a dedicated paraprofessional who knows she is in the right profession. She looks forward to her work in the classroom and will continue to build her professional portfolio. The classes she has taken in her district and her preparation for the Praxis ParaPro Test paid off, as she's received recognition as a Highly Qualified Paraprofessional in her district. Wherever your future takes you as a paraprofessional, know that your commitment to the education of young people and your development as a paraprofessional contribute to education in the 21st century.

CHECKING FOR UNDERSTANDING

1. Describe the educational options available to people interested in becoming licensed teachers. Which option seems most interesting to you and why?

2. Together with your classroom teacher, review the tools used to evaluate paraprofessionals in your school. What kind of questions do these tools include? What kind of information will you share with your mentor regarding your strengths as a paraprofessional?

3. There are many reasons why paraprofessionals take part in professional development activities in their districts. Which professional development opportunities are most interesting to you, and why?

4. What steps must be considered when people apply to colleges and universities?

POINTS OF VIEW

Together with your classroom teacher, complete Table 8-4 that may be used to evaluate your work as a paraprofessional. What are some of the areas you'd like to include on your form? Think about these ideas as you plan your format:

1. If you use an anecdotal format, include a space where the evaluator can include observation notes.
2. Include a section that describes students' actions in the classroom.
3. Include a space where you and your classroom teacher can list goals for future lessons.

A sample is provided below.

Create a reflection guide that will help you think about your work in the classroom. This reflection format will help you organize your ideas on your work as a paraprofessional. Table 8-5 can serve as a model for your reflection journal.

TABLE 8-4 Paraprofessional Evaluation Form

Observation Form Name: _____ Date: _____ Observer: _____	
What did the paraprofessional do in the lesson?	
What did the students do during the lesson?	
Suggestions	
Future Goals	

TABLE 8-5 Paraprofessional Reflection Journal

DATE	LEARNING ACTIVITY DESCRIPTION	AREAS WHERE I WAS SUCCESSFUL IN MY WORK WITH STUDENTS	AREAS WHERE I NEED TO IMPROVE MY WORK WITH STUDENTS

TABLE 8-6 Portfolio Framework

STANDARD I— SUPPORTING INSTRUCTIONAL OPPORTUNITIES	STANDARD II— DEMONSTRATING PROFESSIONALISM AND ETHICAL PRACTICE
a. Have knowledge of and proficiency in basic reading/writing readiness. b. Have knowledge of and proficiency in basic writing/writing readiness. c. Have knowledge of and proficiency in math/math readiness. d. Have knowledge of strategies, techniques, and delivery methods of instruction. e. Assist in delivering instruction according to teacher/provider lesson plans. f. Demonstrate the ability to record relevant information about learners to assist in the learning process. g. Organize and prepare materials to support learning and the teaching process.	a. Have knowledge of and adhere to the distinctions in the roles and responsibilities of teachers/ providers, paraprofessionals, families, and other team members. b. Carry out responsibilities in a manner consistent with all pertinent laws, regulations, policies, and procedures.

STANDARD III—SUPPORTING A POSITIVE LEARNING ENVIRONMENT	STANDARD IV—COMMUNICATING EFFECTIVELY AND PARTICIPATING IN THE TEAM PROCESS
a. Use proactive management strategies to engage learners. b. Support the teacher's behavior management plan.	a. Serve as a member of an instructional team. b. Use effective communication skills (written, verbal, and nonverbal).

PORTFOLIO CORNER

Throughout this book you have collected artifacts for your professional portfolio. Read through Table 8-6, Portfolio Framework, and decide whether your portfolio includes artifacts from each of the four areas. In which areas are your artifacts the strongest? In which areas do you need more materials? How will you improve the areas you feel are the weakest at this time?

REFERENCES

Ansell, S., & McCabe, M. (2003). Off target. *Education Week, 22,* 57–58.

Ashbaker, B., & Morgan, J. (2006). *Paraprofessionals in the classroom.* New York: Allyn & Bacon.

Borich, G. (2004). *Observation skills for effective teaching* (4th ed.). Upper Saddle River, New Jersey: Prentice Hall.

Community Colleges, defined (2006). Retrieved December 18, 2006 from http://www.answers.com/topic/community-college.

Darling-Hammond, L Chung, R., & Frelow, F. (2002). Variation in teacher preparation: How well do different pathways prepare teachers to teach? *Journal of Teacher Education, 53,* 286–302.

Kilbane, C., & Milman, N. (2003). *The digital teaching portfolio handbook: A how-to guide for educators.* Boston: Allyn & Bacon.

Zeichner, K. M., & Liston, D. P. (1996). *Reflective teaching: An introduction.* Mahaw, New Jersey: Lawrence Earlbaum Associates.

Additional selected readings and Paraprofessional electronic resources are available as part of the student Online Companion web site: www.earlychilded.delmar.com.

En español

Objetivos del aprendizaje

Después de leer y reflexionar sobre este capítulo podrá comprender mejor:

- Cómo completar su carpeta profesional
- Tipos de evaluaciones para los educadores
- Tipos de programas de licenciatura para maestros
- Experiencias en desarrollo profesional para paraprofesionales

A medida que usted lea este capítulo, hágase las siguientes preguntas:

1. ¿De qué les sirven a los educadores sus carpetas profesionales?
2. ¿Qué tipos de programas de licenciatura para maestros se ofrecen en su comunidad?
3. ¿Qué debe hacer un paraprofesional para ingresar a un programa de licenciatura?
4. ¿Cómo podrá usted continuar desarrollándose profesionalmente como paraprofesional?
5. ¿Qué tipo de documentos incluirá en su lista para demostrar lo que sabe sobre el desarrollo profesional de educadores?

Para verificar la comprensión

1. Describa las opciones educativas disponibles para las personas interesadas en obtener una licenciatura. ¿Qué opción le parece más interesante y por qué?
2. Junto con el maestro de su clase, haga una revisión de los medios usados para evaluar a paraprofesionales en su escuela. ¿Qué clase de preguntas incluyen? ¿Qué tipo de información compartirá usted con su mentor respecto a sus talentos como paraprofesional?
3. Hay muchas razones para que un paraprofesional participe en las actividades de desarrollo profesional de su distrito. ¿Qué oportunidades de desarrollo profesional le interesan más y por qué?
4. ¿Qué pasos se deben considerar cuando se solicita ingreso a un colegio o a una universidad?

Puntos de Vista

Junto con el maestro de su clase complete la Tabla 8-4 que podría usarse para evaluar su trabajo como paraprofesional. ¿Cuáles son algunas de las áreas que le gustaría incluir? Piense en estas ideas a medida que la vaya completando:

1. Si utiliza un formato anecdótico deje espacio para que el evaluador pueda incluir notas de la observación.

2. Incluya una sección que describa las actividades de los estudiantes en el salón de clases.

3. Deje espacio para poder hacer una lista de objetivos para futuras lecciones junto con el maestro de su clase.

Lo que sigue es un ejemplo.

Haga una guía para reflexionar sobre su trabajo en la clase. Esta hoja le servirá para organizar sus ideas sobre su trabajo como paraprofesional. La Tabla 8-5 le puede servir como modelo para su diario de reflexión.

TABLA 8-4 Hoja de evaluación para paraprofesionales

Hoja de observación Nombre: _____ Fecha: _____ Observador: _____			
¿Qué hizo el paraprofesional en la lección?			
¿Qué hicieron los estudiantes durante la lección?			
Sugerencias			
Objetivos futuros			

TABLA 8-5 Diario de reflexión

Fecha	Descripción de la actividad de aprendizaje	Áreas donde obtuve un buen resultado en mi trabajo con los estudiantes	Áreas donde necesito mejorar en mi trabajo con los estudiantes

Tabla 8-6 Estructura de la carpeta

Estándar I — Apoyar toda oportunidad educativa	Estándar II— Demostrar una conducta profesional y ética
a. Tener conocimientos y habilidad en el alistamiento básico lectura/escritura. b. Tener conocimientos y habilidad en el alistamiento básico escritura/escritura. c. Tener conocimientos y habilidad en el alistamiento básico matemáticas/matemáticas. d. Tener conocimientos de estrategias, técnicas y métodos de enseñanza e instrucción. e. Ayudar a impartir la instrucción de acuerdo al plan de lección del maestro/educador f. Demostrar capacidad para asentar información relevante sobre los educandos para asistir en el proceso de aprendizaje. g. Organizar y preparar materiales para apoyar el aprendizaje y el proceso educativo.	a. Tener conocimientos y aceptar las distinciones en las funciones y responsabilidades de los maestros/educadores paraprofesionales, familias y otros miembros del equipo educativo. b. Cumplir con las responsabilidades de acuerdo a todas las leyes, reglamentos, políticas y procedimientos pertinentes.
Estándar III—Ofrecer un ambiente conducente al aprendizaje	**Estándar IV—Comunicarse eficazmente y participar en el proceso de equipo**
a. Utilizar estrategias de conducción pro-activas para atraer a los educandos. b. Apoyar el plan de control de conducta del maestro.	a. Servir como miembro de un equipo educativo. b. Utilizar destrezas de comunicación (escrita, verbal y no verbal) efectivas.

Para la carpeta

A lo largo de este libro usted ha recopilado documentos para su carpeta profesional. Lea la Tabla 8-6, Estructura de la carpeta, y piense si su carpeta contiene documentos de cada una de las cuatro áreas listadas. ¿En cuáles áreas está el material más importante? ¿En qué áreas necesitará material adicional? ¿Cómo podrá mejorar las áreas en que se siente más débil?

INTERNET RESOURCES

American Federation of Teachers - http://www.aft.org.

American Society for Ethics in Education - http://www.edethics.org.

Bureau of Indian Affairs - http://www.doi.gov (click on Bureau of Indian Affairs).

Community Colleges - http://www.answers.com/topic/community-college.

Council for Exceptional Children (CED) - http://www.cec.sped.org.

Family Education Rights and Privacy Act (FERPA) - http://www.ed.gov and type in "FERPA".

Individuals with Disabilities Education Act - http://www.ed.gov and type in "IDEA".

National Association for the Education of Young Children (NAEYC) - http://www.naeyc.org.

National Clearinghouse for Professions in Special Education - http://www.ideapractices.org.

National Education Association—code of ethics - http://www.nea.org.

National Resource Center for Paraprofessionals - http://www.nrcpara.org.

National School Board Association - http://www.nsba.org and type in "legal issues".

No Child Left Behind Act - http://www.ed.gov and type in "NCLB". For information on NCLB for Spanish speakers, go to http://www.yesican.gov and http://www.yosipuedo.gov.

Praxis ParaPro Test - http://www.ets.org and type in "paraprofessional test".

Recruiting new teachers - http://www.recruitingteachers.org.

Special Education Advocacy—Getting Started, Wrightslaw - http://www.wrightslaw.com/advoc/articles/advocacy.intro.htm.

United for Kids - http://www.partners.utah.edu.

United States Department of Education - http://www.ed.gov. Spanish translations available.

REFERENCES

Ansell, S., & McCabe, M. (2003). Off target. *Education Week, 22,* 57–58.

Ashbaker, B., & Morgan, J. (2006). *Paraprofessionals in the classroom.* New York: Allyn & Bacon.

Boorman, G. (2000). Title I: The evolving research base. *Journal of Education for Students Placed at Risk, 5*(1&2), 27–45.

Borich, G. (2004). *Observation skills for effective teaching* (4th ed.). Upper Saddle River, New Jersey: Prentice Hall.

Borja, R. (2003). Prepping for the big test. *Education Week, 22,* 23–26.

Boyle, M. (2002). *The paraprofessional's guide to the inclusive classroom: Working as a team* (2nd ed.). Baltimore: Paul Brookes Publishing.

Brophy, J. (1998). *Motivating students to learn.* Boston: McGraw-Hill.

Burbank, M.D., McCandless, R., & Bachman, M. (2006). *Collaborative networks and the role of site-based mentors in preparing paraprofessionals.* A paper presented at the Association of Teacher Education, Atlanta Georgia.

Burden, P. (2006). *Classroom Management: Creating a successful learning community* (2nd ed.). Hoboken, New Jersey: John Wiley & Sons, Inc.

Cerebral Palsy Facts (2006). Retrieved July 15, 2006 from http://www cerebralpalsyfacts.com.

Charles, C.M. (2002). *Building classroom discipline* (7th ed.). Boston: Allyn & Bacon.

Community Colleges, defined (2006). Retrieved on December 12, 2006 from http://www.answers. com/topic/community-college.

Corey, G., Corey, M., & Callahan, P. (1993). *Issues and ethics in the helping professions.* Pacific Grove, California: Brooks/Cole.

Cuban, L. (1996). Curriculum stability and change. In P. Jackson (Ed.), *Handbook of research on curriculum* (pp. 216–247). New York: Macmillan.

Cummins, J. (2001). *Negotiating identities: Education for empowerment in a diverse society* (2nd ed.). Los Angeles: California Association for Bilingual Education.

Darling-Hammond, L., Chung, R., & Frelow, F. (2002). Variation in teacher preparation: How well do different pathways prepare teachers to teach? *Journal of Teacher Education, 53,* 286–302.

Department of the Interior (2006). Bureau of Indian Affairs. Retrieved June 14, 2007 from http://www.doi.gov.

Dreikurs, R., Grunwald, B., & Pepper, F. (1982). *Maintaining sanity in the classroom: Classroom management techniques* (2nd ed.). New York: Harper & Row.

Echevarria, J., & Graves, A. (2007). *Sheltered content instruction: Teaching English learners with diverse abilities* (3rd ed.). New York: Allyn & Bacon.

Echevarria, J., Vogt, M., & Short, D. (2004). *Making content comprehensible for English learners: The SIOP model* (2nd ed.). New York: Allyn & Bacon.

Educational Testing Service (2003). *ParaPro assessment study guide, practice and review.* Princeton, New Jersey: Educational Testing Service.

Eggen, P. (1998). *A comparison of inner-city middle school teachers' classroom practices and their expressed beliefs about learning and effective instruction.* Paper presented at the annual meeting of the American Educational Research Association, San Diego, California.

Fisher, L., Schimmel, D., & Kelly, C. (2003). *Teachers and the law* (6th ed.). New York: Longman.

Gallagher, J. (1999). Wuz Up? *In affirming middle grades education,* C. Walley & W. Gerrick (eds.). Boston: Allyn & Bacon.

Gardener, H. (1999). The understanding pathway. *Educational Leadership, 57,* 12–17.

Gay, G. (2000). *Culturally responsive teaching: Theory, research, and practice.* New York: Teachers College Press.

Gestwicki, C. (2007). *Developmentally appropriate practice: curriculum and development in early childhood education,* (3rd ed.). United States: Thomson Delmar Learning.

Gooden, M. (2003). At-risk children: Title I almost 40 years later. *School Business Affairs, 69,* 14–18.

Gregory, G. (2003). *Differentiated instructional strategies in practice: Training, implementation, and supervision.* Thousand Oaks, California: Corwin Press Inc.

Grossman, H. (2004). *Classroom management for diverse and inclusive schools.* Lanham, Maryland: Oxford, Rowman, & Littlefield.

Gutiérrez, R. (2002). Beyond essentialism: The complexity in teaching mathematics to Latinos. *American Educational Research Journal, 39,* 1047–1088.

Hardy, L. (2002). A new federal role. *American School Board Journal, 18,* 20–24.

Hernandez, H. (2001). *Multicultural education: A teacher's guide to linking context, process, and content* (2nd ed.). Upper Saddle River, New Jersey: Pearson.

Heward, W. (2003). *Exceptional children* (3rd ed.). Upper Saddle River, New Jersey: Merrill/Prentice Hall.

Jennings, J. (2002). Knocking on your door. *American School Board Journal, 189,* 25–27.

Kauchak, D., & Eggen, P. (2005). *Introduction to teaching: Becoming a professional* (2nd ed.). Upper Saddle River, New Jersey: Merrill Prentice Hall.

Kauchak, D., & Eggen, P. (2007). *Learning and teaching: Research based methods* (5th ed.). New York: Allyn & Bacon.

Kilbane, C., & Milman, N. (2003). *The digital teaching portfolio handbook: A how-to guide for educators.* Boston: Allyn & Bacon.

Kounin, J.S. (1970). *Discipline and group management in classrooms.* New York: Holt, Rinnhart, and Winston.

Langdon, C.A. (1999). The fifth Phi Delta Kappa poll of teachers' attitudes toward the public schools. *Phi Delta Kappan, 80,* 611–618.

Mehrabian, A., & Ferris, S. (1967). Inference of attitude from nonverbal behavior in two channels. *Journal of Consulting Psychology, 31,* 190–198.

Moll, L., & González, N. (1997). Teachers as social scientists: Learning about culture from household research in race, ethnicity and multiculturalism. P. M. Hall, (Ed.), *Missouri Symposium on Research*

and Educational Policy: Vol. 1 (pp. 89–114). New York: Garland Publishing.

Nance, R. (2007). *Workshop for Sheltered Content Instruction.* The Salt Lake City School District.

National Association for the Education of Young Children (NAEYC). (2006). Retrieved October 8, 2006 from http://www.naeyc.org.

National Education Association (2006). *Code of Ethics of the Education Profession.* Washington, DC. Retrieved July 16, 2006 from http://www.nea.org/aboutnea/code.html.

National Joint Committee on Learning Disabilities (1994). *Learning disabilities: Issues on definition.* A position paper of the National Joint Committee in Learning Disabilities. In Collective perspectives on issues affecting learning disability: Position paper.

National Middle School Association (2006). Retrieved October 8, 2006 from http://www.nmsa.org.

National Resources Center for Paraprofessionals (2005). *The employment and preparation of paraeducators, the state of the art—2002.* Retrieved July 12, 2006 from http://www.nrcpara.org.

No Child Left Behind Act of 2001. Public Law 107–110 (8 January 2002). Washington, DC: U.S. Government Printing Office.

Ogbu, J. (1995). Understanding cultural diversity and learning. In J. Banks & C. Banks (Eds.), *The Handbook of Research on Multicultural Education.* New York: Macmillan Publishing.

Olmedo, I.M. (1997). Challenging old assumptions: Preparing teachers for inner city schools. *Teaching and Teacher Education, 17,* 245–258.

Rueda, R., & Monzo, L. (2000). *Apprenticeship for teaching: Professional development issues surrounding the collaborative relationships between teachers and paraeducators.* Research Report # 8—Center for Research on Education, Diversity & Excellence (CREDE).

Salend, S.J., & Salinas, A.G. (2003). Language difficulties or learning difficulties: The work of the multidisciplinary team. *Teaching Exceptional Children, March/April,* 36–43.

Santrock, J. (2006). *Educational psychology* (2nd ed.). New York: McGraw-Hill. Special Education Advocacy—Getting Started, Wrightslaw—Retrieved February 2, 2006 from http://www.wrightslaw.com/advoc/articles/advocacy.intro.htm.

Shuell, T. (1996). Teaching and learning in a classroom context. In D. Berliner & R. Calfee (Eds.), *Handbook of educational psychology* (pp. 726–764). New York: Macmillan.

Slavin, R. (1986). *Using student team learning* (3rd ed.). Baltimore, Maryland: The Johns Hopkins University, Center for Research on Elementary and Middle School.

Spring, J. (2006). *American Education* (12th ed.). San Francisco: McGraw Hill.

Tribes Learning Community Model (2006). Retrieved February 2, 2006 from http://www.tribes.com.

Turnbull, A., Shank, M., & Turnbull, R. (2002). *Exceptional lives: Special education in today's schools* (3rd ed.). Upper Saddle River, New Jersey: Merrill/Prentice Hall.

Turnbull, A., Turnbull, R., Shank, M., Smith, S., & Leal, D. (2004). *Exceptional lives: Special education in today's schools* (4th ed.). Upper Saddle River, New Jersey: Merrill/Prentice Hall.

United States Bureau of Labor's Occupational Outlook Handbook (2007). Retrieved July 15, 2007 from www.bls.gov.

United States Department of Education (1999). *Digest of education statistics, 1998.* Washington, DC: U.S. Government Printing Office.

United States Department of Education (1999). *Teachers' guide to religion in the public schools.* Washington, DC: Author.

University Neighborhood Partners (2006). Retrieved June 30, 2006 from http://www.partners.utah.edu/boardroles.htm.

Utah State Office of Education (2006). Title 53A—53A-13-101.1 *Chapter 13—Curriculum in the Public School.* Salt Lake City, Utah: Retrieved July 20, 2006 from http://www.usoe.k12.ut.us

Viadero, D. (2003). Staying power. *Education Week, 22,* 24–27.

Villegas, A.M., & Lucas, T. (2002). *Educating culturally responsive teachers: A coherent approach.* New York: State University Press.

Walsh, M. (1999). Appeals court tosses out ruling in Alabama religious-expression case. *Education Week, 18,* 1, 10.

Wiggins, G. (1996/1997). Practicing what we preach in designing authentic assessment. *Educational Leadership, 54,* 18–24.

Zeichner, K.M., & Liston, D.P. (1996). *Reflective teaching: An introduction.* Mahaw, New Jersey: Lawrence Earlbaum Associates.

ADDITIONAL READINGS ON CLASSROOM MANAGEMENT

Fay, J., & Funk, D. (1995). *Teaching with love and logic: Taking control of the classroom.* Golden, Colorado: The Love and Logic Press, Inc.

Parenti, J. (2001). *First year urban teacher.* Philadelphia, Pennsylvania: Teacher for Hire.

Wong, H. (1998). *The first days of school.* Mountain View, California: Harry Wong Publications.

ENGLISH

GLOSSARY

academic learning time The amount of time students spend working on content through independent work or work with classmates.

accountability standards Policies that ensure that students in public schools are being served by the most qualified personnel.

achievement gap Differences in the test performance among groups of people taking standardized tests.

Adequate Yearly Progress (AYP) A part of NCLB that represents the growth each school must demonstrate toward meeting its goals for student performance on standardized tests. If a school is not able to show an appropriate level of growth during two back-to-back years, it is given a rating that indicates its "need of improvement."

administrators School district personnel who oversee the work of the teachers, staff, and students within districts and schools.

advisory periods A period in the daily schedules of many junior high and high schools. Students meet with teachers so that they don't feel lost in a large secondary school. Advisory periods give students regular contact with an adult during each school day.

allocated time The official time that a state or district sets for teaching a specific content area.

alternative forms of assessment Tests that measure student performance through "real life" tasks.

alternative routes to licensure Often shorter than traditional teacher education programs, alternative routes allow people with college degrees to begin teaching without a formal license. In some states alternative programs are guided by state offices of education. Students in these programs must take coursework while teaching in order to earn a teaching license.

Americans with Disabilities Act (ADA) Federal civil rights legislation that protects individuals with disabilities from discrimination in all aspects of life.

anecdotal feedback The thoughts that an evaluator shares based on what he or she saw during a lesson led by a paraprofessional. Oftentimes the notes from the evaluator include a description of what they observed in the classroom with special notes on the strengths and areas for further development.

Annual Measurable Objectives (AMO) Annual Measurable Objectives (AMO) describe the minimum percentage of students who must score well on tests in reading and mathematics. Based upon their students' performance and ability to meet the AMO goals, schools are evaluated to determine if the annual measurable objectives are met.

artifact Sample work product that demonstrates your work as a paraprofessional.

assessing The process of gathering information on a learner's understanding of content.

assessment plans Tools that help educators decide if their lessons are effective and if students have met the goals teachers planned for them.

Attention Deficit Hyperactivity Disorder (ADHD) An exceptionality that often includes behaviors such as hyperactivity, impulsivity, and difficulties paying attention in class. These behaviors occur at high frequencies with high levels of intensity.

Basic Interpersonal Communication Skills (BICS) The language skills people use in social settings. At school, BICS are put into effect in the conversations students have in the hallways, at recess, and in the lunchroom.

behavioral contracts Written guides with specific behavioral objectives in mind that include an outline of the rules and consequences of behaving in a certain way.

bilingual Language programs designed to teach students English through the use of their native language.

body language The nonverbal communication shared through eye contact, posture, gestures, and facial expressions.

Buckley Amendment A term used interchangeably with FERPA regulations. See FERPA.

Bureau of Indian Affairs (BIA) An organization responsible for making changes in American Indian education. The BIA is a group responsible for the administration and management of 55.7 million acres of land held in trust by the US for American Indians, Indian tribes, and Alaska Natives.

cerebral palsy A condition that results in difficulty of movement. While cerebral palsy limits movement and muscle coordination, it doesn't necessarily affect other abilities such as intellectual capacity.

charter schools Schools that exist as independent and state-funded programs that operate as alternatives to public education.

checklists A kind of rating scale that include a set number of questions or areas that an observer looks for when watching a teacher or paraprofessional. Today, many checklists include areas of teaching that link to different types of external standards for evaluating the performance of educators.

classroom management The process of creating and maintaining order in the classroom.

classroom schedules An outline of a day's events.

cognition The ways we think about information.

Cognitive Academic Language Proficiency Skills (CALPS) Language used in more formal settings than BICS, like classrooms and the workplace. CALPS language development may take a number of years to acquire and requires that learners understand both the basic information in content areas such as math, science, history or language arts and more complicated elements of the content.

community colleges Community colleges or junior colleges are two-year programs where students complete an associate's degree in a specialized area of study.

computer assistive technology Technological support provided to students with special education needs.

contacts Interpersonal or physical interactions with students.

cooperative learning A lesson format where students work together for the purpose of learning content within the context of a group.

cultural frame of reference A way of viewing the world based upon one's life experiences, culture, and history.

curriculum The course of study defined by local and national decision makers which includes specific skills, values, and attitudes identified as important by local and national communities.

developmental differences Changes in the students' learning process over the course of their lives.

developmental programs Classrooms where instruction and curriculum choices are geared toward the cognitive, social, and emotional needs of the students.

differentiated instruction Lessons that meet students' needs in many different ways through different activities and ways of testing.

disclosure statements Guides for the content and policies in a class that give students and parents or guardians information on behavior expectations, grading criteria, and curriculum content to be covered in a specific class. They are especially helpful for students who need extra support and planning time.

discovery-based lesson Lessons where educators support students and help them explore content in depth.

district An administrative unit that is legally responsible for the public education of children within specific state boundaries.

due process of law Process, under the law, that requires adequate notice to be given in advance, an explanation of evidence offered, and the participants having an opportunity to respond.

early childhood education Education programs for children usually between 3 and 5 years old. These programs provide children with the chance to explore their environment through touch, sight, sound, taste, and feel.

Educational Testing Service (ETS) A testing company responsible for developing and implementing the standardized tests taken by individuals seeking access to educational institutions.

electronic mail An electronic form of communication using the Internet.

engaged time The time students are focused on their teacher's instruction during a lesson.

English as a Second Language (ESL) Classrooms that are often set apart from mainstream classrooms and provide newcomers to American schools with the support they need to acquire the English language and to adapt to their new environment. Basics skills in reading, writing, and speaking are often very common in these settings.

English Language Learners (ELL) Children learning English for the first time.

exceptionalities Differences present in children who need additional resources to meet their full potential. These children make up 12% of the US student population and are often served in either special education or mainstream classes.

expert groups A type of cooperative learning group where students learn about content and get the chance to share what they know, so that everybody in the group learns the same information.

extrinsic motivators Rewards that are paired with a positive behavior. Tokens, often in the form of points, candy, stickers, or privileges are distributed to students based on positive behavior in educational settings.

Family Education Rights and Privacy Act (FERPA) Federal act that makes school records open and accessible to students and parents. The law also limits the kind of information that can be shared about a student.

federal government National leaders who develop and ensure the implementation of laws and policies related to education.

feedback Information on performance that can be used to increase future learning.

freedom of speech Rights related to the expression of ideas, values, and perspectives.

funds of knowledge The life experiences, ways of approaching work, and learning strategies all children have when entering classrooms.

goal setting An outline for the content to be covered, and the specific learning outcomes a teacher is planning to meet within the lesson.

grade level teaming In middle schools groups of teachers from across content areas such as language arts, history, math, and science work together. Team members plan lessons that connect the content of different areas.

high stakes testing Assessments used to measure students' performance in school-related content areas. Performance results determine if students move from one grade to the next or if a school gets funding.

inclusion Participation of children with exceptionalities in the general education classrooms of their peers with appropriate support and services.

Individualized Education Plan (IEP) A requirement of IDEIA (see below) that lists the goals and services for a child identified as needing special education services. IEPs typically address the child's present level of performance; determines short- and long-term goals; describes the extent to which a child will participate in mainstream classes; identifies dates for services to begin and end, and proposes plans for monitoring the child's growth.

Individuals with Disabilities Education Improvement Act (IDEIA) The major special education legislation in the US adopted originally in the 1970s and reauthorized in 1990 and 2004. IDEIA primarily addresses the policies and procedures related to providing students with special needs with a "free and appropriate" education in the "least restrictive environment".

indoctrinate Promote a personal point of view.

in loco parentis Latin expression meaning *in place of the parents*. A principle that requires teachers to use the same judgment and care as parents in protecting the children under their supervision.

instructional strategies The tools teachers use to teach content to their students.

instructional time The time teachers are directly involved in instruction within a lesson.

I-statements Words or phrases that describe how the person delivering a message is feeling when they deliver a message. I-statements are used to help others understand the perspective of the person delivering a message.

jigsaw A type of cooperative learning where students investigate and explore a specific type of information and then share their information with peers.

learning disability An exceptionality that involves difficulties in acquiring and using information in areas such as listening, speaking, reading and writing, and completing mathematical related assignments.

Least restrictive environment (LRE) A requirement of IDEIA where instruction and curriculum are planned specifically for students with exceptionalities. Least restrictive environments are designed to keep all children within the regular education classroom as often as possible, and to encourage future mainstreaming into traditional classroom settings.

lesson planning A roadmap of goals for student learning, a description of the directions during lessons, and a plan for testing student learning.

local level A group of elected citizens who oversee policies and practices within each school district operation.

logical consequences The natural result of failing to follow the rules or procedures within a classroom.

mainstreaming A policy that became a part of school practices in the 1970s when educators, parent groups, and community members advocated for the movement of students from special education settings to traditional grade level classrooms.

mental retardation An exceptionality that includes intellectual limitations that impact reading, writing, listening, self-care, and interacting with other people.

multiple intelligences An idea that people have skills and abilities related to schoolwork as well as other skills and talents in music, interacting with others, or playing sports.

National Association for the Education of Young Children (NAEYC) The largest professional association for early childhood education.

National Education Association (NEA) Organization that created a code of ethics focused on students and the teaching profession for people who work as educators.

National Middle School Association (NMSA) A professional association for middle school education.

negative reinforcement An action that decreases a behavior.

negligence A teacher's or other school employee's failure to exercise sufficient care in protecting students from injury.

No Child Left Behind Act (NCLB) Federal legislation that addresses the standards or students, teachers, and paraprofessionals working in the public school system.

Office of Indian Affairs An organization whose goal was to promote federal laws in the 1970s and 1980s that supported educational programs that were developed, monitored, and operated by American Indian communities.

paraeducators Paraeducators or paraprofessionals are educators who work under the guidance of classroom teachers to provide students with exceptionalities and language needs with the support to succeed in the classroom.

parent advocacy groups Groups who serve the needs of students, particularly those eligible for special education or English language services. Advocate roles may include writing letters and attending meetings, sharing information on policies and the law, putting forward strategies for asking questions, and providing ideas on how to prepare for school-based meetings where educational plans are identified.

performance assessment A test of the ways that students show their knowledge in a lifelike situation.

portfolio A collection of work samples that showcase one's work.

portfolio assessment A form of testing that gives a picture of performance through a collection of products or "artifacts".

positive reinforcement A reward that maintains or increases a behavior.

Praxis ParaPro Test A standardized test developed by the Educational Testing Service that assesses a paraprofessional's ability to apply their knowledge and skills to classroom situations. The test is divided into six key areas including: a) reading skills and knowledge; b) the application of reading skills and knowledge to classroom instruction; c) mathematics skills and knowledge; d) the application of mathematics skills and knowledge to the classroom; e) writing skills and knowledge; f) the application of writing skills and knowledge to classroom instruction.

preventative measures Practices used by educators that are designed to reduce the occurrence of classroom management difficulties. Examples include building a productive classroom community, creating an interesting curriculum, and implementing effective teaching strategies.

privacy Policies that describe the type of information that may be shared about a student's personal life or academic records.

process The way the student completes a particular assignment or skill.

professional ethics Set of moral standards for acceptable professional behavior

proximity Distance between individuals or objects that allows educators to increase their direct contact with learners by standing near a potentially disruptive student.

Public Law 94-142 The Education of All Handicapped Children Act passed in 1975 specified state and local policies in protecting the rights and educational needs of students with disabilities.

reporting child abuse School district employees have a legal responsibility to report to legal authorities, within the regulations of each state, and within the specific contexts of schools, those situations where there is "reason to believe" that a child has been abused or is in danger.

restatements A way to tell a speaker what they heard in a conversation. Restatements let the listener tell what they heard using their own words and are important because they help both parties in a conversation make sure that the message was heard as intended.

school boards Locally elected officials who determine policies and procedures within a district.

self-reflection In education, self-reflection is how educators think about their work in classrooms. Reflective educators are people who teach, study the results of their teaching, and think about how they'll teach in the future.

shared governance An approach to leadership in a classroom or organization that recognizes each individual as a team member who shares ideas, plans, and responsibilities.

sheltered classrooms Classrooms that are often set apart from mainstream classrooms and provide newcomers to American schools with the support they need to acquire the English language and to adapt to their new environment. Basics skills in reading, writing, and speaking are often very common in these settings.

sheltered content instruction Classrooms that, through changes in curriculum and instruction, include multilingual students who are developing their English skills. The instruction addresses language development in routines and activities of classrooms as well as the actual content of subjects such as math, science, and language arts.

special education Educational services provided to students whose behavior or performance on various tests meets the standards that describe a specific disability.

standardized tests Examinations where the scores of an individual student are compared to a group score that has been developed through a comparison of scores from many people who have taken the same test.

state level Legal decision makers who oversee policies and practices within each state.

teacher-centered instruction Instruction where the teacher carefully specifies goals, presents the content to be learned, and actively directs learning activities. In these formats the teacher directs the lesson in the form of a lecture or class discussion. Students in a teacher-centered classroom are usually passive, waiting for the teacher to directly guide their learning.

teacher preparation programs Programs whose goal is to prepare future teachers in general and special education. These preparation programs work closely with state offices of education to make sure the education they provide meets state and national standards. The coursework in these programs covers many subject areas and requires extensive time working with students in schools and communities. Most programs take between four and five years to complete.

time-out A way of managing behavior that involves moving a student to an isolated part of the classroom or to another room.

Title I Schools A federal education program that provides funding for schools with students from low-income families.

token economies Ways of managing student behavior that include the use of extrinsic motivators such as candy, points, or stickers.

transitional bilingual education Language programs that link a student's knowledge of a new language with his or her native language using gradual progression from the native to the new language.

Tribes Learning Community Model A community building model that includes the strategies educators implement in their classrooms in order to create an environment where students feel included and respected regardless of differences in ability, gender, language, life goals, and interests. The Tribes philosophy encourages classrooms where students are actively involved in their own learning through choices in what they learn and in their opportunities for success.

"withitness" A teacher's awareness of what is taking place in their classroom. Teachers who demonstrate *"withitness"* are aware of the happenings in their classrooms and know what students are doing within the context of a lesson; they know when to change their curriculum and instruction. They can tell what is going on in the classroom at all times, thanks to an ability described by some as "eyes in the back of their heads".

ESPAÑOL

GLOSARIO

administradores Personal del distrito escolar que supervisa el trabajo de los maestros, del personal, y de los estudiantes en los distritos y las escuelas.

ambiente con menos restricciones (LRE) Uno de los requisitos de IDEIA, por el cual la enseñanza y el currículo se planean específicamente para estudiantes con excepcionalidades. Los ambientes con menos restricciones están diseñados para mantener a todos los niños en un salón de clases común en la medida de lo posible, y para alentar su futuro ingreso a un salón de clases tradicional.

aprendizaje cooperativo Formato de lección en que los estudiantes trabajan juntos para aprender contenido en un contexto de grupo.

Asociación Nacional de Educación (NEA según sus siglas en inglés) Organización que creó un código de ética enfocado en los estudiantes y la profesión docente para los que se desempeñan como educadores.

Asociación Nacional de Escuelas Secundarias Medias (NMSA por sus siglas en inglés) Asociación profesional para la educación en las escuelas secundarias medias.

Asociación Nacional para la Educación de Niños Jóvenes (NAEYC por sus siglas en inglés) La asociación profesional más importante para la educación de la primera infancia.

autoridad compartida Estilo de liderazgo de un salón de clases o de una organización que reconoce que cada individuo es un miembro del equipo que comparte ideas, planes, y responsabilidades.

autorreflexión En educación, la autorreflexión se refiere a la actitud de los educadores al reflexionar sobre su trabajo en la clase. Los educadores reflexivos son personas que enseñan, analizan los resultados de su enseñanza y piensan sobre su enseñanza en el futuro.

banco de conocimientos Experiencias de vida, formas de trabajar y estrategias de aprendizaje con el que llegan a la escuela todos los niños.

bilingüe Programas de lengua destinados a enseñar inglés a través del uso de la lengua materna del estudiante.

brecha de rendimiento Diferencias en los resultados de los exámenes entre los diversos grupos de personas que toman exámenes estandarizados.

carpeta Colección de muestras de trabajo que demuestran el desempeño de una persona.

cognición Forma en la que pensamos sobre la información.

colegios de la comunidad Los colegios de la comunidad o colegios menores son programas de dos años en que los estudiantes obtienen un título de asociado en un área de estudio especializada.

Comité de asuntos de habitantes nativos Organización responsable de hacer cambios en la educación de los habitantes nativos. El BIA, según sus siglas en inglés, es el grupo a cargo de administrar y manejar los 55.7 millones de acres mantenidos por los Estados Unidos que pertenecen a los habitantes nativos, tribus indígenas y nativos de Alaska.

con la mayoría *(mainstreaming)* Política que se convirtió en parte de las prácticas escolares en los años 70 cuando educadores, grupos de padres y miembros de la comunidad abogaron porque los estudiantes se trasladaran de las clases de educación especial a las clases regulares.

consecuencias lógicas Resultado natural de no obedecer las reglas o los procedimientos de la clase.

contactos Interacciones interpersonales o físicas con los estudiantes.

contratos de conducta Guías escritas con objetivos de comportamiento específicos que incluyen un bosquejo de las reglas y de las consecuencias de comportarse de cierta manera.

195

correo electrónico Forma electrónica de comunicación por medio de Internet.

crítica anecdótica Las ideas que un evaluador comparte basándose en lo que vio durante la lección conducida por un paraprofesional. A menudo las notas del evaluador incluyen una descripción de lo observado en el salón de clases con notas especiales sobre los puntos más fuertes y los que requieren reforzarse más.

currículo Plan de estudios determinado por las personas que toman decisiones a nivel local y nacional que incluye habilidades específicas, valores y actitudes consideradas importantes por las comunidades locales y nacionales.

declaraciones en primera persona Palabras o frases que describen cómo se siente una persona en el momento en que trasmite un mensaje. Las declaraciones en primera persona se usan para ayudar a los demás a comprender el punto de vista de la persona que transmite el mensaje.

denuncia de abuso a menores Dentro de las regulaciones de cada estado, y dentro del contexto específico de las escuelas, los empleados del distrito escolar tienen la responsabilidad legal de informar a las autoridades legales sobre situaciones donde haya "razón para creer" que existe abuso de menores o que un niño corre riesgo de abuso.

Desorden de hiperactividad con déficit de atención (ADHD por sus siglas en inglés) Excepcionalidad que incluye a menudo comportamientos tales como hiperactividad, impulsividad y dificultad para prestar atención en clase. Estos comportamientos ocurren con gran frecuencia y a un alto nivel de intensidad.

destrezas básicas de comunicación interpersonal (BICS por sus siglas en inglés) Uso del idioma que se hace en un contexto social. En la escuela, este uso tiene lugar en las conversaciones que los estudiantes mantienen en los pasillos, durante el recreo y en la cafetería.

diferencias del desarrollo Cambio en el proceso de aprendizaje de los estudiantes durante el transcurso de su vida.

dificultades de aprendizaje Excepcionalidades que implican problemas en obtener y usar información cuando se escucha, habla, lee o escribe, y para completar tareas de tipo matemático.

distrito Unidad administrativa que es legalmente responsable de la educación pública de los niños dentro de áreas específicas de cada estado.

divulgación de propósitos Lineamientos referentes al contenido y las regulaciones de una clase que dan a los estudiantes y a sus padres o tutores información sobre las expectativas de conducta, el criterio para adjudicar notas y el contenido del currículo a cubrirse. Beneficia sobre todo a los estudiantes que necesitan más apoyo y más tiempo de planificación.

documentos Productos de muestra que sirven como prueba del trabajo de un paraprofesional.

educación bilingüe transitoria Programas de lengua que vinculan el conocimiento de un nuevo idioma a la lengua materna del estudiante basándose en una progresión gradual del idioma materno a la nueva lengua.

educación de la primera infancia Programas de educación para niños entre 3 y 5 años de edad. Estos programas les brindan a los niños la oportunidad de explorar el medio ambiente a través del tacto, la vista, el sonido y el gusto.

educación especial Servicios educativos para los estudiantes cuyo desempeño en varios exámenes coincide con los estándares que indican una dificultad de aprendizaje específica.

Enmienda Buckley Término que se usa también para referirse a la Ley de los derechos de educación y privacidad de la familia.

enseñanza de contenido bajo protección La instrucción que se imparte, a través de cambios en el currículo y en la enseñanza, a estudiantes multilingües que están comenzando a aprender inglés. Las lecciones incluyen el desarrollo del lenguaje relacionado con la rutina y las actividades del salón de clases así como el contenido de materias tales como matemáticas, ciencias y artes del lenguaje.

equipos por nivel de grado Grupos de maestros de enseñanza secundaria en los que profesores de diversas áreas de contenido como artes del lenguaje, historia, matemáticas y ciencias trabajan juntos. Los miembros del equipo planean las lecciones que conectan el contenido de sus áreas respectivas.

escuelas de carta y estatuto o escuelas charter Escuelas que existen en forma y con programas independientes subvencionados con fondos estatales; funcionan como alternativas a la educación pública.

Escuelas de Título I Programa federal de educación que provee fondos para escuelas con estudiantes provenientes de familias de bajos ingresos.

establecimiento de objetivos Guía del contenido a cubrirse y de resultados determinados de aprendizaje que el educador planea lograr en una lección.

estrategias educacionales Medios que los profesores usan para enseñar contenido a los estudiantes.

ética profesional Conjunto de estándares morales adecuados a una conducta profesional aceptable.

evaluación de desempeño Prueba en que los estudiantes demuestran su conocimiento por medio de su actuación en una situación de la vida real.

evaluación de la carpeta Tipo de examen que da una imagen del rendimiento a través de una colección de productos u objetos.

evaluar el proceso de reunir información sobre la comprensión de contenido que tiene un educando.

"estar con los ojos abiertos" La total atención del maestro a lo que ocurre en la clase. Los maestros que "están con los ojos abiertos" son conscientes de lo que pasa en su clase y saben lo que están haciendo los estudiantes dentro del contexto de una lección; saben cuándo cambiar su currículo y enseñanza. Pueden decir qué pasa en la clase en todo momento, y tienen una cualidad que algunos describen como "ojos en la nuca".

estándares de confiabilidad Regulaciones que aseguran que los estudiantes de las escuelas públicas estén a cargo del personal mejor capacitado.

Estudiantes del idioma inglés (ELL por sus siglas en inglés) Niños que comienzan a aprender inglés.

Exámenes de alto riesgo Evaluaciones que se usan para determinar el rendimiento de los estudiantes en las materias escolares. Los resultados de los exámenes determinan si los estudiantes pasan de un grado a otro o si la escuela obtiene fondos.

Exámenes estandarizados Exámenes en los que las calificaciones de un estudiante se comparan con un resultado establecido a través de comparaciones con las calificaciones de varias personas que han tomado el examen.

excepcionalidades Diferencias presentes en niños que necesitan recursos adicionales para lograr su mayor potencial. Estos niños componen el 12% de la población de estudiantes de los EE.UU. y asisten a menudo a clases de educación especial o clases regulares.

formas alternativas de evaluación Pruebas que evalúan el desempeño de un estudiante por medio de tareas "de la vida real".

fuera de clase Método de controlar la conducta en la clase que implica enviar a un estudiante fuera del aula o a una parte aislada de la misma.

gobierno federal Líderes nacionales que desarrollan y aseguran la puesta en práctica de leyes y regulaciones relacionadas con la educación.

grupos de defensa de los padres Grupos que prestan atención a las necesidades de los estudiantes, particularmente los que requieren educación especial o aprendizaje del idioma inglés. Los defensores pueden ejercer muchas tareas como, por ejemplo, escribir cartas y atender reuniones, compartir información sobre leyes y regulaciones, elaborar estrategias para hacer preguntas y brindar ideas sobre cómo prepararse para las reuniones escolares que tratan de planes educativos.

grupos expertos Tipo de aprendizaje cooperativo en grupo en que los estudiantes aprenden sobre contenido y tienen la oportunidad de compartir su conocimiento de modo que todos los integrantes del grupo obtienen la misma información.

horario de clases Guía de lo que se hace durante el día escolar.

inclusión Participación de los niños con excepcionalidades en los salones de clase de sus pares con el apoyo y los servicios apropiados.

indoctrinar Promover un punto de vista personal.

Inglés como segundo idioma (ESL por sus siglas en inglés) Salones de clase a menudo separados de los salones de clases regulares que proporcionan a los recién llegados a las escuelas de los EE.UU. la ayuda que necesitan con el idioma y la adaptación al nuevo ambiente. Habilidades básicas en lectura, escritura y lengua son usualmente muy comunes en estas clases.

In loco parentis Expresión latina que significa *en lugar de los padres*. Principio que requiere que los maestros usen el mismo criterio y cuidado que usan los padres para proteger a los niños que están bajo su supervisión.

instrucción centrada en el profesor Enseñanza en que el profesor fija con cuidado metas, presenta el contenido a ser aprendido y dirige activamente el aprendizaje. En este tipo de formato el profesor dirige la lección en forma de conferencia o discusión. Los estudiantes en una clase centrada en el profesor son generalmente pasivos y esperan que el profesor dirija el aprendizaje directamente.

instrucción diferenciada enseñanza que tiene en cuenta las necesidades de los estudiantes de diversas maneras a través de distintas actividades y formas de evaluación diferentes.

inteligencias múltiples concepto de que las personas tienen destrezas y capacidades relacionadas con el trabajo escolar así como también con otras destrezas y talentos en música, la interacción con los demás o la práctica de deportes.

Juntas escolares Funcionarios localmente elegidos que determinan reglamentos y procedimientos dentro de un distrito.

lección basada en el descubrimiento Lecciones en que los educadores apoyan a los estudiantes y los ayudan a explorar el contenido en profundidad.

lenguaje corporal Comunicación no verbal efectuada a través del contacto visual, la postura, los gestos y las expresiones faciales.

Ley de derechos de educación familiar y privacidad (FERPA según sus siglas en inglés) Ley federal que hace que los expedientes escolares sean accesibles a los estudiantes y sus padres. La ley también limita el tipo de información que se puede divulgar sobre un estudiante determinado.

Ley de personas discapacitadas (ADA según sus siglas en inglés) Legislación federal de derechos civiles que protege a los individuos con discapacidades contra la discriminación en todos los aspectos de la vida.

Ley federal de mejoras en la educación para niños con dificultades de aprendizaje (IDEIA por sus siglas en inglés) La legislación de educación especial más importante de los EE.UU. fue adoptada originalmente en 1970 y reautorizada en 1990 y 2004. IDEIA trata de las políticas y procedimientos relacionados con proveer educación "gratuita y adecuada" en un "ambiente libre de restricciones" a los estudiantes con necesidades especiales.

Ley pública 94-142 Ley de educación de todos los niños discapacitados aprobada en 1975 que especifica políticas locales y estatales para proteger los derechos y las necesidades educativas de estudiantes con dificultades de aprendizaje.

libertad de expresión Derechos relacionados con la expresión de ideas, valores y puntos de vista personales.

lista de control Similar a una escala de clasificaciones, incluye un número determinado de preguntas o áreas en que un observador se concentra al observar a un profesor o un paraprofesional. En la actualidad muchas listas de control incluyen áreas de enseñanza relacionadas con distintos tipos de estándares externos para evaluar el desempeño de educadores.

manejo de la clase Proceso de crear y de mantener orden y disciplina en la clase.

marco cultural de referencia Manera de ver el mundo basada en las experiencias, cultura, e historia personales.

medidas preventivas Prácticas empleadas por los educadores destinadas a reducir las dificultades que puedan surgir en el manejo de la clase. Ejemplos incluyen la creación de una comunidad productiva en el aula, la elaboración de un currículo interesante y el empleo de estrategias de enseñanza eficaces.

Modelo comunitario de aprendizaje de tribus Modelo para la formación de una comunidad que incluye las estrategias que los educadores emplean en la clase para crear un ambiente en el cual los estudiantes se sientan incluidos y respetados independientemente de su diferencias en capacidad, género, idioma, objetivos e intereses. La filosofía de este modelo fomenta clases en que los estudiantes se involucren activamente en su propio proceso de aprendizaje mediante opciones respecto a lo que aprenden y a sus oportunidades de éxito.

motivadores extrínsecos Recompensas que se asocian a un comportamiento positivo. Estas recompensas, a menudo puntos extra, caramelos, pegatinas, o privilegios, se les dan a los estudiantes para premiar un buen comportamiento.

negligencia Fracaso del maestro u otro empleado de la escuela en ejercer el cuidado debido para proteger a los estudiantes y evitar daños.

nivel estatal Las personas que toman decisiones legales y supervisan reglamentaciones y prácticas dentro de cada estado.

nivel local Grupo de ciudadanos elegidos, responsables de supervisar las reglamentaciones y prácticas de cada distrito escolar.

Objetivos anuales mensurables (AMO) Los objetivos anuales mensurables describen el porcentaje mínimo de estudiantes que deben obtener buenas calificaciones en lectura y matemáticas. Se hace una evaluación de las escuelas para determinar si se han alcanzado las metas del AMO basada en el rendimiento de los estudiantes.

Oficina de asuntos de habitantes nativos Organización cuya meta era promover leyes federales en las décadas de los años 70 y 80 que apoyaban programas educativos que desarrollaban, mantenían y operaban comunidades de habitantes nativos.

paraeducadores Paraeducadores o paraprofesionales son educadores que trabajan bajo la supervisión de los maestros de clase para dar apoyo a los estudiantes con excepcionalidades y necesidades lingüísticas para que tengan éxito en el aula.

parálisis cerebral Condición que resulta en problemas de movimiento. Si bien la parálisis cerebral limita el movimiento y la coordinación de los músculos no afecta necesariamente otras habilidades tales como la capacidad intelectual.

período de asesoramiento Período durante el día escolar de muchas escuelas medias y secundarias en que los estudiantes se reúnen con profesores para evitar sentirse perdidos en una de las enormes escuelas secundarias de la actualidad. Los períodos de asesoramiento ponen a los estudiantes un contacto con un adulto durante cada día escolar.

Plan de educación individualizada (IEP por sus siglas en inglés) Un requisito de IDEIA que enumera las metas y los servicios programados para un niño que requiere servicios de educación especial. Esos planes generalmente se refieren al nivel de desempeño actual del niño; determinan metas a corto y largo plazo; explican hasta qué grado el niño participará en las clases regulares; dan las fechas de comienzo y terminación de los servicios y proponen planes para controlar el desarrollo del estudiante.

planes de clase Plan de los objetivos de aprendizaje del estudiante, descripción de las indicaciones a impartir durante las lecciones y plan para evaluar el aprendizaje.

planes de evaluación Instrumentos que ayudan a los educadores para saber si su enseñanza es eficaz y si los estudiantes han alcanzado los objetivos previstos.

premios simbólicos Métodos para controlar el comportamiento del estudiante que incluyen el uso de motivadores extrínsecos; como dulces, puntos extra o pegatinas.

privacidad Regulaciones que indican el tipo de información que puede divulgarse sobre los asuntos personales o académicos de un estudiante.

procedimiento de ley debida Proceso de acuerdo a la ley que requiere que se dé previo aviso, se ofrezca justificación de la evidencia y se brinde oportunidad de respuesta a los participantes.

proceso Modo en que el estudiante desarrolla una tarea particular o una destreza.

proficiencia en el lenguaje académico de destrezas cognitivas (CALPS por sus siglas en inglés) Lengua usada en situaciones más formales que las destrezas básicas de comunicación interpersonal (BICS). Su adquisición puede llevar años y requiere que los que la usan entiendan la información básica en áreas tales como matemáticas, ciencias, historia o artes del lenguaje, así también como elementos más complicados del contenido.

programas de desarrollo Clases en que las opciones de enseñanza y currículo se dirigen a las necesidades cognitivas, sociales y emocionales de los estudiantes.

programas de preparación de maestros Programas cuya meta es preparar a futuros maestros de educación general y educación especial. Estos programas trabajan en conjunto con las oficinas de educación estatales para asegurarse de que la educación que proveen se ajuste a los estándares nacionales y estatales. El trabajo de curso en estos programas cubre muchas materias y requiere un extenso tiempo de trabajo con estudiantes en la escuela y la comunidad. La mayoría de los programas son de cuatro a cinco años de duración.

Progreso anual adecuado (AYP) Un componente de la ley "Que ningún niño se quede atrás" que representa el crecimiento que cada escuela debe demostrar hacia el logro de sus objetivos de rendimiento estudiantil en los exámenes estandarizados. Si una escuela no puede alcanzar un nivel adecuado de crecimiento durante dos años consecutivos, recibe una evaluación que indica "la necesidad de mejoramiento académico."

proximidad Distancia entre individuos u objetos que permite a los educadores incrementar su contacto directo con los educandos al poder ubicarse cerca de un estudiante con problemas de disciplina.

Prueba de Praxis ParaPro Una prueba estandarizada desarrollada por el servicio de pruebas educativas que determina la capacidad de un paraprofesional para aplicar sus conocimientos y destrezas a la enseñanza en el aula. La prueba se divide en seis áreas clave: a) destrezas y conocimientos de lectura; b) la aplicación de las destrezas y conocimientos de lectura a la enseñanza en el aula; c) destrezas y conocimientos de matemáticas; d) la aplicación de las destrezas y conocimientos de matemáticas a la enseñanza en el aula; e) destrezas y conocimientos de escritura; f) la aplicación de las destrezas y conocimientos de escritura a la enseñanza en el aula.

"Que ningún niño se quede atrás" (NCLB por sus siglas en inglés) Legislación federal aprobada en el año 2001 que define estándares en tres áreas: preparación del maestro; rendimiento estandarizado de exámenes para los alumnos de las escuelas públicas; y desarrollo profesional de maestros practicantes.

reacción Información sobre una actuación o desempeño que puede ser usada para fomentar un futuro aprendizaje.

reafirmaciones Modo de informar al hablante de lo que se escuchó en una conversación. Las reafirmaciones permiten que el oyente diga lo que escuchó con sus propias palabras y son importantes porque ayudan a los participantes en una conversación a cerciorarse de que el mensaje fue recibido tal como era previsto.

refuerzo negativo Acción que desalienta un comportamiento.

refuerzo positivo Recompensa que mantiene o fomenta un comportamiento.

retraso mental Excepcionalidad que incluye limitaciones intelectuales que afectan la lectura, la escritura, la audición, el cuidado de uno mismo, o la interacción con los demás.

rompecabezas Tipo de aprendizaje cooperativo en que los estudiantes investigan y exploran un tipo específico de información y de lección para luego compartir la información con sus compañeros.

rutas alternativas para la licenciatura A menudo más cortas que los programas tradicionales de educación docente, las rutas alternativas permiten a las personas con títulos universitarios comenzar a enseñar aunque no tengan una licencia oficial. En algunos estados los programas alternativos dependen de las oficinas estatales de educación. Los estudiantes de estos programas deben hacer el trabajo del curso al mismo tiempo que enseñan para poder obtener una licencia para enseñanza.

salones de clase protegidos Salones de clase separados de los salones regulares donde se proporciona a los estudiantes recién llegados al país el apoyo que necesitan para desempeñarse en inglés y adaptarse al nuevo ambiente. En estos salones se enseña por lo común destrezas básicas en lectura, escritura y lenguaje.

Servicio de pruebas educativas (ETS por sus siglas en inglés) El servicio de pruebas educativas es la compañía responsable de desarrollar e implementar los exámenes estandarizados que toman los individuos que buscan acceso a instituciones educativas.

tecnología de asistencia por computadoras Apoyo tecnológico que se da a los estudiantes con necesidades especiales.

tiempo asignado Tiempo oficial que el estado o el distrito establece para enseñar un área específica de contenido.

tiempo de aprendizaje académico Cantidad de tiempo que los estudiantes emplean para trabajar en un tema de forma independiente o con sus compañeros de clase.

tiempo de concentración Tiempo que los alumnos dedican a concentrarse en las enseñanzas del maestro durante una lección.

tiempo educacional Tiempo de la lección en que los maestros se dedican exclusivamente a enseñar.

INDEX

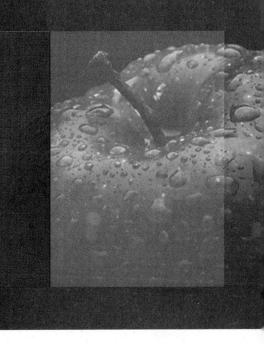